Modern Money and the Rise and Fall of Capitalist Finance

Modern Money and the Rise and Fall of Capitalist Finance examines the true nature of modern money and seeks ideas for an alternative economic system for a just society.

This book suggests that adopting the ideas and institutions of a trust allowed personae to be combined with creditor-debtor relations and, by doing so, led to the evolution of modern money. This also helps explain why modern banking arose in England rather than continental Europe, by conceptualizing modern money as a trust and investigating the inseparable relationship between personae and modern money, because it is more than creditor-debtor relations—it takes the form of a trust.

In explaining how the capitalist credit-money economy differs from previous economies, this book is a significant contribution to the literature on modern money, heterodox economics, and the philosophy of economics and finance.

Jongchul Kim has critically examined the modern concepts of "person" and "property" and applied this critique to an understanding of money and finance. He is currently an associate professor in Sogang University, South Korea.

Routledge Frontiers of Political Economy

Globalization and the Decline of American Power
The Political Economy of the American Fall
Cyrus Bina

Marx and *Le Capital*
Evaluation, History, Reception
Edited by Marcello Musto

Permanent Economic Disorder
Shahzavar Karimzadi

Temporary Economic Crises
Shahzavar Karimzadi

Money and Capital
A Critique of Monetary Thought, the Dollar and Post-Capitalism
Laurent Baronian

Modern Money and the Rise and Fall of Capitalist Finance
The Institutionalization of Trusts, Personae, and Indebtedness
Jongchul Kim

Innovation, Complexity and Economic Evolution
From Theory to Policy
Pier Paolo Saviotti

Economic Growth and Inequality
The Economist's Dilemma
Laurent Dobuzinskis

For more information about this series, please visit: www.routledge.com/Routledge-Frontiers-of-Political-Economy/book-series/SE0345

Modern Money and the Rise and Fall of Capitalist Finance

The Institutionalization of Trusts, Personae, and Indebtedness

Jongchul Kim

Routledge
Taylor & Francis Group
LONDON AND NEW YORK

First published 2023
by Routledge
4 Park Square, Milton Park, Abingdon, Oxon OX14 4RN

and by Routledge
605 Third Avenue, New York, NY 10158

Routledge is an imprint of the Taylor & Francis Group, an informa business

British Library Cataloguing-in-Publication Data
A catalogue record for this book is available from the British Library

ISBN: 978-0-367-51047-3 (hbk)
ISBN: 978-0-367-51050-3 (pbk)
ISBN: 978-1-003-05221-0 (ebk)

DOI: 10.4324/9781003052210

Typeset in Bembo
by Apex CoVantage, LLC

I am deeply grateful to my parents, Yoo-ho Ja and Young-gil Kim, and two great teachers, Jonathan Nitzan and Ted Winslow. Thanks to their help and advice, I have been able to pursue my own research.

The following chapters in this book reproduce my prior publications with some revisions.

Chapter 1: Kim, Jongchul. "Money is Rights in Rem: A Note of the Nature of Money." *Journal of Economic Issues* 48, no. 4 (2014): 1005–1019.

Chapter 3: Kim, Jongchul. "How Modern Banking Originated: The London Goldsmith Bankers' Institutionalisation of Trust." *Business History* 53, no. 6 (2011): 939–959.

Chapter 4: Kim, Jongchul. "Modern Politics as a Trust Scheme, and its Relevance to Modern Banking." *Journal of Economic Issues* 47, no. 4 (2013): 807–826.

This work was supported by the Ministry of Education of the Republic of Korea and the National Research Foundation of Korea (NRF-2021S1A5A2A01061947)

Contents

Figures

Tables

Introduction

This introduction explains how the main concepts of this book—property, legal personae, trusts, the hybridity of money and credit, and the hybridity of property and debt—can be embedded into a coherent theory of money.

Persona, Property, Trusts, and Modern Money

The dominant group of social scientists in a particular time period either explicitly or implicitly share a common philosophical perspective that can allow them to work together even if they are researching different subjects. What if it is the perspective that conventional social scientists share is problematic?

Modern Western philosophy, the system that present conventional social science currently follows, has developed two main concepts: person and property. The modern concept of the person originated from the Greek term *persona*, which originally referred to the masks that actors wore on stage. Modern Western philosophy and law have developed this term into a philosophical and legal concept, whereby a person means an independent subject having both reason and free will. A person is not equivalent to a human being but rather something that is conceptually created and becomes effective "by law." For example, not all human beings were treated as "persons" in the West during early modern times. At that time, a married woman was not legally considered a person. She could not defend herself in court, requiring her husband to represent her instead.[1] Nowadays something that is not actually a human being can legally be considered a person: a business corporation (hereafter referred to as "a limited liability joint-stock corporation").

The concept of person is fundamental to the ontology of three identities: the modern nation-state, business corporations, and personal identity (individualism). The modern nation-state and business corporations retain their identities despite changes in their constituents. They are more than just collectives because they make contracts with their members. Because only separate entities can make contracts with one another, the group and its members must be treated as separate. In fact, the modern nation-state and business corporations are assumed to have their own identities, capable of enjoying their own rights and responsibilities independent of those of their members. An individual in

DOI: 10.4324/9781003052210-1

modern society is also assumed to retain her identity and remain the same person despite aging and changing in appearance over time.[2]

The concept of person is paired with the concept of property. The term *property* derives from the Latin *proprius* meaning "one's own, or something private or peculiar to oneself;" thus, the property of man originally meant human attributes such as body, life, liberty, and action.[3] In the first half of the seventeenth century in England, however, the term *property* was broadened to mean not only those human attributes but also material objects such as land owned by a person.[4] This metamorphosis created the ideology of the "birthright" of an Englishman to have property—not only liberty but also land. This ideology had a direct political impact when the English Parliament used the ideology in its struggle against the Crown, finally achieving victory in the Glorious Revolution of 1688.

With this metamorphosis, the dominant group of early modern Western philosophers, which included John Locke and G. W. Friedrich Hegel, regarded the essence of human existence as a simple relationship between person and property. It regarded all the attributes of human beings and their possessions—such as body, labor, life, liberty, and land—as property, and presupposed the concept of a person who could possess these properties in exclusivity. This conceptualization was widely shared among British intellectuals in the seventeenth century, and Locke is their representative who made these widespread ideas of person and property into a coherent theory. Then in the nineteenth century, Hegel took over the conception.[5]

This book argues that the above three personae—the modern state, business corporations, and individuals—would not so much be naturally-given objective phenomena as the products of a modern ontological and political project. For Friedrich Nietzsche and Alfred North Whitehead who criticized modern Western philosophy, the idea of the person is one of the significant mistakes that modern Western philosophy made when it is seduced by language. Our language takes the form of "subject and predicate." When modern Western philosophy has mistakenly assumed that reality has the same "subject-predicate" structure as language, we separate the subject from the predicate, or the "doer" from the "doing."[6] Seduced by language, modern Western philosophers mistakenly assumed that this imagined abstract subject—the doer—which is separate from the predicate, is the self that creates the "doing." Rene Descartes' proposition, *cogito, ergo sum* (I think, therefore I am), which kickstarted modern Western philosophy, is just such an example. Descartes thought that because "doing (for Descartes, thinking)" is occurring, there should be a subject that creates "the thinking." This mistake of assuming that reality mirrors the subject-predicate linguistic structure is represented in the modern philosophical ideas of person and property: a person is equivalent to a subject, and property is equivalent to a predicate. As Nietzsche and Whitehead argued, however, "the doing is everything: there is no substratum or doer behind the doing."[7] In other words, there is no separation between the doer and doing, between subject and predicate, and between person and property—the essence of human existence does not take the form of person and property.

The modern concepts of person and property have not remained a mere tool for understanding society; they have become a dominant way of constructing a society. Here, epistemology has become ontology, in that men have created the world in the way in which they have interpreted it. This book argues that the modern concepts of person and property have constituted the ontological nature of modern money.

Currently, there is no academic endeavor that theorizes how the modern ideology and institutions of person and property constitute the essence of modern money. This lack of theorization is preventing us from fully understanding the nature of modern money. For example, the credit theory of money, which has recently become popular among heterodox scholars, argues that money is credit, i.e., creditor-debtor relations.[8] Unfortunately, this theory neglects the distinctive nature of the capitalist creditor-debtor relations, which are different from their pre-modern form. Although creditor-debtor relations have existed for millennia, their ubiquity in modern times is unprecedented. What has made them so widespread? What differentiates their capitalist form from their pre-capitalist one? This book argues that modern money is more than creditor-debtor relations. It argues that modern money is both *the combination of creditor-debtor relations with the above three personae* and *the combination of creditor-debtor relations with property*.

These combinations are known as a trust. In the past, I have argued that a trust is central to an adequate understanding of the capitalist institutions of modern banking, business corporations, and representative democracy. However, whenever I present this argument to academic audiences, their response is almost always one of two kinds. If the audience consists of social scientists, most of them simply do not know what a trust is. Therefore, I have to explain everything, from the ABCs of a trust to its broader social implications, and there is rarely enough time to explain everything in sufficient detail. By contrast, if my audience consists of lawyers, they often only want to define a trust in its technical legal sense and resist extending this legal concept into an interdisciplinary social science concept with broader social implications. Their resistance is understandable when one realizes that law schools in the United States train lawyers as practitioners rather than legal theorists. For them, no Ph.D. in law is available (except at Yale University), and they rarely have a chance to study in the program of the Doctor of the Science of Law (J.S.D.) or the Doctor of Juridical Science program (J.S.D.) because only a few schools offer this program, and they mostly offer it to international students. Practitioners are not concerned with the origins and evolution of a trust, the social and moral motives behind it, or how its evolution has affected or shaped society. In spite of this resistance, however, attempts to extend a trust into an interdisciplinary concept are nothing new. In the late seventeenth century, Locke argued that representative democracy is a trust, and in early eighteenth-century England a joint-stock corporation was legally considered a trust.[9]

Legal textbooks define the trust in two ways. According to one definition, the trust is a double-ownership that makes it possible for two exclusive ownership claims to exist simultaneously over the same asset—legal ownership claimed by trustees and equitable ownership claimed by beneficiaries. According to the other definition, the trust is a hybrid between property and debt. The trusted property is the trustees' property because they obtain its legal ownership. But, at the same time, it is the trustees' debt because they must pay benefits to beneficiaries permanently.

The foremost motive of a trust has been for the owner both to enjoy privileged property rights and to avoid the legal responsibilities attached to these property rights. A property owner avoids legal responsibilities by transferring legal ownership of the property to trustees, while retaining its equitable ownership, thereby continuing to enjoy the benefits of ownership. Since the early thirteenth century, the landed class in England have used the concept of the trust—and its feudal form, the *use* of land—for various reasons, such as when an individual wanted "to escape from his creditors; or feared that a felony conviction would result in the loss" of his property and lands.[10] However, the most important external force that the trust or *use* intended to avoid was feudal duties and paying taxes to the rulers or the state.

It has always been the rich and powerful who have used the trust. The motivations that led to the invention of the *use* were, as Sir Edward Coke described in 1594, "fear and fraud: fear in times of troubles and civil wars to save their inheritances from being forfeited; and fraud to defeat due debts, lawful actions, wards, escheats, mortmains, etc."[11] However, these fears regarding inheritance were unjustifiable according to the feudal principle of land tenure, which stated that a contract was made between two individuals—a king and a lord—and not between a king and a lord's family.[12] The inheritance of land to the lord's descendants was justified only when the duties and services of a tenant were also transferred to a descendant. Thus, in traditional English law, if an inheritor in a direct or collateral line did not exist, or if an inheritor was underage and thus could not perform those duties and services when the landowner died, the Crown took the land as *bona vacantia* [unclaimed goods].[13] To avoid this taxation, landowners or tenants would transfer the ownership of the land to a number of feoffees but allowed their heirs to retain an equitable interest in the land. Even in the present day, tax avoidance is the motive that "dominates all others in the context of the creation of trusts in modern law,"[14] and is effectively fraudulent. This book argues that in modern times this scheme of the trust has been extended to the three capitalist institutions of modern banking, business corporations, and representative democracy.

In order to enjoy privileged property rights without taking social responsibilities, a trust uses two schemes: a hybrid scheme of ownership as seen in Figure 1 (a), and a specific governance scheme as seen in Figure 1 (b). In a hybrid scheme of ownership, a trust is a combination between property rights and creditor-debtor relations; i.e., a hybrid of property (property rights) and debt (contractual rights).[15] As seen in the above case of the lord who wanted to unlawfully leaves land to descendants, the trusted land is a hybrid of property and debt. It is a *property* of the trustees because the trustees took legal

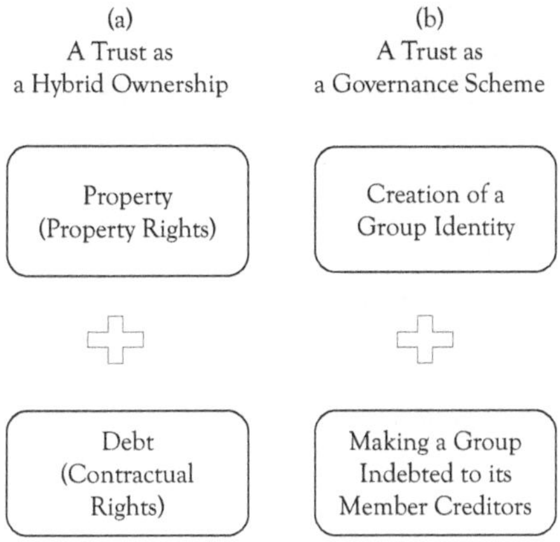

Figure 1 A Trust

ownership of the land, but it is also a *debt* of the trustees (in other words, a *credit* given to trustees) because the trustees must pay a dividend to the beneficiaries of the trust regularly and in perpetuity. By contrast, the settlers and beneficiaries are no longer legal owners; instead, they become *creditors* who can demand a dividend and can avoid the responsibility of returning the land to the king. However, the settlers and beneficiaries simultaneously remain *equitable owners* according to whose order the trustees must use the land. To sum up, a trust is a Janus-faced creation that constantly turns its face to enjoy the benefits and reduce the costs of property and debt. Due to the hybridity, double-ownership is established whereby legal ownership is enjoyed by the trustees, and equitable ownership is enjoyed by the settlers and beneficiaries. Arguably, modern money could be said to have originated from this hybrid and double-ownership when adapted to finance.

A trust is also a governance scheme that creates a personified group and governs it by making it a debtor to its members. By creating such a permanent personal identity of a trust and making it a debtor, the original owner and their descendants can enjoy equitable ownership *permanently*. This governance scheme has been extended to modern personified groups including business corporations and nation-states. When an individual, such as a king, dies, his/her debt obligations are canceled as well. Through a trust, however, debts can be maintained permanently when they are owed by the imaginary group of a trust, such as the modern state, whose identity and obligations are maintained permanently through replaceable representative politicians.

This concept of a trust is largely absent in classical works, including those of Karl Marx and Max Weber, on the origin and nature of capitalism. However, some scholars in the twentieth century, including Ronald Stanley Neale and Frederic Maitland, have argued that the central role of a trust is in the origin and nature of capitalism. Neale argued that the class of landowners and the legal nature of their ownership of land—particularly regarding trusts—provided the legal and institutional framework "which alone made possible the development of industrial capitalism in England," and that the bourgeoisie of the eighteenth century merely borrowed a trust from the landowners almost intact.[16] Maitland also argued that the essence of capitalism cannot be explained through the concept of contract, but rather through a specific form of ownership and collective—a trust.[17] He further argued that the effects of a trust extend across the economy and politics, from the creation of joint-stock arrangements with limited liability to the idea of trusteeship that informed the justifications for imperialism.[18] This book develops these two theorists' *intuitive* arguments into a coherent and complete argument covering the three capitalist institutions mentioned earlier: modern money, limited liability joint-stock corporations, and modern nation-states. By doing so, this book offers a new theory of capitalism that characterizes the nature of capitalism as a trust.

Figure 2 briefly describes what I have explained so far. The ontology of person-property constitutes the philosophical background of trusts, and the specific forms of trusts are the three capitalist institutions.

Table 1 shows the double-ownership in the three capitalist institutions. A trust has never been used to explain modern banking—a perplexing omission, since modern banking and the law of a trust have originated from the same historical context in the same time period and have identical mechanisms. As a trust, modern banking establishes a double-ownership scheme. Two groups in modern banking—a bank and the bank depositors—are the exclusive owners of the same cash kept safely in the bank's vaults. To prevent

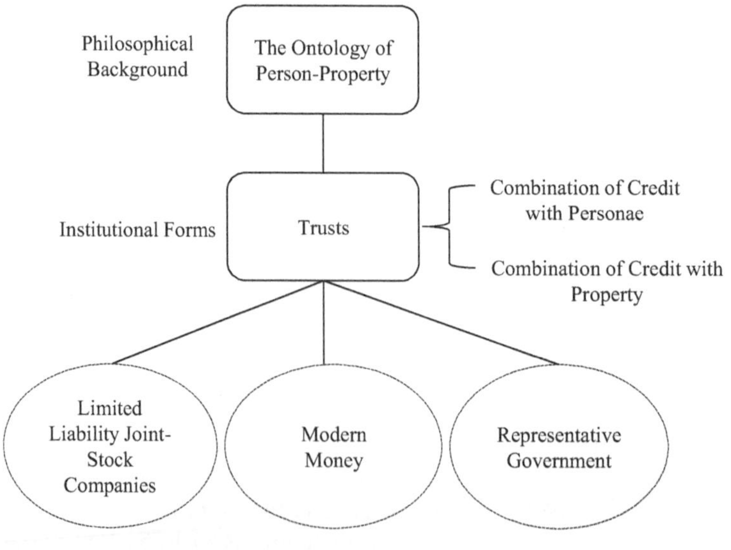

Figure 2 The Outline of Main Concepts of the Book

Table 1 Double Ownership in the Three Trusts

Trust schemes / *Double-ownership*	*Modern banking*	*Representative democracy*	*Joint-stock corporations*
Legal owners	Bank	The state or the people (represented by elected politicians)	Corporation (represented by managers)
Equitable owners	Depositors	People	stockholders

a misunderstanding, I am discussing demand-deposit-taking rather than time-deposit-taking. In demand deposits, a single quantity of cash creates two cash balances of the same amount: one for the bank and the other for the depositors. Consequently, the loaning of demand deposits to third parties by commercial banks create a money supply, which is a mechanism through which private bankers create money. This double-ownership scheme was constructed because commercial banking is a hybrid between a loan transaction (by which depositors are creditors to a bank) and a deposit transaction (by which depositors have property rights). On the one hand, it is a deposit transaction because the depositors expect the bank to keep their money safe and have a right to withdraw the money at any time on demand, meaning that the depositors retain practical ownership of the money. On the other hand, modern banking is also a loan transaction, in which the ownership of a loan is transferred from creditors to debtors, i.e., from depositors to a bank. Thanks to this transfer, banks can lend deposits in their own names to third parties as well as attain and retain the ownership title to the loans.

"The principle of shareholder irresponsibility" in corporate law can be considered another typical example of a trust. In limited liability joint-stock corporations, double-ownership is established: equitable ownership enjoyed by shareholders, and legal ownership possessed by the corporations themselves. Furthermore, the hybridity of property and debt is also established. On the one hand, in corporate law, shareholders are not legal owners of a corporation's assets because corporate law assumes that the shareholders have transferred the property rights of the assets to the corporation. Since shareholders do not have property rights in the assets, corporate law does not ask the shareholders for any form of legal responsibility for a corporation's use of the assets. Here, shareholders are essentially *creditors* who transfer legal ownership of the money to debtors and thus no longer take any responsibility for the debtors' use of the money. Here, the corporation is the *debtor* to its shareholders, as it pays a regular dividend. On the other hand, however, major shareholders are *owners*, controlling the corporation through their voting rights for electing and dismissing directors and deciding important managerial issues.

Likewise, representative democracy can be considered a trust, establishing double-ownership. On the one hand, according to the modern doctrine of public trust, representative politicians possess the legal ownership of sovereignty. They decide the interests of the people and have absolute power to govern people according to these interests. Therefore, unless this created interest betrays the will of the people, people cannot overthrow a representative government.[19] On the other hand, sovereign power is entrusted by—or borrowed from—its equitable owner, people. Public trustees have been charged with a moral and legal obligation to exclude their own interests and promote the will of the people. Consequently, under this doctrine, the power to rule over people is a hybrid, double-ownership scheme. On one hand, it is the representative politicians' property because they decide what the interests of the people are; on the other hand, it is borrowed power that ultimately belongs to people.

Interestingly, the concept of the trust arose out of the violation of the Roman legal principle that strictly divided property rights from creditors' rights. This principle considered any mixing of these two rights to be a crime. Among Western countries during early modern times, England was the least affected by Roman law and had developed its own legal tradition distinct from that of Continental Europe. My discussion of the trust helps explain why representative democracy, the modern business corporation, and modern banking originated from and have developed most successfully in Anglo-American countries, where the culture of trusteeship predominates. Furthermore, my study contributes to extending the concept of the trust beyond its narrow legal boundaries, opening the door to an interdisciplinary study that spans both economics and politics.

If the trust is central to understanding the capitalist institutions of modern banking, corporations, and representative democracy, two questions arise: First, if these three seemingly unconnected phenomena can be defined by the same concept, how similar are their natures? Second, did they evolve together and mutually contribute to each other's evolution? To the best of my knowledge, no one has thus far examined these two questions together. By studying these questions in conjunction with each other, one can understand the nature of capitalism, since it should arguably be understood as something in which an ethos has evolved and transmuted into diverse forms: here, the ethos is a trust, and the diverse forms are the three capitalist institutions.

Money Economy Versus Credit Economy

Money shortage has been considered a major social problem in capitalism, causing trade stagnation and underemployment. Money is often hoarded privately and thus often disappears from the economy. Thus, monetary expansion has therefore been considered indispensable for solving debt crises: when financial crises occur and thus the hoarding propensity of money by private investors becomes intense, creating money and pouring it into the economy has always been considered the optimal solution for rescuing a highly indebted economy suffering liquidity shortages. The capitalist money economy initially developed two major methods to create more money. Historically, the first method was to colonize other countries around the world, loot their gold and silver, and mint it into money. The second method is to transform credit claims into money by granting creditors property rights. This book will examine how this second method developed.

The first method exacted physical violence on the people of colonized countries. The second method is also socially and morally repugnant for several reasons. First, it makes whole societies indebted, in that it puts whole societies into captivity, fastened with the chains of debt. This indebtedness forces societies to pursue exponential growth. Highly indebted social actors including governments, business corporations, and individuals, tend to push their economy to grow exponentially since growth will allow them to accrue income by which they can then pay off the growing interest on their debt. They also tend to look at everything around themselves as a potential source of income, urgently feeling to need to repay the interest and principals of their growing debt. The second reason is that it grants privileged rights to bankers and financiers who are engaged in the process of money creation. They enjoy having the power to decide where this created money is allocated and, by doing so, decide which industry the resources of a society are allocated to. When they make these decisions, their only concern is pecuniary, with other social values including helping the poor and preserving the environment largely rendered irrelevant. The third reason is that it contributes to worsening inequality. Groups of capitalists and industries that can initially borrow newly created money at cheap rates can also acquire social resources before other people and industries, thereby gaining an advantage over others when winning competition in business. Furthermore, the bankers, financiers, and those who can initially borrow money at cheap rates have the power to impose inflation taxes on society since the newly created money will eventually cause inflation. All these privileges that they enjoy have contributed to growing inequality. Finally, it has created an economic cycle of boom and bust. Resources are overexploited during boom times and then wasted during a recession. This unsustainable drive to exploit natural resources has now reached an ecological tipping point with the effects of anthropogenic climate change.

Nevertheless, there have been economic systems throughout history where money shortages were never a problem. According to David Graeber, credit and money economies have been alternating across the Eurasian continent for the last 5,000 years.[20] A credit economy is an economy where credit instruments, such as bills of exchange, are the dominant medium of exchange, while a money economy is an economy where the medium of exchange is money, such as coins or fiat money. According to Graeber, the money economy, which includes the current capitalist money economy, predominated during periods of widespread warfare and plunder or during periods of ruthless materialism and self-interest, while the credit economy tended to dominate during periods of relative peace or across networks of trust without the violent intervention of the state.[21] In a credit economy, monetary expansion was not required because money was stockpiled in temples or a public bank and *rarely* used as a medium of exchange. Moreover, a credit economy does not pour money into the economy to solve debt crises; rather, it directly restructured the social relationship between creditors and debtors. For example, the Babylonian and Sumerian civilizations had a highly developed credit economy, and peasant debts were often canceled by emperors during periodic "redemptions." This cancelation of consumer debt was often seen as recovering the relationship of equality, strengthening social order, and contributing to the maintenance of the credit economy. This way of recovering equality between rich creditors and poor debtors differed from the way a money economy treated debt crises: a money economy would pour money into the economy so that the *rich creditors could still be repaid*. Thus, in a money economy, a society can escape from debt crises but will have to maintain and cultivate inequality between rich creditors and poor debtors. A similar phenomenon happened in recent quantitative easing measures that were introduced to save the global financial system after the financial crisis of 2008. Quantitative easing has now worsened inequality within developed countries—mainly by inflating the prices of assets, such as stocks and real estate. It has also worsened inequality between the developed countries that implemented it and the rest of the world, because wealth is transferred to developed countries for free and disproportionately from low-income countries.[22] This mechanism will be discussed in more detail in Chapter 7.

Structure of the Book

The remainder of this book is structured as follows. Chapter 1 discusses the origin of the legal concept of property and argues that it was strongly intertwined with the birth of a money economy. It also argues that the legal concept of property was created in the image of money during the late Roman Republic. The later part of this book demonstrates that contemporary banking, including commercial and shadow banking, creates money by mirroring credit in the image of property. Consequently, this book argues that money and property have tended to mirror each other historically.

Chapter 2 analyzes the modern ontologies of person and property and refers particularly to John Locke, whose ideas have constituted the philosophical foundation of modern Western society. The chapter demonstrates that Locke's concept of property ontologically restores the Roman legal concept of property, which was created during the later Roman Republic. According to Nietzsche and Whitehead, modern Western ontology mistakenly assumes that reality has the same structure as the linguistic structure of subject-predicate. This chapter shows that Locke's ontology of person-property makes the same mistake.

Chapter 3 demonstrates that the mistaken idea of property constitutes the ontological foundation of modern money. As a demonstration of this, the chapter analyzes how a trust, which is a hybrid between property and debt, contributed to the development of modern money in late-seventeenth-century England.

Chapter 4 analyzes how the governance scheme of trusts, which creates personified groups—such as the modern state and business corporations—and makes them debtors, contributed to the evolution of modern bank money into *de facto* national currency in early modern England. It examines why the concept of legal personae and trusts is critical to our understanding of modern money. Credit economies that existed before capitalism created institutions to protect debtors or often revived the social order by canceling consumer debts. The capitalist credit economy, by contrast, considers strict debt obligations to be both a supreme moral good and a way of securing social order. It creates a political scheme to ensure that debt obligations are strictly fulfilled. This scheme is a trust. The trust transforms the debts of individuals, whose death can cancel their debt obligations, into the debts of imaginary groups, such as the modern state, whose identities and obligations are permanently maintained by replaceable trustees. The chapter further argues that modern banking could not have developed without this politics of trusts.

Chapter 5 uses the notions of property and trusts to explain the nature of shadow banking in the twentieth and twenty-first centuries. As examined, the legal concept of property was created in the image of money during the late Roman Republic. This chapter argues that shadow banking creates money by mirroring credit in the image of property. That is, it is a social institution by which financiers obtain the privilege of enjoying both contractual rights and property rights. Moreover, it argues that this privilege ultimately led to the financial crisis of 2008.

Chapter 6 discusses two cases of combining creditor-debtor relations with a social institution of persons: limited liability joint-stock corporations and quantitative easing. It argues that this combination is a trust and a capitalist method through which property rights can be enjoyed while avoiding legal responsibilities.

Chapter 7 examines the nature of the post-neoliberal form of finance. The neoliberal form of finance started to fall after the financial crisis of 2008, and the answer to the question of what a post-neoliberal form of the economy would look like revolves around the debate on the nature of current inflation. In the twentieth century, inflation skyrocketed when the capitalist economy was in crisis and experienced a qualitative change. If we examine the nature of current inflation, we can better understand the economic contradictions that the post-neoliberal form of finance creates. Recently, political struggles have occurred between two opposing ideologies: sound finance and fiscal and monetary expansionism. Currently, expansionists appear to have almost won this ideological struggle. However, this chapter demonstrates that expansionism has also worsened inequality within and between countries as shall be seen in the case of quantitative easing.

I conclude the book in Chapter 8 by commenting on a potential policy that could reform the current financial system from a new perspective. My comment is brief and incomplete, but it offers a direction for future research. The current discourse focuses on how to externally regulate the greedy and ill-behaved finance sector by adding more regulatory schemes and governmental intervention. However, what this book discusses infers that we need a reform policy in a more fundamental way. One principle for this reform policy would be to prevent all financial investors from enjoying both property and contractual rights simultaneously. The book ends with a discussion of an alternative principle of wealth redistribution, which is named "cooperative basic capital."

Notes

1 Pateman, "Self-Ownership," 23.
2 Locke, *The Works*.
3 Olivecrona, "Appropriation," 219.
4 Pipes, *Property*, 30–31.
5 The philosophical controversy over the concept of the person revolves around the question as to whether we can reasonably say that there is something unchanging by itself, but which undergoes change over time. For example, in early modern times, two Western philosophers, Locke and David Hume, dissented in this controversy. Locke argued that every man has a personal identity; i.e., a "person" that retains the same identity over time, despite the aging process. By contrast, Hume refuted this argument, saying that no "person" continues over time. Most of the early modern Western philosophers including Hegel were on Locke's side. Furthermore, the ontological idea that individuals and groups are believed to have their own personal identities is culturally specific. Non-Western societies have developed different ontologies. For example, in Buddhism, all existences are considered to have no intrinsic personal identity: "All existences are empty" is written in the Heart Sutra. In Buddhism, having a personal identity is the result of Karma that an individual's ignorant behavior has facilitated and which a Buddhist tries to ultimately overcome.
6 Nietzsche, *Genealogy*, 45; Whitehead, *Process*, 167.
7 Nietzsche, *Genealogy*, 25.
8 Ingham, *Money*.
9 Ireland, "Corporate Law," 40; Pennington, "Shares," 141.
10 Martin, *Modern Equity*, 8.
11 Chudleigh's case (1594) 1 Co Rep 113b at 121b.
12 Macfarlane, *Modern World*, 59–72.
13 Martin, *Modern Equity*, 9.
14 Martin, *Modern Equity*, 43. Recently, however, to protect their tax base, many jurisdictions, including the U.K., are enacting rules that make traditional trust structures less effective vehicles for tax avoidance.
15 Maitland argues that a trust is the hybrid of property and debt (Maitland, *Collected Papers*, 314.)
16 Neale, "Bourgeoisie," 95–101.
17 Maitland, *Collected Papers*.
18 Maitland, *Collected Papers*.
19 Goodhart, "English Contributions," 671–688.
20 Graeber, *Debt*.
21 Graeber, *Debt*, 213.
22 Hudson, "Quantitative Easing."

Bibliography

Goodhart, A. L. "English Contributions to the Philosophy of Law." *Columbia Law Review* 48, no. 5 (1948): 671–688.

Graeber, David. *Debt: The First 5,000 Years*. Brooklyn, NY: Melville House Publishing, 2011.

Hudson, Michael. "U.S. 'Quantitative Easing' is Fracturing the Global Economy." Working Paper, *Levy Economics Institute of Bard College* (2010).

Ingham, Geoffrey. *The Nature of Money*. Cambridge, UK: Polity Press, 2004.

Ireland, Paddy. "Corporate law and the Myth of Shareholder Ownership." *Modern Law Review* 62, no. 1 (1999): 32–57.

Locke, John. *The Works of John Locke, Vol. II*. London: W. Sharpe and Son, 1823.

Macfarlane, Alan. *The Making of the Modern World*. London: Palgrave, 2002.

Maitland, Frederic. *The Collected Papers of Frederic William Maitland*, edited by H.A.L. Fisher, Vol. 3. Cambridge: Cambridge University Press, 1911.

Martin, Jill. E. *Modern Equity*. London: Sweet & Maxwell Ltd., 2001.

Neale, Ronald. "The Bourgeoisie, Historically, Has Played a Most Revolutionary Part." In *Feudalism, Capitalism and Beyond*, 95–101. London: Edward Arnold, 1975.

Nietzsche, Friedrich. *On the Genealogy of Morality*. Indianapolis: Hackett Publishing Corporation, Inc., 1998.

Olivecrona, Karl. "Appropriation in the State of Nature: Locke on the Origin of Property." *Journal of the History of Ideas* 35, no. 2 (1974): 211–230.

Pateman, Carole. "Self-Ownership and Property in the Person: Democratization and a Tale of Two Concepts." *The Journal of Political Philosophy* 10, no. 1 (2002): 20–53.

Pennington, Robert. "Can Shares in Companies Be Defined?" *The Corporate Lawyer* 10, no. 7 (1989): 141.

Pipes, Richard. *Property and Freedom*. Toronto: Random House of Canada, 2000.

Whitehead, Alfred North. *Process and Reality*. New York: Free Press, 1978.

1 Money and Property

This chapter analyzes how the legal concept of property was created in the image of money during the late Roman Republic. It identifies that the concept of property rights from its origin is intertwined with the concept of money. The latter part of this book demonstrates that contemporary banking, including commercial and shadow banking, creates money by mirroring credit in the image of rights in rem. Consequently, this book argues that the development of money and the legal concept of property has been intertwined; that is, money and rights in rem have tended to mirror each other historically.

Roman law strictly divided property rights (rights *in rem*) from contractual rights (rights *in personam*). However, this traditional division was undermined by a new legal conception of property, described by Wesley Hohfeld in the early twentieth century.[1] He suggested that property rights (rights *in rem*) be understood as a kind of rights *in personam*, and that the difference between these two rights is merely quantitative. Rights *in personam* avail against *one or a few definite* persons, while rights *in rem*, by contrast, avail against persons who constitute a *very large and indefinite* class of people.[2] Under the influence of this new conception of property, sociology and economics have begun to understand property as a bundle of rights consisting of any claims, including rights, duties, privileges, and liabilities.

A similar reduction has occurred in conventional monetary theory. In conventional monetary theory, the function of money that fundamentally distinguishes money from credit—finalizing creditor-debtor relations—has come to be regarded as outdated. Thus, it is no longer included in the famous triad of the functions of money: (i) a medium of exchange; (ii) a unit of account; and (iii) a store of value. That is, the difference between money and credit is no longer a major concern of conventional monetary theory. This trend has even extended to a heterodox theory of money. The post-Keynesian school of economics—including the theories of Geoffrey Ingham and L. Randall Wray—argues that money is credit and that the difference between money and credit is merely quantitative. Ingham argues that traditional credit instruments, such as bills of exchange, are claims against a single or small number of definite debtors who issue or transfer them, and that by contrast, money, such as gold coins and cash, are claims against everyone in a society.[3]

DOI: 10.4324/9781003052210-2

The reduction of rights *in rem* to rights *in personam* and of money to credit has a similar motive. The blurring of the line between property rights and contractual rights in the twenty-first century reflected the doctrine of the welfare state that dominated in the Golden Age of capitalism after World War II. At that time, by reducing rights *in rem* to rights *in personam*, legal theorists, "sought to undermine the notion that property is a natural right, and thereby smooth the way for welfare state intervention in regulating and redistributing property."[4] Similarly, credit theorists of money sought to undermine "the ideological naturalization of money," a belief that money is "based on the value of a supposedly natural commodity," and thus smooth the way for welfare state intervention in producing, regulating, and redistributing money.[5]

However, after the late 1970s, when neo-liberalism began to emerge and the natural rights of property owners began to be re-emphasized, legal and institutional economic theorists have rediscovered the classical distinction between property and contracts.[6] For example, E. G. Furubotn and R. Richer distinguish relative property rights (what this book calls "contractual rights") from absolute property rights (what this book calls "property rights") and examine how the latter should be distributed to solve negative externalities and increase efficiency.[7]

However, this rediscovery has not yet successfully applied to the understanding of finance. Thus, under this influence of the twentieth century's conception of property as a bundle of rights, institutional economists' effort to explain the nature of modern money is not very successful. For example, recently, Gunnar Heinsohn and Otto Steiger have tried to use the notion of property to explain how modern banks create money.[8] However, unfortunately, because they cannot distinguish between property rights and contractual rights, they fail to offer an accurate analysis of how modern commercial banks transform contractual credit claims to money. Two heterodox schools of economics, Post-Keynesian and Austrian, have also suffered from the twentieth century's concept of property. Because they failed to distinguish between property and contract, they have emphasized only one side of the two and have failed to notice the hybrid nature of the bank deposit of modern banks. To prevent a misunderstanding, I am here discussing demand deposit-taking rather than time deposit-taking. In fact, these two groups of heterodox economists agree with the fact that modern banks create money with loan-making activities: when a bank loans money to a borrower, it opens a demand deposit account for a borrower and then makes new deposits into the account. However, these two schools disagree with what the modern bank loans to the borrower. Post-Keynesian economists argue that what the modern bank loans to the borrower is the *bank's debt*,[9] while Austrian school of economists argue that it is the *deposit* that the bank embezzles from its original depositor.[10] Due to this basic disagreement, these two schools have ignored and ceased to learn from each other. However, this mutual ignorance is unfortunate because both schools' arguments have their own basis in truth, even if they are partially true. Arguably, these two schools capture only one side of the same coin but fail to capture the whole picture.

Contrary to this Post-Keynesian claim, what the modern bank loans to the borrower is more than the bank's debt. It is both the bank's debt and the bank's property. Under the present law, depositors in demand deposits are creditors to a bank. Because the bank opens a demand deposit account for a borrower and makes new deposits into the account, the borrower become a depositor. Here, because the borrowers are depositors, what the bank loans to the borrowers is the bank's debt in which the bank becomes the *debtor* to the borrowers. But at the same time, what the bank loans to the borrowers is the deposits newly created by the contract between the bank and its original depositors, and thus the bank enjoys the *property rights* of the newly-created deposit and thus can loan to the borrowers. Here, the bank becomes the *creditor* of the borrowers. Thus, what the modern bank loans to the borrower is a hybrid between *property rights* (newly created deposit) and *contractual claims* (banks' debt). Post-Keynesian economists fail to identify this mutual indebtedness and the coexistence of two disparate legal categories, property and debt, in the modern banks' money-creating activity.

Austrian school of economists acknowledges that the bank has a property right on what it loans to the borrower. However, these economists wrongly argue that the bank embezzles this property right from the original depositor. Contrary to Austrian economists' argument, as shall be seen in Chapter 3, the bank does not embezzle it, because the original depositor allows the bank to use his/her deposits in the bank's name and discretion. Thus, the money the bank loans to the borrowers is not the deposits embezzled from the original depositors but the deposits newly created by the contract between the banks and the original depositor. Because the bank and the original depositor contract to loan "what they do not actually own" to a borrower, what the bank loans to the borrower is *the bank's debt* to the borrower as well. Here, Austrian school of economics fail to identify this mutual indebtedness between the bank and the borrower and the coexistence of two disparate legal categories, property and debt, in the modern banks' money-creating activity. As a result, the two schools fail to understand that the creation of modern money by commercial banks entails the process of making a hybrid between property and contract and between *property rights* (newly created deposit) and *contractual claims* (banks' debt).

Furthermore, the post-Keynesian reduction of money to credit seems to seriously limit one's understanding of the nature of modern money. As shall be seen, modern money was institutionalized when it maneuvered around the division between money and credit and between rights *in rem* and rights *personam*. This book will analyze how this maneuver became one of the main causes of the financial crisis of 2008. Thus, it is crucial to understand the difference between money and credit and between rights *in rem* and rights *personam* if one is to understand the nature of modern finance and the cause of the financial crisis.

This study makes three analogies: an analogy between money and property, an analogy between credit and rights *in personam*, and an analogy between the capitalist money and the hybrid of rights *in rem* and rights *in personam*. The second analogy is self-evident because credit transactions belong to rights *in personam* at law.

The later chapters of this book examine the third analogy, between the capitalist money and the hybrid of rights *in rem* and rights *in personam*. This analogy only emerged relatively recently with the advent of capitalism. Capitalist money is generated when the law grants creditors, who can enjoy rights *in personam*, with rights *in rem*. This hybridity between rights *in rem* and rights *in personam* is an essential characteristic of modern money. Here, modern money includes, among other things, the bank money of commercial banks, MMF shares, and repos. This book further defines the capitalist money as a trust, because a hybrid of rights *in rem* and rights *in personam* by law is a trust. This hybridity is far more than a reduction of rights *in rem* to rights *in personam* and of money to credit. It is a Janus-faced creation that constantly changes its face to enjoy the benefits and reduce the costs of both sides.

This chapter analyses how the first analogy of money and rights *in rem* has been historically constructed. That is, it analyzes how money and rights *in rem* began to have a similar pattern and began to mirror each other. This first analogy has a relatively long history that began in a society in which a new concept of property—*dominium* or rights *in rem*—was first settled at law, and in which money became a predominant medium for social relations. These two phenomena emerged simultaneously in the late Roman Republic. Money is not necessarily the same thing across time and societies. But when the first analogy was settled—that is, when money and rights *in rem* began to have a similar pattern and mirror each other—money, in the modern sense, more or less emerged. That is, money became something that modern economics characterizes as having four functions: (i) a medium of exchange; (ii) a unit of account; (iii) a store of value; (iv) and a finalization of debt.

1.1. Analogy

Through this book, I hope to shed new light on the nature of money because the analogy is not a mere metaphor. It is a real historical construction, in which the development of the legal concept of rights *in rem* and money are intertwined. I argue that money in the modern sense must be understood as a historical construction of both law and the economy, especially the legal concepts of property and money.

The analogical argument that money is rights *in rem* grows out of a philosophical perspective that considers analogy to be a real force rather than a mere metaphor. This perspective differs from the modern scientific tradition, especially Newtonian scientific materialism, in which analogy is no longer considered a real force explaining causal relations between phenomena. According to A. N. Whitehead, this abandonment of analogy is unfortunate, and it happened because the Newtonian physical world consists only of inanimate matter—senseless, valueless and purposeless.[11] However, nature purged of these properties is, according to Whitehead, no longer nature. In the Whiteheadian perspective, nature consists of organic actual entities that have feelings and intentions, and thus when they intend to be alike, they attempt to share a similar pattern. In ancient Greek philosophy, analogy is also a real force that organizes the physical world. For example, in Plato's philosophy, a thing attempt to share a similar pattern with another thing when it wants to be like that other thing. Furthermore, analogy is a critical methodological device in legal doctrine, which recognizes that not all possible future contingencies can be captured in statutes or codes, and that rules and legal principles can be transposed to similar circumstances.

As shall be seen, money and rights *in rem* share many similar patterns. The historical development of these similar patterns can be explained, arguably, by analogy. That is, a society has constantly constructed them in each other's image. A similar analogical approach is used by Orlando Patterson (1982) in explaining why the Romans invented the legal concept of rights *in rem*. The Roman concept of rights *in rem* haunted Western law for two thousand years. This Roman understanding of property as a relation between persons and things is a metaphysical *fiction*, as Patterson argues, because it raises the metaphysical question of "how a person's rights can be established as a direct relation between the person and a thing *without the consent of others persons*."[12] Metaphysically, according to Patterson, any form of rights cannot be established without consent of other people. For Patterson, all forms of rights are basically a relation between ourselves and everyone else. If a person can exert her absolute power over her possessions, she can do so because everyone else agrees to refrain from interfering with them and allows her to treat them in any way she likes.[13] Nevertheless, according to Patterson, the metaphysical fiction of rights *in rem* was made into a law in the late Roman Republic. His explanation of how this happened is as follows. The Romans wanted absolute psychological power over a thing. The "thing" in the minds of the Romans was a slave. The Romans needed a new concept of property that allowed them to distinguish slaves from other persons, as slaves became the most rapidly expanding source of wealth in the late Roman Republic. This need could not be fulfilled by the existing concept of property because it regarded property as a set of relationships between persons. Thus, the Romans invented a new concept of property that imitates the image of the relationship between master and slave, where the slave was conceived of as "above all a res (thing), the only human res."[14] Patterson's hypothesis is supported etymologically and economically. Etymologically, the word *dominium*, meaning "absolute private property," denoted slave-master when it first appeared in the third century BC. And economically,

> [i]t can be no accident that the shift in the meaning of "dominium" for slaveholding to the holding of all objects of property in an absolute sense perfectly correlates with the changeover of the Roman economy from one in which slaves were simply one of many objects of property to a society

> in which slaves became one of the two most important sources of wealth and objects of property.[15]

In fact, the image of the masters of slaves fits the image of rights *in rem*. The Roman masters could do anything against their slaves, including killing them without any interference, because slaves were socially dead; they were forcefully ripped from all the social relations that made them human beings.[16] A slave was no longer someone's child, friend, or relative, and thus could no longer be protected by them. If the masters killed non-slaves, they would have to face revenge from the victims' relatives and friends. Analogically, rights *in rem* also grant an owner with the power to rip a thing away from all social relationships with others, thereby allowing the owner to exert absolute power over the thing without any interference of other people.

This book agrees with Patterson's analogical argument but offers another hypothetical analogy about the invention of the idea of rights *in rem*. It argues that the "thing" on the minds of the Romans was slaves *as well* as money. The word *dominium* appeared in the late Roman Republic when hundreds of thousands of slaves were pouring into Italy and Rome became a genuine slave society. Interestingly, in the same period, Roman soldiers not only captured slaves but also plundered precious metals, such as gold, silver, and bronze. Precious metals were also pouring into Italy, coined by those captured slaves, and changed the Roman Republic into a genuine money economy in which coined money became "essential to the life of Roman cities at all social levels."[17] The Romans needed to create a new concept of property that encompassed both new forms of wealth—money *and* slaves. The image the Romans found in coined money was that of the lordship of a king or God. Money can endow its possessor with the ability to cancel any ongoing moral obligations to others, that is, to be totally independent of creditor-debtor relations. Metaphysically it means that by possessing money, its possessor can get everything

Table 1.1 Analogy between Slaver-Masters, Property Owners, and Money Holders

Roman masters' absolute power over slaves	*Property's image*	*Money's image*
• the power to rip slaves from their social relations • slaves are socially dead; they are no longer someone's child or friend and are no longer protected by them • the power to kill slaves without the consent of others • the lordship of a king or God	• the power to rip property from its social relations with other people and thus from its social obligations and duties to others • absolute rights on property, free from interference • the lordship of a king or God	• Finality: the function of finalizing creditor-debtor relations • the power to be free from any obligations to other people • the power to live outside of social relationships • the lordship of a king or God

from society but live outside of social relations because money allows its possessor to cancel any obligations to others. This ability can only be possessed by a king or god. This godlike or king-like image seems to have been one reason, for which Emperor Tiberius declared it "a capital offence to take a coin with the image of Augustus into a brothel or lavatory."[18] This image of a king or god was realized in the new concept of property. *Dominium*, or rights *in rem*, is absolute power over a thing, and this power can only be possessed by a king or God.[19] Thus, this is a reason why this absolute power of property has troubled medieval jurists who thought that if such rights existed, only God could have them.[20] The above table summarizes analogical aspects between slaver-masters, property, and money.

1.2. Property was Created in the Image of Money

So far, I have discussed the godlike image of a "thing" in money and property. Now I will examine what "thing" implies. In order to do so, I first look at the nature and role of "thing" in money (alternatively called money-thing or the thingness of money).

The thingness of money is closely associated with finality—the function of finalizing creditor-debtor relations. As mentioned above, this finality fundamentally differentiates money from credit. Both money and credit can function as media of exchange and be denominated by the same unit of account. Nonetheless, because of its association with finality, the concept of money is the opposite of the concept of credit, which is associated with debt. The transfer of a credit instrument creates a creditor-debtor relation. By contrast, money is anything that is generally acceptable in the *final* settlement of creditor-debtor relations. This finality is closely associated with the "thingness" of money. Precious metals, such as gold and silver, have often been used for coinage because their thingnesses themselves are supposed to have intrinsic precious value. And because of the precious thingness, out of which it was made, money was supposed to have a natural power to settle debt finally. This supposition has been criticized by the credit theory of money, which argues that it is not the intrinsic value of the thing but institutional settings—such as the state's power to tax—that originated money and led to money's famous triad.[21] According to the credit theory of money, the recent immaterial money in electronic and digital form demonstrates that the origin and power of money has nothing do to with the thingness of money.[22] The theory abandons the importance of thingness entirely for an understanding of the origin and nature of money, and argues that money is merely an abstract unit of measure.[23] Here, because both debts and cash are denominated by this unit of measure, the fundamental difference between money and debt (credit) disappears.

Is thingness really useless for an adequate understanding of the nature of money? One can refute the idea that money functions because the thingness of gold and silver is intrinsically valuable. However, one can still assume that a certain way of institutionally imposing a social meaning on the thingness would explain the nature of money. The thing of money has been *socially* empowered to finalize creditor-debtor relations and to cancel any ongoing moral obligations to others. I will look at how this empowerment was socially used in the Roman Republic, and then at how this image of empowerment was recreated by the Romans in the new concept of property—rights *in rem*.

The history of money demonstrates that the thing in money does not need to be made of valuable materials. Mere paper is enough to take the mythical power of money institutionally. Interestingly, the thing in rights *in rem* does not need to be any tangible material either. The legal concept of property as rights *in rem* was developed by natural rights theorists when they resettled the concept on the basis of Roman law around 1400.[24] In natural rights theory, property includes not only material, but also immaterial attributes. All the attributes of a person—including labor, body, and liberty—are treated as a *res* (thing) which the person can own and transfer to other persons.

David Graeber's recent research helps one understand how different ways of institutionalizing the thingness of money creates different kinds of money.[25] In primitive communal societies, which Graeber calls the human economy, mutual obligations between people were not transformed into the idea of debt, according to which everyone *must* pay what she owes. At that time, the modern idea that money can finally settle debt also did not exist. Rather, one important social implication and role of money in the human economy was to acknowledge the impossibility of clearing one's debt. For example, when murder was committed and threatened to cause social discord, a community's leaders arranged reconciliation. The murderer was advised to pay something precious that expressed "just how badly you feel about having just killed his brother in a drunken brawl, and how much you would really like to avoid this becoming the basis for an ongoing blood-feud."[26] However, this money did not mean to extinguish what the murderer owed, because the debt could not be paid in full by anything other than a life.

According to Graeber, the role and social use of money changed significantly when the human economy was transformed into the credit economy and where the idea of debt became dominant.[27] When the idea that a debt must be repaid with an interest, which implies a penalty when delaying a return, became a dominant morality in the credit economy, money became socially empowered to finalize debts.

The role and social use of money changed further, according to Graeber, when the credit economy was transformed to the money economy. The money economy began when coinage was invented around the sixth century BC. One of the main purposes of this invention was to solve debt crises. Some societies tried to mitigate debt crises by distributing to the population coined money, which was endowed with the capability of finalizing one's debt. Roman coinage had the same motive and role. Debt crises in Rome took a form of conflict between the aristocracy and the poor. To prevent the debt peonage of poor peasants to aristocrats and to maintain a free peasantry, Roman society chose the military option of distributing loot plundered from other societies. In the earlier, ancient credit economy, gold, silver, and bronze had been stockpiled in temples. However, now they were plundered by Roman soldiers, minted by slaves captured in war, and distributed to soldiers and the population on a massive scale. Here, coinage became a solution to debt crises.[28] As Graeber writes,

> [t]he traditional date of the first Roman coinage—338 BC—is almost exactly the date when debt bondage was finally outlawed (326 BC). . . . The entire Roman Empire, at its height, could be understood as a vast machine for the extraction of precious metals and their coining and distribution to the military.[29]

In addition to the general military option of distributing coins, coins were also used directly when a debt crisis occurred. For example, in 33 AD, when the moneylenders of Rome attempted to call in all debts, debtors were threatened with having to sell off their land in a rapidly falling market. To solve the debt crisis, Emperor Tiberius provided the debtors with an interest-free loan of one hundred million sestertii.[30] Money was also the direct solution to the debt crisis of the 80s BC. Two measures were implemented. One was the stabilization of the exchange rate between silver *denarii* and copper *asses* by the praetor Gratidianus, and the other was debt reform by L. Valerius Flaccus, which allowed debtors to pay off their debts at a rate of one *as* on the silver *sestertius*.[31] At that time, one *sestertius* was valued at four *asses*. Interestingly, according to historian Michael Crawford, such political interventions did not occur when currency shortages occurred in 63, 49, and 44 BC. The lack of intervention in these instances implies that *coinage was a political measure to solve debt crises rather than an economic measure to encourage commerce*. Even though coinage in Rome played an important role as a medium of exchange, this economic function was not its primary purpose. It was instead "an accidental consequence of the existence of coinage, not the reason for it."[32]

Coinage in the Roman Republic and Empire was a substitute for an old solution to debt crises. Previously, in Babylonian, Sumerian, and other ancient civilizations, debts were cancelled without using money. Rural debts owed by peasants were simply cancelled by the emperor in a periodic "redemption" or "year of jubilation."[33] By contrast, the Romans tried to solve debt crises by introducing coinage. Plundered money was distributed to soldiers, who were the sons of poor farmers, and it allowed them to be free from debt bondage. The difference from the old solution was that money allowed the Romans to solve debt crises *even when creditors were still repaid*, that is, even when creditors' rights were still guaranteed.

The argument that the concept of rights *in rem* was created in the image of money is hypothetical and speculative. I try to persuade readers by explaining social contexts suggesting the plausibility of the argument. I do not argue that such social contexts inevitably lead a society to creating the concept of rights *in rem*, because within the same contexts a society could choose to prevent such a godlike image of money and ownership from becoming predominant.

If the concept of rights *in rem* was created in the image of an object, this object should be essential to everyday life of the Romans. That is, the object should be so essential to their daily existence that people would project the image of the object onto the new legal concept. The candidates for such objects can include slaves, land, and money. The analogy of slaves and rights *in rem* is discussed by Patterson, and I accept his analogy here. Land has been one of the most essential objects to everyday life for a long time. From land, however, it is unlikely that people would draw the idea of an individual's absolute property rights, because land is hardly owned and cultivated by "an" individual. Land was usually possessed by a family rather than an individual, and it was cultivated cooperatively by many people. Land has often been owned by various people at the same time. While its rights of use and cultivation belong to one person, its legal ownership often belongs to another. Today, however, land has become an object of property to which absolute rights are attached. This happened because the concept of absolute property rights was (often violently) applied to land. The process of this application—the legal enclosure of land—in early modern times entailed violence against peasants, and this demonstrates that it is difficult to draw the idea of an individual's absolute property rights from land. Instead of land, I suggest money as a good candidate to be the object from which rights *in rem* are derived. Money is a perfect object of individual *dominium*. It can even be put into an individual's pocket.

Historically, money became essential to everyday life in big military empires such as the Roman Empire, where its armies could plunder large amounts of precious metals from neighboring countries.[34] If money is to be essential to everyday life, it should be coined of various denominations so that it can be used to buy commodities of various prices. In particular, large quantities of money of small denominations should be coined, so that ordinary people could use it as the main means of procuring the products of everyday life and so that the previous credit economy could be replaced by a money economy. Bronze coinage in the Roman Republic had such a small denomination, and it was coined in extraordinarily large quantities because the army under the Republic was originally paid in bronze.[35] After bronze, silver coinage was introduced, and, by end of the republic period, gold coinage had been produced regularly. In the late period of the Republic when the concept of *dominium* was created, money of small and big denominations became the dominant medium of social relations.

Notes

1 Hohfeld, "Fundamental Legal Conceptions."
2 Hohfeld, "Fundamental Legal Conceptions," 718.
3 Ingham, "Revisiting the Credit Theory"; Wray, "Introduction."
4 Merrill and Smith, "Property and Law," 364.
5 Ingham, "Revisiting the Credit Theory," 130.
6 Merrill and Smith, "Property and Law."
7 Furubotn and Richter, *Institutions and Economic Theory*.

8 Heinsohn and Steiger, *Ownership Economics.*
9 Wray, *Modern Money Theory*, 84.
10 Rothbard, *Mystery of Banking.*
11 Whitehead, *Process.*
12 Patterson, *Slavery*, 32.
13 Graeber, *Debt*, 200.
14 Patterson, *Slavery*, 32.
15 Patterson, *Slavery*, 32.
16 Graeber, *Debt*, 168–169.
17 Crawford, "Money and Exchange," 42.
18 Crawford, "Money and Exchange," 47.
19 Graeber, *Debt*, 205.
20 Graeber, *Debt*, 205.
21 Ingham, "Revisiting the Credit Theory"; Wray, "Introduction."
22 Ingham, "Revisiting the Credit Theory."
23 Wray, "Introduction," 9.
24 Graeber, *Debt*, 206.
25 Graeber, *Debt.*
26 Graeber, *Debt*, 60.
27 Graeber, *Debt.*
28 Graeber, *Debt*, 228–229.
29 Graeber, *Debt*, 230–231.
30 Crawford, "Money and Exchange," 46.
31 Crawford, "Money and Exchange," 45.
32 Crawford, "Money and Exchange," 46.
33 Graeber, *Debt*, 64–65 & 81–87.
34 Graeber, *Debt.*
35 Crawford, "Money and Exchange," 47–48.

Bibliography

Crawford, Michael. "Money and Exchange in the Roman World." *The Journal of Roman Studies* 60 (1970): 40–48.

Furubotn, E. G. and R. Richter. *Institutions and Economic Theory. The Contribution of the New Institutional Economics.* Ann Arbor, MI: University of Michigan Press, 2001.

Graeber, David. *Debt: The First 5,000 Years.* New York: Melville House Publishing, 2011.

Heinsohn, Gunnar and Otto Steiger. *Ownership Economics.* New York: Routledge, 2013.

Hohfeld, Wesley N. "Fundamental Legal Conceptions as Applied in Judicial Reasoning." *Yale Law Journal* 26, no. 8 (1917): 710–770.

Huerta de Soto, Jesús. *Money, Bank Credit, and Economic Cycles.* Auburn, AL: Ludwig von Mises Institute, 2009.

Ingham, Geoffrey. "Revisiting the Credit Theory of Money and Trust." In *New Perspectives on Emotions in Finance: The Sociology of Confidence, Fear and Betrayal*, 121–139. New York: Routledge, 2012.

Merrill, Thomas W. and Henry E. Smith. "What Happened to Property and Law?" *Yale Law Journal* 111 (2001): 357–398.

Patterson, Orlando. *Slavery and Social Death: A Comparative Study.* Cambridge. MA: Harvard University Press, 1982.

Rothbard, Murray N. *The Mystery of Banking.* Auburn, AL: Ludwig von Mises Institute, 2008.

Whitehead, Alfred North. *Process and Reality*. New York: Free Press, 1978.
Wray, L. Randall. "Introduction to an Alternative History of Money." Working Paper No. 717, *Levy Economics Institute of Bard College* (2012)
Wray, L. Randall. *Modern Money Theory: A Primer on Macroeconomics for Sovereign Monetary Systems*. New York: Palgrave Macmillan, 2012.

2 Person and Property—Mistaken Ideas

This chapter analyzes John Locke's ontologies of person and property, which has constituted the philosophical foundation of modern Western society. This chapter demonstrates that Locke's concept of property ontologically restores the Roman legal concept of dominium, which was created in the late ancient Roman Republic. According to Friedrich Nietzsche and Alfred North Whitehead, modern Western ontology mistakenly assumes that reality has the same structure as the linguistic structure of subject-predicate. The chapter identifies that Locke's ontology of person-property makes the same mistake, and by identifying this mistake in Locke's ontology of property, this chapter advances an ontological critique that sheds new light on the understanding of the modern concept of property.

The ancient money economy transformed into a credit economy during the Middle Ages, and the law of property rights was abolished.[1] This greatly improved the lives of ordinary people because "the nexus between war, bullion, and slavery [in the money economy] was broken, and conquest and acquisition for their own sake were no longer celebrated" and because there occurred "a widespread movement to control, or even forbid, predatory lending."[2] One of the great theoretical contributions that David Graeber makes is that he corrects our misunderstanding of the Middle Ages. We have a skewed perception that the Middle Ages were little different from the Dark Ages: full of superstition, intolerance, and oppression because we're used to thinking that the Middle Ages was something that only happened in Western Europe.[3] However, according to Graeber, the greatest accomplishments of the Middle Ages in the high level of ordinary people's lives were made in China and the Islamic world where highly developed liberal markets based on credit were commonplace. Although even in the Middle Ages of Western Europe "oppressed medieval serfs might have been, their plight was nothing compared with that of [slaves in Roman Republic and Empire]."[4]

In the seventeenth century in England, however, a money economy and the law of property rights had reemerged. In other words, the modern era began when natural-right theorists resettled the concept of property based on Roman law, and its quintessence was Locke's natural-right theory of property. Locke's concept of property restored the Roman legal concept of *dominium*, and this chapter identifies this fact.

DOI: 10.4324/9781003052210-3

Many intellectuals in seventeenth-century England mistakenly assumed that reality has a subject-predicate structure, identical to linguistics. Locke was a thinker who propounded a coherent theory to this common sense. This chapter identifies that Locke's concept of property makes the same mistake. This identification helps us to advance an ontological critique that sheds new light on the understanding of the modern concept of property.

Scholars have not analyzed Locke's mistake in detail and have therefore been unable to understand why Locke adopted the peculiar concept of private ownership rights that is akin to the Roman legal concept of *dominium*. This chapter argues that this can be traced to the confusion between reality and language.

The remainder of this chapter is structured as follows. Section one shows that Locke's theory of property makes the mistake of assuming that reality has a subject-predicate structure. Section two identifies that Locke's theory of property is akin to the Roman legal concept of *dominium*. It also argues that this analogy between Locke's theory of property and *dominium* occurs as a result of Locke's ontology of person-property, that is, because Locke's theory of property mistakenly presupposes a doer—person—who can claim an exclusive private realm and thus creates a strict distinction between the private and the common. Section three examines an analogy between property, slavery, and money. This analogy arises when we frame human nature in terms of the ontology of person-property, where a person has an absolute sovereign power over property.

2.1. Is Locke's Ontological Formula of "Person-Property" a Case of the Linguistic Structure of "Subject-Predicate"?

Nietzsche criticizes the idea that doing can be separated from the doer. In his *On the Genealogy of Morality*, he criticizes modern Western philosophy for mistakenly presupposing the doer as the cause of doing. On this view, this mistake occurs because modern philosophers wrongly assume that reality shares a structure with language, a subject-predicate structure. For example, we say "lightning flashes." If we believe that reality has this subject-predicate structure, we mistakenly set up "lightning" as the subject who causes the act of "flashing."[5] However, in reality, there is only the event that "lightning flashes." That is, there is no "doer" separate from its "doing"—the doing is everything, and the doing itself is the subject.[6]

This section locates this same mistaken distinction between subject and predicates in Locke's ontological formula of person-property, where a person is the analogue to a subject, and property is the analogue to a predicate. Locke expresses his ontological formula for person-property when offering his theory of property in his *Second Treatise of Government*. His formula implies that the nature of man can be characterized in terms of a relationship between person and property. The following text from Locke provides an example of the formula. Here, the term "possessions" is equivalent to the term "property."[7]

> [A]ll men are naturally in . . . a state of perfect freedom . . . [and] dispose of their possessions and persons as they think fit.[8] Man in that state have an uncontrolled liberty to dispose of his person and possessions[9]; By the same act, therefore, whereby any one unites his person, which was before free, to any commonwealth, by the same he unites his possessions, which were before free, to it also[10]; [H]e be absolute lord of his own person and possessions.[11]

In the below text, Locke lists actions, labor, estates, possessions, and property separately. However, for Locke, property represents all the others. Thus, the following sentences also describe his ontological formula of "person-property":

> [It] is . . . a liberty to dispose and order freely as he lists his person, actions, possessions, and his whole property within the allowance of those laws under which he is[12]; man . . . [is] master of himself, and proprietor of his own person, and the actions or labour of it[13]; It cannot be supposed that they should intend, had they a power so to do, to give any one or more an absolute arbitrary power over their persons and estates[14]; Their persons are free by a native right, and their properties, be they more or less, are their own.[15]

Locke presents his ontology of person-property the most concisely in the sentence that "Every man has a *property* in his own *person*."[16] However, most scholars have mistakenly interpreted the term *property* in the sentence to be an abstract noun meaning "ownership of" or "right to own." For example, in his "Locke on Property," J. P. Day interprets this sentence to mean "Every man has right to own his person."[17] Karl Olivecrona also interprets it as saying "[H]is own person is exclusively his own,"[18] and James Tully interprets it to say that "the right in one's person is exclusive."[19] These interpretations are grammatically implausible, as Locke prefixes property with the indefinite article "a." This means that property cannot be a general, abstract noun but must be a common noun, meaning a concrete object that is capable of being possessed. However, this grammatical rule is ignored by modern scholars to produce the interpretation of the term to mean "ownership." To make their misinterpretation grammatically consistent, some modern scholars remove the article. Judith Richards, Lotte Mulligan, and John K. Graham write: "Locke was being consistent in maintaining his argument that each man, having property in his person, possessed property more satisfactorily protected within rather than outside political society."[20]

Scholars have also misinterpreted the term "person" in this sentence. Modern libertarians identify it with the term "man" and thus believe that the sentence implies "self-ownership."[21] However, Locke consistently and clearly distinguishes between "person" and "man" in both his *Second Treatise of Government* and *An Essay Concerning Human Understanding*.[22] This interpretation also contradicts Locke's main argument that a person and property can be transferred to someone else. If someone has sole ownership over herself, she cannot transfer any part of herself—whether her property or person—to someone else.[23]

Crawford B. Macpherson mistakenly conflates "person" with "personality" here. For Macpherson, "personality" here includes labour, body, and liberty.[24] He interprets the sentence to state that "Everyone has ownership of his personality, that is, ownership of body, labour, liberty and so on." Similarly, Carole Pateman interprets the term "person" to refer to a bundle of property including labor, body, and liberty.[25] Accordingly, she interprets the sentence as "Everyone has ownership of his bundle of property including body, labor, liberty and so on." Both scholars' interpretations are mistaken, because they contradict Locke's clear intention to distinguish "person" from "property."

Locke proceeds to write: "[E]very man has a property in his own person: this nobody has any right to but himself."[26] Here, the demonstrative "this" signifies the noun of the previous sentence—"a property." If the term "this" means "the right to possess," the phrase "any right to" becomes an unnecessary repetition. Thus, the word "this" and the antecedent "a property" cannot be an abstract noun but a common noun, meaning "something capable of being possessed." Locke then discusses what this "something capable of being possessed" is, asserting that it is "labour and work." He argues that if labor—a property existing within a person—is mixed with external nature, then the mixed part of nature becomes the exclusive property of the person. Thus, the phrase "a property" in the sentence that "Every man has *a property* in his own person" refers to the word "labour," where this is treated as a thing capable of being possessed and transferred.

Some scholars would interpret the demonstrative "this" to signify "person" rather than "property." However, this interpretation does not match with Locke's argument. He writes, there is "something that is a man's own but can be mixed, annexed, or joyned with Nature." This is certainly not the person but the property. That is, what a laborer mixes with Nature is labor—the individual's property—not his person. Thus, the demonstrative "this" refers to the antecedent property. To ensure, let us see Locke's own writings:

> [E]very man has a property in his own person: this nobody has any right to but himself. The labour of his body, and the work of his hands, we may say, are properly his. Whatsoever then he removes out of the state that nature hath provided, and left it in, he hath mixed his labour with, and joined to it something that is his own, and thereby makes it his property. . . . For this labour being the unquestionable property of the labourer, no man but he can have a right to what that is once joined to.[27]

The sentence that "this nobody has any right to but himself" is paraphrased at the end of this paragraph into this form: "for this labour being the unquestionable property of the labourer." Locke later writes, "lives, liberties, and estates, which I call by the general name property."[28] Even though he omits labor in this list, labor is certainly property that no one has any right to but the laborer and that can be mixed with nature.

Locke's concept of person exhibits the following five characteristics: (1) equality; (2) continuity; (3) the self as an owner; (4) exclusive territoriality; and (5) extensibility of its exclusive territory.

First, Locke's person is defined as equal among men. Man's attributes and assets make each man different. That is, the appearance of a person's unique body, his/her social status, religion, wealth, and so on, make him/her different from others. However, when these attributes are made separate from the individual, what remains is an abstract person that is equal for everyone. This concept of person contributes to the ideology that everyone is equal before the law.[29]

Second, Locke's abstract person maintains its identity continuously across time. Locke writes, "This personality extends itself beyond present existence to what is past [. . . I]t becomes concerned and accountable, owns and imputes to itself past actions, upon the same ground and for the same reason that it does the present."[30] For Locke, every man has a "personal identity" that "has existed in a continued duration more than one instant,"[31] and this personal identity allows a man to experience reward, punishment, and guilt. If a man is punished for a past wrongdoing, it is because the man in the past is the same man as the one facing punishment, that is, because the man has personal identity. For Locke, the property of a man, including body and assets, changes over time, and therefore, it cannot be the basis of a man's identity. However, "person" is abstract and immutable, so it can be used as a basis for a man's identity.

Third, a "person" is defined as "the owner of property." Locke writes in *An Essay Concerning Human Understanding* that "Person [. . .] is a forensic term appropriating actions and their merit."[32] For Locke, actions and merit are property. In this text, Locke uses the word "appropriate," a word that comes from the Latin root *propri*. The word "property" comes from the Latin *proprius*, meaning "to belong to one's own." Therefore, the term "appropriate" refers to the act of making something a *proprius*, that is, making something a property. Thus, the "person" is the self who owns property. Here, Locke's ontological formula of person-property can be seen again.

Fourth, for Locke, "person" is a man's exclusive territory. In his *Second Treatise of Government*, Locke writes that "being a part" is the same as "being a property." However, these two are generally not considered to be the same. As J. P. Day notes, if a man is a member of a golf club and belongs to this club, we would not say that he/she is the property of the club.[33] The member would become the club's property only when no one can interfere with the club no matter how harshly it treated the member. However, equating "being a part" with "being a property," Locke assumes that "person" has exclusive territoriality.

Fifth, this exclusive territory can be expanded. That is, the more property that an individual owns, the greater the exclusive territory of that person becomes. Locke sees this expansion as a process whereby an individual realizes his free will. For example, if a man mixes his labor with some land, the mixed part becomes the property of the man, and the exclusive territory of his person is thereby expanded. Likewise, for Locke, if a man transfers his liberty to representative politicians to establish a political society, the exclusive territory of his person becomes expanded from the private to a public realm. In this way, Locke justifies representative democracy.

Here, it becomes clear that the linguistic distinction between subject and predicate appears in Locke's formula of person-property. That is, person is the analogue to subject, and property is the analogue to predicates. Both Locke's person and the linguistic subject are vacuous subjects, devoid of any characteristics, and what characterizes them is property or predicates. Certainly, Locke's person cannot exist without its particularizing properties, as a proper sentence can only be completed when predicates particularize a linguistic subject. However, Locke conceptualizes person as a vacuous subject that needs property to be made particular, defining property in unusually wide terms to include not only assets but also body, labor, liberty, and life.

Both Locke's person and the linguistic subject maintain their identities continuously over time. The philosophical controversy over this enduring identity of subjectivity has long revolved around the question whether we can reasonably maintain that there is something unchanging in itself that nevertheless undergoes change over time.[34] For example, in early modern time, Locke and David Hume dissented in this controversy. As noted, Locke argued that everyone has a personal identity, that is, a "self" that retains the same identity and continues over time, even though everyone ages and changes.[35] Hume rejected this argument, maintaining that there is no such self that continues over time. Most early modern Western philosophers, including G. W. F. Hegel, were with Locke. They assumed that, from birth, there is a subject called "I" such that "I" considers its life to be made up of the results and experiences of what the subject "I" chooses freely.[36]

Whitehead criticizes the Western philosophical concept of person. Like Nietzsche, Whitehead's process philosophy does not presuppose a fundamental subject that experiences becoming. One of the most original contributions of Whitehead's process philosophy is that it does not distinguish between the experiencer and the experience, the aware and the awareness, or the doer and the doing. According to Whitehead, like Nietzsche, this distinction originates in the structure of language, which abstracts the doer from the doing in the form of the subject-predicate linguistic proposition. Thus, Whitehead considers the becoming or experience itself as an actual entity and identifies no actual entity that undergoes becoming.

Whitehead argued that philosophers can no longer adhere to the concept of enduring subjectivity due to two main reasons. The first reason is modern scientific achievements such as those that were made in the field of quantum physics. Whitehead proposed that the ultimate unit existence of the universe—actual entities in Whiteheadian terms—would have a quantum-physical characteristic. In quantum physics, a particle does not exist continuously in time and space but occupies spatial and temporal extension *all at once*, like pulses or vibrations. Thus, the achievements of quantum physics refute both the conventional view that entities exist continuously in time and space and Locke's concept of person, which maintains its subjectivity continuously in time and space.

We are surrounded by enduring things such as trees, rock, and humans. How does Whitehead explain this endurance if he rejects the subjective endurance of actual entities? For Whitehead, an enduring object is a society that comprises actual entities. Although an actual entity becomes itself all at once without spatial and temporal endurance, its realization generates its own individual space-time continuum. He claims that, because actual entities generate their own space-time continua "successively," they facilitate the spatial and temporal continuity of the world. Thus, Whitehead stated, "Temporalisation is not another continuous process. It is an atomic succession. Thus time is atomic (i.e., epochal), though what is temporalised is continuous and divisible."[37] In this case, Whitehead used the term "epochal." An epochal becoming or epochal temporalization is not a divisible nor continuous process but occurs "as a whole and at once without spatiotemporal division or continuity." When a group of actual entities become a society, i.e., inherit a certain identity of character successively, enduring objects like trees and stones are formed. Therefore, Whitehead stated, "[Their] physical endurance is the process of continuously inheriting a certain identity of character transmitted throughout a historical route of actual entities."[38] Early modern philosophy, including Locke's, mistakenly regarded this successive repetition of a certain identity of character as an ontologically primary fact and assigned it the name of "the subject" or "person." However, as demonstrated by quantum physics, the idea of personal identity in which the subject remains unchanged while undergoing changes through time is a grave intellectual mistake; rather, as claimed by Whitehead, the subject is epochal.

The second reason for Whitehead's rejection of the concept of enduring subjectivity is Zeno's paradox, which holds that, if a "becoming" occurs with continuity, it cannot be completed. If the process of A becoming B is continuous or divisible, then before A can become B, A must first complete the becoming process halfway. Before A can complete the becoming process halfway, it must complete a quarter of the process. Before A can complete a quarter of the becoming process, A must complete one-eighth of the process, and so on. Thus, "we are involved in an infinite regress,"[39] and this infinite regression renders a "becoming with continuity" impossible. There are two ways to avoid this infinite regression. One is to deny the fact that something (*res vera*) is becoming. The other is to accept the fact that every act of becoming is not divisible into earlier and later sections,[40] i.e., that becoming is epochal. An epochal becoming refutes Locke's concept of person that maintain its subjectivity continuously in time and space.

Why does Locke consider property not only "things that can be owned" but also "a man's attributes including body, labour, liberty and life"? In other words, why does Locke formulate the ontology of person-property in his *Second Treatise of Government*? Whitehead and Nietzsche would critically observe that Locke mistakenly applies the linguistic structure of subject-predicates to understand reality and human nature. However, he would not agree that he had made this mistake. Rather, he simply accepts the dominant perspective of the elites of his time, who thought that human attributes such as liberty and the body are property. For example, before Locke, Thomas Hobbes, in *Leviathan*, published in 1651, regards life, limbs, assets, and the means of life as property.[41] Locke's contemporaries spoke of the Protestant religion as their "property," and Richard Baxter, a contemporary Puritan leader, also said that men's lives and liberties are the chief parts of their property.[42] These facts means that the dominant group of elites in Locke's times had the ontology of person-property that has been discussed so far, and Locke just follows suit.

Even though the word "property" has two meanings in modern English—attributes and things—it originally referred only to the former,[43] remaining close to its etymological roots in the Latin *proprius*, meaning "one's own or something private or peculiar to oneself;" thus, originally, the property of an individual meant human attributes, such as body, life, liberty, and action.[44] In the first half of the seventeenth century in England, however, the term "property" was broadened to mean not only the attributes of a man but also material objects.[45] This metamorphosis created the ideology of the "birth right" of Englishmen to have property—liberty and land—which had a direct political impact when Parliament used this ideology in its struggle against the Crown.

Locke was among those who theoretically justified the metamorphosis. Locke's logic runs as follows. Labor, an inherent attribute of a man, is man's property. If a man mixes this property with part of nature, this part also become a property of that man. This property formation does not require any agreement from other people because mixing a man's person's own property with external nature is sufficient to make the mixed part the man's property. Here, an external object is treated like a unique attribute of a man: just as labor is an inherent property that a man possesses from birth, external objects mixed with labor become another inherent property of the man. Thus, for Locke, property includes not only labor, life, and liberty but estates as well.[46]

Here, Locke tends to conflate the two senses of "property"—attributes and things. This conflation may lead him to conceptualize property in two ways. One is to treat the right to possess things as "natural." Locke assumes that the right to possess things is the same as the right to possess the natural attributes of human beings; therefore, the right to possess things is considered to exist prior to the establishment of social institutions or a consensus. I refer to this as the propertization of things. This propertization contributes to forming the modern ideology of human rights, in which human beings are assumed to have the birthright to possessing property—understood as not only liberty and the body but also goods.

The other is to treat all the attributes of a person, including labor, body, and liberty, as things that the person can own and transfer to other persons. I refer to this as the propertization of the attributes of human beings. This propertization presupposes the concept of the abstract person: after having turned all the attributes of a man into separable and transferable property, what remains is the abstract subject that retains its identity as the owner of property. Through this process, Roger Cotterrell argues, the idea of property contributed to the generation of the modern ideology of human equality.[47] Property—attributes and things—makes human beings different from each other. However, by considering human beings as separable from their property, modern Western law treats them as the same and equal to each other. This is the origin of the concept of "person" in modern law.[48] The two propertizations—that of human attributes and that of things—are, like two sides of the same coin, the two sides of Locke's concept of property. However, current scholars cannot account for why these two propertizations occur simultaneously in Locke's concept of property because their analyses overlook Locke's ontology of person-property.

2.2. Locke's Ontological Formula of "Person-Property" Creates a Peculiar Concept of Ownership Rights

Locke's property ontologically restores the Roman legal concept of property—*dominium*—which was created in the late Ancient Roman Republic and has rarely been found in any legal systems other than those of Ancient Rome and modern Western society. In spite of the close relation between Locke's concept of property and the Roman legal concept of *dominium*, the ontological similarity between the two remains underappreciated. To understand what the Roman legal concept is, it is helpful to compare it with its opposite, i.e., rights in *personam*. The Roman legal concept of *dominium* is now called "rights in *rem*," where the Latin *rem* means thing. Rights *in rem* implies that an owner's rights are established as the direct relation with that thing without the agreement of other people. These rights are in contrast to rights in *personam*, where the Latin *personam* means person. For rights in *personam*, a person's rights are established because other contractual parties agree. For example, if a person has the right to dispose or use a piece of land at will, it is because other people involved in the land implicitly or explicitly agree to this. However, the Roman legal concept of rights *in rem* and Locke's concept of property reduce this matter of a "people-to-people" relationship to one of "people-to-things." According to these concepts, for example, the right to dispose and use land at will is established by a direct ownership relationship between the person and the land and does not need any form of agreement of other persons.

Here, both the concept of rights *in rem* and Locke's concept of property assume that owners form a relationship with other people *indirectly* through "things," that is, through "*rem*" or "property." Moreover, it is assumed that for both rights, the owner communicates with an unspecified number of people in society by telling them simply "no," that is, "not to interfere with the *rem* or property an owner owns." Thus, the way in which an owner cultivates relations with other persons in a society by means of these rights is "negative, simple, exclusive and indirect." Rights in *personam*, on the other hand, are exercised between particular contractual parties, and the contents of the rights are also specified in detail through contracts.[49] Thus, the way by which an individual has an interpersonal relationship through rights *in personam* is "concrete" and "direct." If I can use something at my disposal, it is because people in a society have allowed me to do so, either implicitly or explicitly, not because I have formed a direct relationship with it. The question of how to allocate assets between people is, in fact, a matter of the relationships between people. Thus, the legal concept of "rights in *personam*," rather than "rights in *rem*," has been commonly used to regulate asset allocation between people in various civilizations, except in Ancient Rome and the Western modern societies that inherit the Roman legal system. In fact, it is a fiction that my right to things needs no tacit or explicit agreement with others.[50] However, this fiction became a reality when it was made into law in the late Roman Republic and in its descendants.

Why is there such a strong analogy between Locke's theory of property and the Roman legal concept of *dominium*? Arguably, this is because Locke's theory of property mistakenly presupposes a doer—person—who can claim its own exclusive private realm and thus creates a strict distinction between the private and the common. According to Locke, the realm of person-property is wholly private, meaning that the person is an absolute sovereign in relation to this property; no one can interfere with the private domain of this person, while other areas outside of the domain of the person are held completely in common. Locke argues that nature is given to man in common and that the mixing of labour transforms this communal asset to the absolute private property of a person.

By contrast, considering reality in terms of "doing" or "event," Whitehead would refute Locke's dichotomy of the private and the common. According to Whitehead, the universe is in some way both entirely private and entirely public. An actual entity creates itself by using all the other past existences in the universe as its data. That is, all the data that the entity uses to create itself are not generated by the entity itself but are what the common universe offers. There is nothing that the actual entity can own exclusively, and the only new thing that this actual entity adds to the universe is a new assemblage of the data. In this respect, we can say that the creation of an actual entity belongs wholly to the common realm. However, the actual entity reinterprets these data from its own private perspective. Thus, there can be no existence that is independent of this private creation and perspective. In this respect, we can say that all existences in the universe can be considered the wholly private domain of an actual entity that reinterprets and reorganizes them from its own private perspective.

As a result, for Whitehead, Locke's strict dichotomy of the private and common realms does not hold.

Locke repeatedly argues that a man's body and labour are exclusively his. However, this view is not a universal notion, historically speaking. For example, during the Chosun Dynasty in Korea, people sought to minimize their own bodily harm even when committing suicide, which is why hanging was the most common form of suicide, as it was believed that a person's body was given from the parents and did not belong to the individual at all. Can the air that I breathe into my lungs be exclusively "mine"? There is no clear distinction between my "private realm" and the "environment" surrounding me. Moreover, most of the components of the human body are replaced with new ones over the course of three years, and the parts of the brain, which are replaced least often, are replaced with new ones in ten years. All the elements that make up a person's body are given by nature, and thus we cannot say that the body is "exclusively mine." More appropriately, to put it in Whiteheadian terms, the body is "the closest environment to me" or an assemblage of what nature offers a person.

By contrast, in Locke's ontology of person-property, what constitutes the essence of man is not any relationship between men but a relationship between a person and property. Thus, in Locke's ontology, we are ontologically separated from each other, and even when someone forms a relationship with others, this relationship is ontologically secondary, meaning that it does not affect the essence of that person. Thus, for Locke, what constitutes the essence of a person—that is, property—would be exclusively that person's possession.

Furthermore, Locke's ontology of person-property does not look for the cause of an event in a complex relationship but rather as a result of the free choice of the hypothetical subject, person. Thus, Locke's ontology exaggerates the subject's responsibilities, and often making a matter of responsibilities into moral corruption, i.e., sin. For example, Locke treats wage-laborers as free property owners who have labor as their property and can choose wage contracts voluntarily and freely. Thus, for Locke, if laborers do not engage in wage labor contracts and thus suffer from poverty, they have the sole responsibility for that. In fact, when Locke was asked to become a member of England's Board of Trade in 1697 to present his views on the rise of unemployment, he responded that this rise was not caused by lack of job opportunities or excess population but by the *moral corruption* of the poor.[51]

2.3. An Analogy between Property, Slavery, and Money

If we frame human nature in terms of the ontology of person-property, where a person has an absolute sovereign power over property, we can establish a strong analogy between property, slavery, and money. We already find that there is a strong analogy between property and slavery. This analogy arrived when the Roman legal concept of property was invented. Legal theorist Orlando Patterson's theory about the origin of the legal concept of property demonstrates this analogy, as explained in the previous chapter. According to Patterson, for rights in *rem*, *rem* was a slave, and the image of the masters of slaves fits the image of rights *in rem*.[52] Likewise, in modern times, an analogy between slavery and property was found in natural-right theorists who resettled the concept of property on the basis of Roman law in the fifteenth century. They used their theory to justify slave ownership in early modern times. According to this theory, liberty is transferable: it can be sold, swapped, loaned, or voluntarily surrendered. Thus, as Graeber writes, "there could be nothing intrinsically wrong with, say, debt peonage, or even slavery. And this is exactly what natural-rights theorists came to assert."[53] For them, slavery was justifiable because it was an equal exchange between liberty and life: slaves gave up their liberty to get back their lives instead. Thus, "In fact, over the next centuries [beginning in the fifteenth century], these ideas [of natural rights] came to be developed above all in Antwerp and Lisbon, cities at the very center of the emerging slave trade."[54]

Locke opposed slavery. However, his natural right theory, where a people can freely transfer their own property, bears within it a vestige of slavery. He describes a particular case in which a man becomes a slave because he has committed a crime for which he would be sentenced to death.[55] When a man's life is forfeited due to his crime, according to Locke, someone to whom the law gave a power to forfeit the man's life could delay to complete the sentence and make the man a slave instead. Locke argued that this form of slavery inflicts no injury to the enslaved. If the slave does not want to be treated harshly by the master, Locke assumes that the slave can choose to give up his life. Here, Locke sets up an equal exchange between life and liberty. The master takes the liberty of the enslaved in return for the life of the enslaved. If the slave no longer wants to be a slave, he can give up his life.

Our examination of how the analogy between property and slave was established at the late Roman Republic gives us another chance to examine the relationship between property and money. Locke would deny this analogy, as he clearly distinguishes between the origin of money and the origin of property and blames money rather than property for wealth inequality. According to Locke, the concept of property exists from the beginning of the natural state, i.e., from the beginning of mankind, but money was only introduced much later, after the barter system was fully developed. However, contrary to Locke's assertion (and also contrary to Karl Menger's theory of origin of money), as the recent findings of anthropologists demonstrates, money did not become a dominant medium of exchange due to the development of barter.[56] Rather, the social motivations for inventing coin money were associated with war-making.[57] Furthermore, contrary to Locke's assertion, property and coin money originated almost concurrently. Historically coined money was created *immediately before* the legal concept of property was invented. The legal concept of property was invented in the late Roman Republic (around the first or second century BC), marking its first appearance in history. Coinage appeared only a little earlier, in the sixth century BC, in Lydia; the first Roman coinage was invented in 338 BC to pay mercenaries.[58]

The previous chapter already identified an analogical relation between property and money. The *rem* on the minds of the ancient Romans was money *as well* as slaves. The Romans needed to create a new concept of property that would encompass both new forms of wealth—money *and* slaves.

Locke imputes the cause of the inequality of wealth not to the institution of property rights but only to money. Contrary to this claim, it is more appropriate to attribute the wealth inequality of the Ancient Roman Empire not only to money but also to laws of property. In Ancient Rome, a large land was concentrated in the hands of a few aristocrats, such that many farmers became vagabonds. This inequality was even more severe in the colonies of the Roman Empire. For example, in Northern Africa under Roman rule, six landowners owned half of Northern Africa,[59] and the law of property protected their ownership. Likewise, the extreme inequality of wealth in the early modern West is largely due to the emergence of the concept of property rights. The Christian world in Europe during the Middle Ages abolished property rights and usury and thus lowered the extreme exploitation that the landowners of the Ancient Roman era committed against the majority of peasants.[60] However, as the Roman legal concept of property reappeared in the fifteenth century, the violent theft of free peasants' land that occurred during the Ancient Roman Empire reoccurred from the last third of the fifteenth century and continued to the end of the eighteenth century.[61] The nobles appropriated common lands, claimed property rights for the land where the serfs lived and cultivated, and tore down serfs' houses. As in Ancient Rome, huge lands were concentrated in the hands of a few nobles, and many independent farmers became vagabonds. Because Locke lived during this period, he would have clearly witnessed that the concept and institution of property rights caused this tragedy. However, he made the concept of property immune from criticism. His view is very different from Karl Marx's that argues that the modern ideology of absolute private property contributed to creating the modern form of slavery: the property-less proletariat.[62]

Why is the analogy between property, slavery, and money established? A reason is that Locke's theory of property frames human nature in terms of the ontology of person-property and assumes that a person has an absolute sovereign power over property. Locke's property rights and *dominium*—the power of a slave master—grants a person with the power to rip property or slaves away from all social relationships with others, thereby allowing the person to exert absolute power over property or slave without any interference of others. Likewise, money grants its owner with the same power with which the owner can cancel ongoing moral obligations to others and become independent of them. However, this power of slave-masters, money-holders, or property owners is ontologically unjustifiable, as discussed so far. As mentioned earlier, "being a part" is not the same as "being a property." As J. P. Day notes, a member of a golf club would become the club's property only when no one can interfere with it no matter how harshly it treated the member.[63] Nonetheless, Locke frames the relationship between person and property as the exclusive possessive relationship. Why? A reason is that Locke frames reality with the linguistic structure of subject-predicate. Whitehead points out that the ontology of subject-predicates is "the doctrine of . . . subjects qualified by their *private* predicate. This is doctrine of subject with *private* worlds of experience. If this granted, there is no escape from solipsism."[64] That is, the ontology of subject-predicates contributes to creating the dichotomy between the private and the public realms and then leads us to think that the experiences or attributes of a person is the *private* realm exclusively possessed by the person.

2.4. Linear or Recurrent

This chapter argues that Locke's propertization of human attributes, where labor is treated like a thing that can be separated from a laborer and mixed with external objects, is unreasonable because there can be no subject that can exist independently of its activity. As Nietzsche argues, there is nothing behind activity, and activity—here labor—is itself a subject, as "the doing" is everything. This mystical idea that human attributes can be separable is sometimes used in language, such as in the linguistic expression "I entrust you with my liberty." Strictly speaking, this expression does not mean that "I treat my liberty like an object and hand it over to you" but rather implies that "I obey you like your slave." Because language has a subject-predicate structure, it cannot help but to treat predicates, which are all activities and characteristics that describe a subject, as something capable of being separated from the subject. In Locke's ontology of person-property, which mistakenly represents reality in the linguistic form of subject-predicate, predicates are made into something capable of being separated from a subject. Here, Locke's notion of "property," which includes labor, body, life, and liberty, is mistakenly made into something capable of being separated from a man and capable of being transferred to someone else.

Locke argues that when a laborer mixes his inborn attribute, labor, with external objects, this mixed part becomes like the attributes that he owns from birth. This chapter analyzes the ways in which this propertization of things is unreasonable: labor and liberty cannot be separated from an individual and mixed with external objects or transferred to others. Locke argues that representative government is established when people give up their liberty to representative politicians, and through this establishment, people extend their exclusive territory of private sovereignty to the public realm. However, giving up liberty to politicians does not mean the extension of people's free will and its realization in representative government. Rather, critically speaking, this constitutes nothing less than a promise to "obey" the representative government like a slave.

This chapter has also argued that Locke's theory of property creates a peculiar concept of private ownership rights that is akin to the Roman legal concept of *dominium*. It argues that this analogy between Locke's theory of property and the Roman legal concept of *dominium* and an analogy between property, slavery, and money could occur if we mistakenly presuppose a doer—person—who can claim its own exclusive private realm and thus create a strict distinction between the private and the common.

For Locke, the idea of personal identity is the basis for justifying the system of reward and punishment. Because the idea of personal identity assumes the continuity and preservation of the self, this continuity accumulates all past happenings, including wrongful acts, and prevents any salvation before the end of the continuity.[65] As long as society is based on the idea of identity, guilt and the past are inexpiable, and debts are not forgiven unless the exact amount of punishment or payment is given to restore original equality. Historically, the rich have used the ideology of strict debt obligations to exploit the poor's land and labor,[66] and, as Nietzsche argues, the powerful have used the ideology of strict sense of guilt to control the weak.[67]

Locke's concept of personal identity replaced the cyclical concept of the self that had been the dominant concept from ancient times to the Middle Ages.[68] A prime example is the Ancient Mesopotamian belief that the god Marduk destroys the world on the last day of the year and re-creates it on the first day. It was a circular worldview in which the world and beings were believed to be newly created every year. This circular concept of the self was replaced by the modern linear concept of the self, and a representative example of this linear concept is Locke's concept of personal identity.

To conclude, Locke's ontology of person-property is a modern philosophical and political project that creates the "person," grants it inordinate privileged rights, such as private property on land, and reduces the matter of responsibility into a matter of guilt and sin. Here, it is assumed that a person's right is established not because other persons agree implicitly or explicitly but because this right is natural—that is, it belongs exclusively to that person without others' agreement. Where a social problem arises, the notion of person attributes it to the sin they committed. The notion is less concerned with analyzing and improving the complex relations involved in the social problem than with reducing it to the problem of moral corruption of persons.

Nevertheless, the concept of personal identity is not historically universal. Mankind has long believed that its existence—like the seasonal recreation of nature—periodically disappeared and was recreated. As mentioned, this circular concept of the self resolves the problem of sin and debts in a healthier way by periodically cancelling sins and consumer debts. By this means, ancient people periodically sought to return to an original and balanced order created by the gods, periodically resetting their social relations to solve social problems.[69] However, the modern ideology of personal identity prevents this traditional solution. Modern subjects enjoy the inordinate privilege of property rights but, in return, make themselves suffer from the accumulated records of their guilt and debts.

Notes

1 Graeber, *Debt*, 251–252.
2 Graeber, *Debt*, 251.
3 Graeber, *Debt*, 251–252.
4 Graeber, *Debt*, 252.
5 Nietzsche, *Genealogy*, 25.
6 Nietzsche, *Genealogy*, 25.
7 The underlines in the following sentences are mine.
8 Locke, Second *Treatises*, §4.
9 Locke, *Second Treatise*, §6.
10 Locke, *Second Treatise*, §120.
11 Locke, *Second Treatise*, §123.
12 Locke, *Second Treatise*, §57.
13 Locke, *Second Treatise*, §44.
14 Locke, *Second Treatise*, §137.
15 Locke, *Second Treatise*, §194.
16 Locke, *Second Treatise*, §27.
17 Day, "Locke on Property," 208.
18 Olivecrona, "Appropriation in the State of Nature," 223.
19 Tully, *A Discourse on Property*, 105.
20 Richards, Mulligan, and Graham, "'Property' and 'People'," 37.
21 Rothbard, *Ethics of Liberty*, 21 & 49.
22 Flew, 'Locke," 61.
23 Pateman, "Self-Ownership," 28.
24 Macpherson, "Locke," 551.
25 Pateman, "Self-Ownership," 26.
26 Locke, *Second Treatise*, §27, my underlines.
27 Locke, *Second Treatise*, §27, my underlines.
28 Locke, *Second Treatise*, §123.
29 Cotterrell, "Power"; Kim, "Identity and the Hybridity of Modern Finance," 427.
30 Locke, *The Works of John Locke, Vol. II*, 69.
31 Locke, *The Works of John Locke, Vol. II*, 68.
32 Locke, *The Works of John Locke, Vol. II*, 69.
33 Day, "Locke on Property," 216.
34 Davis, *The Theory of the Individual*, 12.
35 Locke, *The Works of John Locke, Vol. II.*
36 This prejudice in modern Western philosophy originated in Descartes' *Meditations* (i.e., the Cartesian subject).
37 Whitehead, *Science*, 129.
38 Whitehead, *Science*, 111.
39 Whitehead, "Time," 63.
40 Whitehead, *Process and Reality*, 68.
41 Hobbes, *Leviathan*, 226.
42 Olivecrona, "Appropriation in the State of Nature," 219.
43 Olivecrona, "Appropriation in the State of Nature," 219.
44 Olivecrona, "Appropriation in the State of Nature," 219.
45 Pipes, *Property and Freedom*, 30–31. Even though people today think this extension strange, this was common in seventeenth-century England (Olivecrona "Appropriation in the State of Nature," 219). For example, Hobbes in his *Leviathan* considered life, limbs, assets, and the means of life as property (Hobbes, *Leviathan*, 226). Locke's contemporaries spoke of the Protestant religion as their "property," and Richard Baxter, a contemporary Puritan leader, also said that men's lives and liberties are the chief parts of their property ("Appropriation in the State of Nature," 219).

46 Locke, *Second Treatise*, §123.
47 Cotterrell, "Power."
48 Similarly, for Hegel, at the first stage of historical evolution, the self begins as an abstract single person (G. W. F. Hegel, *Philosophy of Right* (Oxford: The Clarendon Press, 1962), §35). As in Locke's theory of person, this abstraction of person is possible because Hegel *propertized the attributes of a person*. For Hegel, property includes not only that which is external to a person but also things inside a person, such as his or her productive capacity and body. Thus, for Hegel and Locke alike, a laborer is a property owner because he or she has property—labour, his or her productive capacity—in his or herself, and because this property can be alienated.
49 Merrill and Smith, "What Happened to Property and Law."
50 Patterson, *Slavery*, 32.
51 Qtd. In Bourne, *Life of Locke*, 178.
52 Patterson, *Slavery*, 32–34.
53 Graeber, *Debt*, 206.
54 Graeber, *Debt*, 206.
55 Locke, *Second Treatise*, §23.
56 Graeber, *Debt*; Kim, "Money is Rights *in Rem*."
57 Graeber, *Debt*.
58 Graeber, *Debt*, 225–228.
59 Avila, *Ownership*, 159.
60 Avila, *Ownership*.
61 Marx, *Capital 1*.
62 Marx, "Critique of the Gotha Program," 526.
63 Day, "Locke on Property," 216.
64 Whitehead, *Science*, 152. Italics is mine.
65 Eliade, *The Myth*.
66 Graeber, *Debt*.
67 Nietzsche, *Genealogy*.
68 Eliade, *The Myth*. According to Eliade, in the Middle Ages, the cyclical concept of the self was popular among ordinary people, even though some elites were already familiar with a linear concept of the self.
69 Eliade, *The Myth*.

Bibliography

Avila, Charles. *Ownership: Early Christian Teaching*. Wipf and Stock, 2004.

Bourne, H. R. Fox. *The Life of John Locke*. Vol. II. London, 1876.

Cotterrell, Roger. "Power, Property and the Law of Trusts." *Journal of Law and Society* 14, no. 1 (1987): 77–90.

Davis, J. B. *The Theory of the Individual in Economics: Identity and Value*. London: Routledge, 2003.

Day, J. P. "Locke on Property." *The Philosophical Quarterly* 16, no. 64 (1966), 207–220.

Eliade, Mircea. *The Myth of the Eternal Return*. Princeton: Princeton University Press, 1954.

Flew, Antony. "Locke and the Problem of Personal Identity." *Philosophy* 26, no. 96 (1951): 53–68.

Graeber, David. *Debt: The First 5,000 Years*. Brooklyn, New York: Melville House Publishing, 2011.

Hobbes, Thomas. *Leviathan*. Oxford: Oxford University Press, 1996.

Kim, Jongchul. "Identity and the Hybridity of Modern Finance: How to Specialise the Modern Ownership of Property, Trusts and Finance." *The Cambridge Journal of Economics* 38, no. 2 (2014): 425–446.

Kim, Jongchul. "Money Is Rights in Rem: A Note on the Nature of Money." *Journal of Economic Issues* 48, no. 4 (2014): 1005–1019.

Locke, John. *The Works of John Locke, Vol. II*. London: W. Sharpe and Son, 1823.

Locke, John. *Two Treatises of Government*. New York: Cambridge University Press, 1960.

Macpherson, Crawford B. "Locke on Capitalist Appropriation." *The Western Political Quarterly* 4, no. 4 (1951): 550–566.

Marx, Karl. *Capital*. Vol. 1. Harmondsworth, Middlesex: Penguin Classics, 1992.

Marx, Karl. "Critique of the Gotha Program." In *The Marx-Engels Reader*, edited by Robert C. Tucker, 2nd ed. New York: Norton, 2002.

Merrill, Thomas W. and Henry E. Smith. "What Happened to Property and Law?" *Yale Law Journal* 111 (2001): 357–398.

Nietzsche, Friedrich. *On the Genealogy of Morality*. Indianapolis: Hackett Publishing Corporation, Inc., 1998.

Olivecrona, Karl. "Appropriation in the State of Nature: Locke on the Origin of Property." *Journal of the History of Ideas* 35, no. 2 (1974): 211–230.

Pateman, Carole. "Self-Ownership and Property in the Person: Democratization and a Tale of Two Concepts." *The Journal of Political Philosophy* 10, no. 1 (2002): 20–53.

Patterson, Orlando. *Slavery and Social Death: A Comparative Study*. Cambridge, MA: Harvard University Press, 1982.

Pipes, Richard. *Property and Freedom*. Toronto: Random House of Canada, 2000.

Richards, Judith, Lotte Mulligan, and John K. Graham. "'Property' and 'People': Political Usages of Locke and Some Contemporaries." *Journal of the History of Ideas* 42, no. 1 (1981): 29–51.

Rothbard, Murray. *The Ethics of Liberty*. New York: New York University Press, 1998.

Tully, James. *A Discourse on Property: John Locke and his Adversaries*. Cambridge: Cambridge University Press, 1980.

Whitehead, Alfred North. "Time." In *Proceeding of the Sixth International Congress of Philosophy*. New York and London: Longmans, Green & Co., 1927.

Whitehead, Alfred North. *The Science and the Modern World*. New York: The New American Library, 1948.

Whitehead, Alfred North. *Process and Reality*. New York: Free Press, 1978.

3 The Origin of Modern Money—Modern Money as a Trust

This chapter demonstrates that the mistaken ideas of person and property constitute the ontological foundation of modern money. To demonstrate this, the chapter analyzes how a trust—a hybrid between property and debt—contributed to the origin of modern bank money in late-seventeenth-century England and argues that modern money is a trust.

In the previous chapter, I argued that the modern ideology of person-property is a modern philosophical and political project that creates a "person" granted with the inordinate privilege of property rights. In return for this privilege, this ideology makes the person take full responsibility for the accumulated and never-forgotten records of all its guilt and debts.[1] As the sense of guilt and sin were strengthened, the obligation of debt repayment also became stricter in modern times. In fact, abolishing the medieval usury law and imposing the strict obligation of debt repayment regarding consumer debt has ushered in a new era in which the rich use such strict debt obligations to exploit the land and labor of the poor. However, ontologically human beings who do not have godlike perfection neither deserve such inordinate property rights nor can take such full responsibility for the never-forgotten records of guilt and debt. The rich and powerful have themselves devised institutional schemes of enjoying the inordinate privilege of property rights *while avoiding the responsibilities* that are attached to the privilege. I argue that this scheme is a trust.

The current legal practice of filing certain economic transactions into two different legal categories, property or contract, is clearly a Roman concept. In this sense, our modern era is an extension of Roman times, but with an important difference: we now freely mix property rights and contractual rights, or freely grant the privileges of property rights to creditors. This mixture is a trust, and the trust is central to the nature of modern banking and finance.

Going further to the seventeenth century, this chapter analyzes how a trust played a central role in originating modern banking. London goldsmith bankers in the second half of the seventeenth century were the first bankers in the West to loan the funds deposited with them in the form of transferable paper money.[2] This chapter argues that this innovation, which ushered in the era of modern banking, was a trust. The trust is a double-ownership scheme: two

DOI: 10.4324/9781003052210-4

individuals are the *exclusive* owners of one and the same thing: one *at law*, and the other simultaneously *in equity*. Similarly, in goldsmith banking, two groups—the borrowers of the bankers' notes and depositors—were the *exclusive* owners of one and the same cash that was kept safely in the bankers' vaults; and one amount of cash created two cash balances of the same amount, one for the borrowers and the other for depositors. This double-ownership remains a central feature of the present banking system. Demand deposits with commercial banks are exclusively owned by two exclusive groups simultaneously—depositors who have originally deposited and borrowers to which the bank loans its noes. This is the money creation mechanism of modern banks.

To include goldsmith bankers' money under the concept of trusts extends our understanding of the cultural and political motives behind modern money. Goldsmith banking and trusts, as shall be demonstrated, originated from the same historical context and motive and were uniquely English phenomena. Goldsmith banking and later joint-stock banking have grown within the context of the legal and political culture of trusts in England. Thus, arguably, understanding the legal and political implications of trusts is critical to understanding the legal and political implications of modern money. Moreover, including goldsmith bankers' money within the concept of trusts helps explain the origin and nature of modern money. This explanation is the main focus of this chapter.

The present literature of the credit theory of money overstates the role of the development of transferable credit instruments in originating modern money, and, as a result, it often mistakenly believes that modern money evolved from simple credit instruments, bills of exchange. This overstatement and the consequent mistake are made by Geoffrey Ingham in *The Nature of Money*.[3] He argues that two pre-existing economic developments were necessary for the origin of modern money. (1) The first was the evolution of bills of exchange into pure credit instruments and their depersonalization (that is, the emergence of the bills "payable to X or *bearer*"). Transferable credit instruments, such as promissory notes, drawn orders, and bills of exchange, in seventeenth century England used two types of clauses: "payable to X or order" and "payable to X or bearer."[4] The order clause of the bills required specifying a payee when they were transferred; while the bearer clause of goldsmith bankers' notes did not. Thus, the bearer clause of the notes let the bankers payable to whoever presented them. (2) The second was the emergence of deposit banking. He believes that the integration of these two developments—deposit-bankers' loaning their deposits in the form of depersonalized credit instruments—transformed simple credit instruments, bills of exchange, into money.

This account offered by Ingham, however, has some critical weaknesses. Historically the depersonalization of bills of exchange was not a necessary condition for the origin of modern money, and modern money cannot be considered to evolve from the bills of exchange. In the second half of the seventeenth century, when English goldsmith bankers introduced paper money, bills of exchange with a *bearer* clause were known and transferred, but were not the custom among merchants. Rather, as explained later, the custom tended to establish the rule of endorsements in the formula "payable to X or order" to improve the negotiability of bills of exchange. Even common law differentiated the bills of exchange between a bearer clause and an order clause and discouraged merchants from using the bills with a bearer clause. For example, a common law court in *Hodges v. Steward* in 1692 did not give a bearer of a bill with "payable to X or bearer" the same creditor's right as the first holder.[5] The court's view can be accepted as an adequate description of reality. Common law courts carefully observed the custom of merchants, and they had been trying to adopt the customs into the common law since the early seventeenth century.[6] Furthermore, even the full practical development of the *transferability* of bills of exchange with an *order* clause was not a precondition for the origin of modern money. In England during the latter half of the seventeenth century, bills of exchange "tended . . . to be used for single transactions rather than pass[ed] from hand to hand."[7] Economic historian R. Richards also confirms that in England the transferability of bills of exchange developed in parallel with the development of goldsmith banking rather than prior to it.[8]

Simple credit instruments, such as bills of exchange, cannot evolve into modern money because the former differ by nature from the latter. Unlike bills of exchange, modern money is inherently self-contradictory because it is not only credit but also money, as shall be seen. The concept of money is contradictory to the concept of credit. The transfer of a credit instrument creates a creditor-debtor relation in which the transferor becomes a debtor and the transferee becomes a creditor. The transfer imposes a payment obligation on a transferor. In contrast, money is defined as anything that is generally acceptable in *final* settlement of a debt.[9] The following passage, written by an anonymous writer in 1695 accurately differentiated paper money from paper credit:

> Paper credit ever was and will be useful for the carrying on of Trade and Dealings, viz. Bonds, Mortgages, Bills, or what else is used, only as a pledge to gain time for the payment of Money . . . but the Bills you propose, are designed . . . not only to discharge Debtors, but also Debts finally, and by Law, therefore such Notes and Bills . . . deserve the Name of Paper Money.[10]

For a credit instrument to become money, a transferor must be free from the payment obligation. That is, to become money, credit must stop being credit. Thus, the becoming of credit into modern money is logically impossible and has never occurred historically. Rather, the origin of modern money should be found in the innovation of goldsmith bankers, who made their paper money self-contradictory by making it simultaneously into money and credit. And the transferability of modern money should also be understood as part of goldsmith bankers' innovative scheme rather than as something that evolved from the transferability of bills of exchange.

This chapter argues that the two characteristics of goldsmith bankers' money—self-contradiction and transferability—must be understood as parts of one and the same scheme, a trust. Both characteristics are essential to a trust. The trust is self-contradictory because it is simultaneously a credit transaction and not a credit transaction. The chapter argues that this self-contradiction explains the self-contradictory nature of goldsmith bankers' money. And it also argues that the transferability of bankers' paper money should be considered the same thing as the transferability of the beneficiary's rights in a trust. Finally, the chapter further argues that, like the transferability and self-contradiction of trusts, the transferability and self-contradiction of goldsmith banking helped satisfy property owners' desire to keep their interest in property free from the Crown's interference.

The chapter begins by comparing goldsmith bankers' promissory notes with bills of exchange in order to clarify the distinctive form of creditor-debtor relations that goldsmith bankers exploited. The chapter then examines how bankers exploited the trust scheme to create the self-contradictory nature of modern money. It finally examines how this innovation on the part of bankers shared the identical concept, motive, and historical context as the origin of trusts.

3.1. Bills of Exchange and the London Goldsmith Bankers' Notes

Goldsmith bankers began their role of financial intermediaries as *creditors*. Around the early seventeenth century, some London goldsmiths began to exchange foreign and domestic coins, and they exploited the discrepancies in the weights and values of the coins.[11] A State document of 1628 divided the goldsmiths into two kinds. The first were "working goldsmiths" who traditionally kept precious metal and worked in it; and the second were "exchanging goldsmiths"—those who carried on the business of money-exchanging, bullion dealing, and dealing in plate and jewels. The document also notes that this development of division was, at the time of its writing, a fairly recent innovation among the goldsmiths.[12] Using the profit earned from this money exchange, those exchanging goldsmiths began to loan money to private persons and to *discount* various debt instruments, including bills of exchange and government debts like tallies.[13] After the Civil War, and especially after the Restoration of 1660, goldsmith bankers were transformed from creditors into *the biggest debtors* in London, and soon afterwards in all of England, as they started massively taking deposits and issuing paper money.

Goldsmith bankers issued notes in the form of loans, usually when discounting bills of exchange. The Bank of England replicated goldsmith bankers' discounting business as a means of issuing the Bank's paper money. This discounting business marked a striking difference between the Bank of England and the Continental public deposit banks of the late seventeenth century. Merchants in Amsterdam, for example, were legally obliged to present their bills of exchange to the Bank of Amsterdam, where the debts of the bills were cleared among merchants; and for this clearance the deposited funds of the merchants in the Bank were used. Thus, the financial role of public deposit banks on the Continent was to *clear* the creditor-debtor relations of bills of exchange. In contrast, the discounting business of the Bank of England and goldsmith bankers, as shall be seen, *transformed and extended* those creditor-debtor relations.

Goldsmith bankers' notes often used the bearer clause. In contrast, the merchant custom for the bills of exchange in seventeenth century England often used the order clause. Here, we compare the bills of exchange payable to "X or *order*" with the goldsmith bankers' promissory notes payable to "X or *bearer*." The time periods for this comparison are the second half of the seventeenth century and the early eighteenth century.[14]

Before examining the differences in the creditor-debtor relationships of goldsmith bankers' notes and bills of exchange, we need to address a potential misunderstanding about the concept of transferability. This misunderstanding arises from the idea of the identity of the objects being transferred, which may have coined the term "transferability." When we make a payment by offering a banknote to another person, we tend to focus on the object—the banknote—that is now being transferred and tend to emphasize that the identity of the object being transferred as being the same object that was originally created. Unfortunately, this way of thinking can lead to us mistakenly defining transferability as the object-centered way: transferability is assumed to be *the object's ability to be transferred* to others. For example, assume that you transfer a $100 bank note to the phone company to pay your telephone bill. The phone company will receive $100 money from your bank when the company brings the note to the bank. Is this $100 that the phone company receives the same $100 money that you originally possessed? We can also assume that this transfer happens in the form of an electronic money transfer that does not need the delivery of a paper money. In our example, $100 will be debited from your bank account, and $100 will be credited to the bank account of the telephone company. Is it correct to say that the latter $100 is the same thing as the former $100? Does the bank not redefine credit-debit relations by debiting $100 from you and then crediting $100 to the phone company?[15] Before the transfer occurs, the bank creates a creditor-debtor relationship with you, then when the transfer occurs the bank redefines the same creditor-debtor relationship with the phone company rather than with you. The fallacious idea of "the transfer of identity" had already been refuted by the early modern Common Law Court. The Court in *Williams v. Field* (1694) considered every transfer to be *a making of a new contract* by declaring that endorsement is "the drawing of a new bill."[16] In other words, each transfer is a redefinition of a creditor-debtor relationship rather than the transfer of the same thing. The transferee has the same degree of creditor's right as that of the transferor, not because the same thing is transferred to a new holder, but because the original debtor reproduced or redefined the same relationship with a new holder as with the previous one. This means that we are able to define transferability in a relation-centered rather than an object-centered way. A transfer is a redefinition or a reproduction of the same relationship. For this redefinition, of course, a transferee does not need to go to the original debtor to get permission since the redefinition is already permitted by the original parties of a bill or note when the debt instrument is issued.

In this chapter, I discuss seven differences in the creditor-debtor relations of goldsmith banker's notes and bills of exchange: (1) the number of debtors, (2) finality, (3) the distance between original debtors and transferees, (4) demandability, (5) the expansion of credit, (6) usuriousness, and (7) mutual indebtedness.

[1] The first difference was the number of debtors involved in the transfers of the notes or the bills. As a bill of exchange was transferred from hand to hand, its transferors became additionally included as liable parties. Figure 3.1 describes how the transfers of a typical bill of exchange that was used for international trade would redefine creditor-debtor relations.

In part (a), merchant Tom in London purchased a bill of exchange from merchant-banker John in London and then paid Paul with the bill. The purchase of the bill was an imposition on John of a debt obligation. Here, the drawer of the bill, John, was the original debtor of the bill. To settle this debt obligation, however, John ordered merchant-banker Jack in Amsterdam to honor the bill and pay Paul. If Jack accepted the bill and promised to pay the sum of money, he was re-established as the new debtor to Paul. And then John, according to the common law, was re-established as a warrantor to Paul.[17] A warrantor here was someone who would be liable when Jack could not pay. Here John and Jack composed a group of debtors to Paul. In part (b), Paul used the accepted bill as a means of payment by endorsing it to Martin. Here, Paul became, according to the common law, another warrantor to Martin,[18] and the group of debtors to Martin was expanded to include Paul. In part (c), the second endorsement by Martin to Carly added another warrantor, Martin, to the group of debtors of the bill.

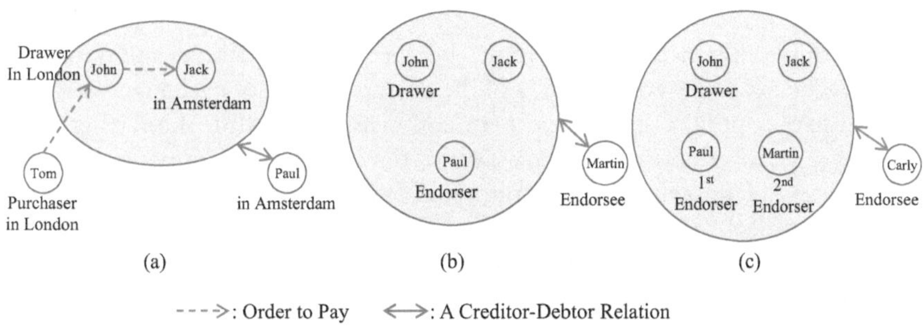

Figure 3.1 The Redefinitions of Creditor-Debtor Relations by Endorsements in Bills of Exchange

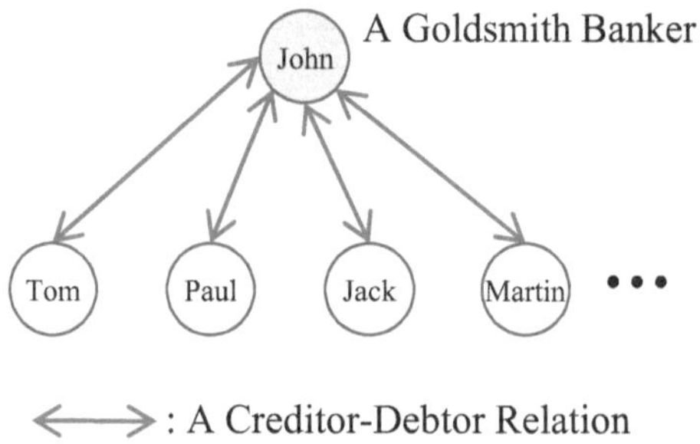

Figure 3.2 The Redefinitions of Creditor-Debtor Relations by the Transfers of Goldsmith Bankers' Notes

In contrast, as seen in Figure 3.2, goldsmith banker John remained the sole debtor as his note transferred between Tom, Paul, Jack, and Martin. When John issued a note payable to Tom and bearer, John became an original debtor to the holder of the note, Tom. Even when Tom transferred the note to Paul, John still remained the only debtor to Paul. Why were transferors free from the debt obligation of the note? To explain the reason, we need to discuss the second difference between notes and bills of exchange.

[2] The second difference was that goldsmith bankers' notes enjoyed finality legally. Only when the transferor endorsed debt instruments could transferees sue the transferor, because the common law regarded a transfer of debt instruments without endorsement as a plain sale rather than the making of a debt contract.[19] Common law courts made this legal distinction between a sale and a debt contract because they wanted to establish the rule of endorsements for the negotiability of bills of exchange. The bankers' notes exploited a loophole in this common law distinction. Because bankers' notes payable to bearer did not necessarily require endorsement in transfer, their transferors were no longer legally liable for the notes.[20]

[3] The third difference was the distance between original debtors and transferees. The necessary consequence of the transfer of bills of exchange was that transfers, continuously making new contracts, led a bill to be farther and farther removed from its original debtor, the drawer. This growing distance was legally acknowledged by common law courts. In *Lambert v. Pack* (1700), the court declared that when a holder of a bill made a charge on an endorser, "there is no need to prove the drawer's hand . . . though it be a forged bill."[21] The addition of liable parties through endorsements as described above was largely due to the growing distance between the original debtor and the transferees.[22] In order for a debt to be transferable without the diminution of value, transferees should possess at least the same degree of confidence in an

original debtor as transferors. However, this requirement was rarely possible due to the growing distance which involved the original debtors in other countries. Endorsements were premiums to supplement the diminution of value by adding the previous parties to a group of debtors.[23]

In contrast, transfers of bankers' notes did *not increase the distance between their original debtors—goldsmith bankers—and transferees*. Goldsmith bankers' notes circulated mainly in the London community, where transferees knew the bankers' reputation well.[24] Important London goldsmith bankers were famous, and their reputations were well known in the community.[25]

[4] The fourth difference was demandability. A demand clause was widely used in bankers' notes: the holders of the notes could demand payment from the bankers at any time, i.e., could end the creditor-debtor relation with the bankers on demand or at short notice. This liquidity was what made the notes most attractive to small investors.[26] In contrast, bills of exchange generally had a fixed payment date, usually three months after the acceptance of the bills, and a demand clause was rarely used.[27]

The demandability of bankers' notes was not characteristic of credit transactions. What essentially differentiates credit transactions from other economic transactions is the transfer of the present availability of funds against their future availability. But "payable on demand" did not entail this transfer: the holders of the notes enjoy the present availability of funds. Thus, these are not credit transactions. In contrast, bills of exchange payable in a fixed period—usually in three months—were credit transactions because the creditors ceded the present availability during the period. The demandability of goldsmith bankers' notes—and the legal enjoyment of finality—seemed to be the reason that contemporary merchants regarded payment with notes as *actual payment* finalizing their debt obligations. Demandability seemed to give the holders of the notes the impression that their notes were equivalent to gold that was safely kept in goldsmith's vaults. In *Tassell and Lee* v. *Lewis* (1695) a common law court described how goldsmith bankers' notes were considered among merchants in comparison to bills of exchange: "The notes of goldsmiths . . . are always accounted among merchants as ready cash, and not as bills of exchange."[28]

In contrast to merchants' opinion, however, common law courts regarded the bankers' notes as credit. In *Ward v. Evans* (1702), in which the endorsee sued the first endorser of a goldsmith banker's note, Chief Justice Holt stated:

> I am of opinion, and always was (notwithstanding the noise and cry, that is the use of Lombard street, as if the contrary opinion would blow up Lombard Street) that the acceptance of such a note is not actual payment.[29]

What made goldsmith bankers' notes "a promise to pay" rather than actual payment was the fact that the bankers maintained a fractional reserve. The cash ratio varied, according to contemporary financier Richard Cantillon, from 10% to around 66%, depending on the practice and conduct of his clients.[30] This fractional reserve in part broke the direct representation between the notes being circulated from hand to hand and the cash kept in vaults. And it then in part transformed the notes into paper credit.

[5] Here the fifth difference between notes and the bills of exchange occurred: *the expansion of liquidity*. By maintaining a fractional reserve (and by mutually accepting other London goldsmith bankers' notes at par), the goldsmith bankers were able to create liquidity.[31] By contrast, in the case of bills of exchange there was no liquidity creation—the credit amount of the bills was exactly the same as the sum that the purchasers of the bills trusted in the drawers.

[6] The sixth difference was that while goldsmith bankers' notes were usurious, bills of exchange were not. As mentioned, goldsmith bankers issued their promissory notes mainly to those who brought bills of exchange to discount them. This discounting business of goldsmith bankers assumed a distinctive character from the business of Continental Europe. According to R. de Roover, the dealing, negotiation, or exchange of bills of exchange on the Continent was *not a type of a loan*; rather it was a type of *speculation* that exploited the discrepancies in rates of exchange that occurred when the bills were used for international trade.[32] Thus, because it was not usurious, theologians did not oppose the dealing.[33] By contrast, the discounting business of goldsmith bankers in England, according to Roover, was *a type of loan*, and a discounting rate is a form of interest rate.[34] This usurious characteristic of the discounting business by the goldsmith bankers seemed to be one of the reasons why contemporaries labeled the bankers as usurers. Thus, the development of discounting in England required the Church to relax the usury restriction,[35] with England the first country in Western Europe to relax its usury restrictions.[36]

Due to this usurious characteristic, Chief Justice Holt objected to treating the bankers' promissory notes under the same rules as bills of exchange in the cases of *Clerke v. Martin* in 1702 and *Buller v. Crips* in 1703. In *Clerke v. Martin*, Holt complained that attempts to sue on goldsmith bankers' notes in the form of actions on the merchant customs "amounted to the setting up a new sort of specialty, unknown to the common law, and invented in Lombard Street, which attempted in these matters of bills of exchange to give laws to Westminster Hall."[37] The traditional view regarded Holt's decisions as reactionary and unthinking objections to mercantile innovations. However, the legal theorist James Rogers refuted this traditional view by arguing that there were justifiable reasons for Holt's decisions.[38] As mentioned, common law courts adopted both the custom of merchants into the common law, beginning in the early seventeenth century, and shorter and simpler pleadings for actions on bills of exchange. The main reason for these adoptions was that the courts regarded bills of exchange as more than just simple loan transactions. The bills were for trade that would promote people's well-being and were therefore called bills of *exchange*. Thus, the court had distinguished the special commercial rules governing bills of exchange from the general principles of usurious obligations. For Holt, goldsmith bankers' promissory notes were mere usuries, did not grow in the custom of merchants, were not related to trade, and could not, therefore, be treated in the same manner as bills of exchange. Holt argued that if common law treated goldsmith bankers' loan business in the same manner as bills of exchange, it would be unfair to debtors and give underserved advantages to creditors.[39] To sum up, Holt believed that goldsmith banking is a usury, which parasitically exploits a proportion of the profits that merchants had to earn. Holt's decision was the medieval legacy that treated commercial loans and usury differently. The medieval law supported bills of exchange because they were commercial loans that promoted commerce, while it outlawed usury because it exploited the poor. For Holt, goldsmith bankers' promissory notes were suspected of being usurious and could not, therefore, be treated in the same manner as bills of exchange. However, Parliament overrode Holt's decision in 1704 by issuing the Promissory Notes Act when Parliament began to be controlled by the moneyed interests of financiers.

[7] The seventh and final difference was that goldsmith bankers established mutual indebtedness with their borrowers, unlike for the loaners and borrowers for bills of exchange. When goldsmith bankers would loan their notes to a person, this person would become a debtor to the bankers and this debtor would become the first holder of the notes. However, because the bankers' notes were bankers' promises to pay, the bankers would also become debtors to the note holders.

3.2. Methods of Maintaining a Fractional Reserve

The discounting business of goldsmith bankers shares some of the effects created by recent asset-backed securitization. First, these two—goldsmith bankers' discounting business and assets-backed securitization—contribute to standardizing debt instruments, thereby improving the transferability of the instruments. For example, in order to finance debts, a bank or a non-bank intermediary, such as the General Motors Acceptance Corporation, transfers, in trust, the pool of mortgage or automobile debts to a separate trust company, and the trust company then transforms the pool of debts into more standardized forms of security[40]; consequently, this standardization allows for improved transferability. Similarly, goldsmith bankers transformed the pool of bills of exchange that were issued for irregular sums into more standardized debts that were issued for round sums and were more easily transferable (see Figure 3.3).[41]

Second, the issued transferable debts in the two cases are secured by the pools of the bills of exchange and mortgage debts, respectively, rather than by a specific bill or mortgage. As a result, it is now "asset-backed" rather than

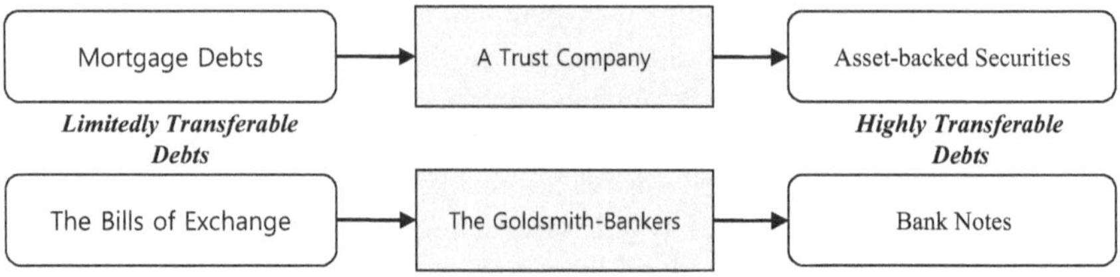

Figure 3.3 A Trust Company and the London Goldsmith Bankers

"collateralized." This discounting business contrasts with the bankers' early lending, which was typically collateralized (or pawned) by jewelry.

In addition, the pooling of debt allows the trust company to get a *statistical* view of the debts collected. This would also have held true for the goldsmith bankers' discounting business. The risk of a specific bill would be completely unpredictable to a person who did not have a thorough knowledge of the bill or the skills to deal with them. However, when pooled, the risk of total bills of exchange would become more or less expectable based on the previous default rate in a debt pool. It is expected that, like in the case of the present asset-backed securitization, this statistical attitude would allow the goldsmith bankers to make a more distant or impersonal relationship with a specific merchant's bills of exchange than in the early discounting business.

Goldsmith bankers' discounting business contributed to transforming the creditor-debtor relations of bills of exchange into those of modern bank money. In the last section, I compared these two creditor-debtor relations.

Permanent Indebtedness & Liquidity

Another method that goldsmith bankers exploited to maintain a fractional reserve was a scheme that made it possible to turn a *long-term* or *permanent loan* for a debtor into a *short-term loan for* a creditor. From the standpoint of a holder of a goldsmith banker's debts—the banker's notes and deposits—credit was offered to the banker in the short-term because the holder could easily transfer the banker's debts to others or convert them into metal coins, either on demand or at short notice. From the standpoint of the bankers, however, the credit could be—and usually was—considered a long-term credit that the bankers would not have to repay provided the bankers' debts were transferred from hand to hand between the creditors. Furthermore, a portion of the pool of credits to the bankers remained permanently in the hands of the bankers unless all the creditors requested conversions simultaneously. This portion would then become permanent capital that the bankers would not need to repay. It was permanent indebtedness that allowed bankers to maintain a fractional reserve and to create money out of "thin air." Arguably, the pooling and transferability of their debts allowed bankers to create short-term debt relations with a creditor while simultaneously creating permanent debt relations with the wider community. This scheme seemingly enhanced the security of the bankers' debts from both sides. From the standpoint of the debt holder, liquidity and transferability could create the impression that the holder was easily able to avoid a default risk of the debts. From the standpoint of the bankers, the appearance of long-term or permanent indebtedness due to transferability enabled bankers to make a permanent or long-term investment. This scheme allowed prominent goldsmith bankers at the time, such as Alderman Edward Backwell, to earn record profits: long-term investment in the Crown was the only exception to the usury law that prohibited interest rates above 5% or 6%. Bankers would charge an interest rate in excess of 10% on loans to the Crown.

However, this seemingly secure scheme was, in fact, insecure. Illiquidity in the form of bank runs and other liquidity crunches could easily be caused by external agitation or the defaults of goldsmith bankers' large debtors. For example, "the Great Fire in 1665 and [the] subsequent appearance of the Dutch at Chatham caused many goldsmiths to stop payment, and while most of them later reopened there were frequent failures among them."[42] Charles II defaulted in 1672 on the money that goldsmith bankers loaned him. This default, called the Stop of the Exchequer,[43] resulted in the failure of many London goldsmith bankers and made their notes unacceptable during the 1670s.

3.3. The Nature of the London Goldsmith Bankers' Deposit-Taking

The bankers could exploit these methods—the pooling of debts and permanent indebtedness—because depositors transferred to the bankers an authority to re-invest deposits at the bankers' discretion in the bankers' names. This transfer was a loan transaction in which the legal ownership of the loaned property was transferred to a debtor. If depositors, rather than bankers, had retained ownership of the loans, bankers could not have enjoyed the benefits of permanent indebtedness and a fractional reserve, simply because this arrangement would not have allowed the discounted bills to be pooled as assets belonging to the bankers.

During the Cromwellian period, depositors transferred authority to lend their funds to goldsmith bankers and allowed the bankers to own the debt claims of the loan.[44] This transfer of ownership differentiated these bankers from other early modern financial intermediaries in England. The latter intermediaries, such as money-scriveners or notaries, lent customers' funds at their own discretion. But after a money-scrivener had arranged a mortgage, the customers took over the debt claim of the loans.[45]

Goldsmith bankers' deposit-taking was self-contradictory because it was simultaneously a loan contract and not a loan contract. Because deposits were repaid on demand, the ownership of deposits practically remained in the hands of depositors. But bankers lent deposits at their own discretion and in their own names, and they attained and retained the ownership title of the loans. Here the ownership of deposits was transferred from depositors to bankers because a person—in this case, the goldsmith banker—could lend property in his or her name only when he or she had ownership of it. How could the ownership of the thing simultaneously be *transferred* and *not transferred*?

Under Continental civil law traditions "rights *in rem*" were strictly divided from "rights *in personam*," as seen in Table 3.1. In a loan transaction, the rights of a creditor are the rights against a person (rights *in personam*). The creditor cedes legal ownership of the property to a debtor until a maturity date and, in exchange, obtains a debt claim that goes against a person. At the maturity date, the creditor can oblige the debtor to fulfill an obligation to repay principal and interest. In a deposit transaction, by contrast, the rights of a depositor are "rights *in rem*" (the rights against a thing) because the depositor retains legal ownership over the deposited property. Due to this strict distinction, the above-mentioned contradictory nature of bank deposits in modern banking has long been an embarrassing enigma to Continental legal theorists. A safekeeping service has long been considered distinct from loan-making, and thus depositaries have been able to charge a safekeeping fee to depositors. Additionally, there has been a protracted moral and legal debate as to whether depositaries' attempts to utilize deposited funds for their profit constitute a crime. In the strict Roman law tradition, an honest depositary of fungible things, such as money and grain—known traditionally as an "irregular deposit"—had to keep 100% *tantundem* of deposits in order to honor the right of depositors to withdraw the deposits *at any time on demand*, while an honest depositary could not issue transferable receipts of deposits to a value greater than the amount that he kept. This rule existed even in the common law tradition. During the 1860s in the United States, grain elevators issued deposit receipts larger than the amount that they kept, by lending the receipts to speculators in the Chicago wheat market. Resultant dislocations in wheat prices and bankruptcies in the wheat market were settled when the over-issue was treated as fraudulent and illegal by common law courts.[46] However, an exception was made in common law with regard to demand deposits with banks. In 1848, in *Foley v. Hill and Others*, the House of Lords *finally* declared that demand deposits with banks were loans to the bankers. Here, in addition to the issue of deposit receipts to depositors, bankers were *legally allowed* to (over-) issue deposit receipts to third parties in the form of a loan.

Table 3.1 Deposits versus Loans in Roman Law

	Legal Category	*Ownership*	*Purpose*	*Temporality*	*Reserve*
Deposits	Rights *in rem*	Not transferred	Safekeeping	Withdraw on demand	100%
Loans	Rights *in personam*	Transferred	Interest-gaining	Fixed specific period	No reserve

Throughout Western history, private banks on the Continent abused the belief of depositors by loaning deposited funds to one of their customers. Governments on the Continent established public deposit banks to exact credit for public expenses, and particularly for international wars. However, these abuses by private and public deposit banks were frequently the object of public accusation. *Unlike the Bank of England*, the Continental public deposit banks were strictly prohibited from loaning deposited funds to private individuals.[47] The Bank of Amsterdam, which was a highly respected Continental public bank during the seventeenth century, was established to put an end to the abuse of deposited funds and maintained a 100% reserve ratio for more than 150 years after its foundation in 1609.[48] Thus, on the Continent, where both bills of exchange that were payable to the bearer and deposit banking developed earlier than in England, the combination of deposit and loan never developed as freely as in the case of goldsmith bankers and the Bank of England.

During the seventeenth century, one justification for interest-gaining on a loan was what economics today calls opportunity cost.[49] Demand deposits with goldsmith bankers did not entail an opportunity cost because they were paid at any time on demand. In spite of this lack of opportunity cost, interest-gaining was one of the purposes of goldsmith bankers' demand deposits. This coexistence of two disparate purposes—interest gaining, which characterizes a loan transaction, and liquidity, which characterizes a deposit transaction—was well described by an anonymous contemporary author in *The Mystery of the New Fashioned Goldsmiths or Bankers* in 1676:

> This new practice giving hopes to everybody to make Profit of their money until the hour they spent it, and the conveniency as they thought, to command their money when they please, which they could not do when lent at interest upon personal or real Security.[50]

The self-contradictory nature of goldsmith bankers' demand deposit taking[51] was a result of the double-ownership scheme of goldsmith banking. This double-ownership differs from fragmented or shared ownership. While in fragmented ownership each owner has exclusive ownership of only part of the property, in double-ownership each owner has exclusive ownership of the whole property. While in shared ownership each owner cannot use or sell a shared property without the consent of other owners, in double-ownership each owner has the free right to use and sell the property without the consent of the other owner.

Economists' Understandings of Goldsmith Bankers' Deposit-Taking

Economic historians regard goldsmith bankers' deposit-taking as a loan transaction, usually without providing logical reasons for it.[52] However, a recent debate between Austrian economists of the "free banking school" raises some issues relevant to the nature of the bankers' deposit-taking. This study identifies these issues as: the fungibility argument, the legal-impossibility argument, the certificate argument, and the fraud argument. The debate pits the fractional-reserve free banking school (hereafter fractional-reserve school), especially Lawrence White, against the so-called 100% reserve free banking school (hereafter full-reserve school), which includes M. Rothbard, Jesús Huerta de Soto, Hans-Hermann Hoppe, and J. Hűlsmann.

Fungibility Argument The fungibility of money units allows depositaries to return deposits in genre rather than in specie. The fractional-reserve school argues that this fungibility makes modern deposit-taking, including that of goldsmith bankers, a loan transaction by effectively transferring ownership of deposits from depositors to depositaries.[53] In contrast, the full-reserve school argues that fungibility does not entail the transference of ownership and that therefore modern deposit-taking with fractional-reserve is a fraud betraying the traditional safekeeping principle of deposit-taking.

In Western European history, the idea of fungibility was often used, unsuccessfully, to justify the depositories' personal use of deposited funds. In England around the late sixteenth and early seventeenth centuries, the same rationale—the maxim that "money has no earmark"—was often used in common law courts to characterize the deposit-taking of money as a loan transaction. For example, in *Bretton v. Barnet* in 1598, Justice Walmseley

> took a difference between goods and money: for if a horse be delivered to be redelivered, there the property is not altered, and therefore a detinue lies, for they are goods known: but if money be delivered, it cannot be known, and therefore the property is altered, and therefore a debt will lie.[54]

The maxim of "no earmark" was no longer used in *Foley v. Hill and Others* in 1848 when common law courts finally settled the issue of bank deposits as loans to banks. Instead of the maxim, it adopted the *bankers' custom* that bankers considered themselves debtors.[55] Lord Cottenham in that case did not explain why the maxim was no longer used, but the reason can be inferred from the earlier decision made in *Miller v. Race* (1758), where the fungibility argument was dismissed as justification for why a bona fide holder of money for valuable consideration can keep the ownership of the money that had previously been stolen. As Lord Mansfield declared in that case: "It has been quaintly said, 'that the reason why money can not [*sic*] be followed is, because it has not earmark:' but this is not true."[56] An implication of this declaration was that the fungibility of monetary units did not result in a transfer of ownership. This implication can be applied to banks' deposit-taking: fungibility does not entail the transfer of ownership in deposits from depositors to banks. Even though the court did not explain why fungibility does not result in the transfer of ownership, it is easy for us to reason it out. As legal theorist Benjamin Geva rightly argues, "Fungibility of money . . . explains the depositary's right to mix the deposited money instead of keeping it separate. It does not necessarily explain the depositary's right to use the money."[57] A depositary is still required to keep an equivalent amount of money deposited.

Legal Impossibility Argument For the full-reserve school, deposit-taking is so distinct from a loan transaction that an economic transaction cannot be both a deposit transaction and a loan transaction. For this school, if an economic transaction has these characteristics simultaneously, double-ownership titles would be established on the same fund. But, according to this school, this double-ownership is from the juridical point of view impossible because "two individuals cannot be the exclusive owner of one and the same thing at the same time."[58]

In contrast, the fractional-reserve school does not acknowledge the establishment of double-ownership in modern banking. This lack of acknowledgement, as Huerta de Soto argues, repeats the mistake that the currency school made when it played a leading role in establishing the Peel's Act of 1844, which founded the modern banking system.[59] The Act did not realize that an "on demand" clause made demand bank deposits constitute a part of the money supply, much as bank notes do, and thus that bank deposits with a fractional reserve—"issuing" unbacked deposits—have "exactly the same economic nature and produce . . . the same damaging effects as the issuance of unbacked banknotes prohibited" by the Act.[60]

Certificate Argument For the full-reserve school, unbacked modern bank notes, including those of goldsmith bankers, are basically the receipt or certificate.[61] In contrast, for the fractional-reserve school, bankers' notes were promissory notes that have differed by nature from deposits-certificates. To justify the latter argument, White insists that the circulating deposit-certificates, which had a bearer clause and were backed by a 100% reserve, and thus upon which the bank notes would be modelled, never existed.[62]

It seems to be true that in Western history deposit-certificates did not circulate freely *outside* the circle of depositors of an issuing bank before goldsmith bankers exploited both fractional-reserve deposit banking and transferable notes payable to bearer. However, this historical fact does not exclude the possibility that bank notes with a fractional reserve have had the characteristics of deposit-certificates. The following is the oldest preserved sample of a London goldsmith banker's note.

> November 28, 1684.
> I promise to pay unto ye Right Honorable Lord North and Grey or bearer ninety pounds at demand.
> For Mr. Francis Child & myself John Rogers.[63]

This sample demonstrates the coexistence of disparate characteristics: "promise" can be considered a loan characteristic;[64] and "at demand" is certainly the characteristic of deposit-certificate that provides the holder of the bankers' notes the present availability of deposited funds. The form that the notes originally took, according to economic historian A. Feavearyear, was the same as the above example, having the clause of "a *promise* to pay the named person, *on demand*, or with so many days' notice."[65] To conclude, the following facts seems to have occurred together. First, goldsmith bankers' notes with a fractional reserve were basically deposit-certificates. And, second, the certificates were a hybrid from the beginning, having characteristics of both loans—"promise"—and deposit-certificates—"on demand."

More specifically, the banknotes were promissory notes at law but were deposit certificates in essence. Legally, the notes that goldsmith bankers issued to depositors and borrowers were credit instruments—promissory notes. Promises to pay in seventeenth century England were referred to as "notes," and common law courts regarded the bankers' notes as promissory notes. And when Parliament issued the Promissory Note Act in 1704, the act regarded goldsmith bankers' notes as promissory notes. Most economic historians also assert that bankers' notes were promissory notes by which bankers became debtors to their depositors. For example, David Richards, a historian, argued that, during the Cromwellian period, depositors transferred authority to lend their funds to goldsmith bankers and allowed them to own the debt claims of the loan.[66] Because the law regarded the notes goldsmith bankers issued to their depositors as credits to the bankers, the bankers could loan deposits to third parties in their name for their profit-gain. But at the same time, the notes were practically deposit certificates since they offered to depositors and borrowers the rights to withdraw their deposits at any time on demand. This withdrawal on demand is not characteristic of promissory notes, as mentioned, since promissory notes usually have a fixed maturity date until which creditors have to wait for being repaid by their debtors.

Fraud Argument The full-reserve school argues that modern bankers commit two kinds of frauds. The first fraud is embezzlement committed by a bank against depositors. According to Rothbard, modern bankers, including the London goldsmith bankers, fraudulently use the money entrusted to their care for their own gain.[67] This rebuke of goldsmith bankers for embezzlement is incorrect because bankers loaned deposits to third parties with the explicit or implicit permission of depositors. Economic historian Richards confirms that rich depositors *fully authorized* the bankers to use deposited money as loans to third parties.[68]

The second fraud, according to the full-reserve school, is made by a bank and its depositors against third parties. When depositors allow a bank to loan their deposits to third parties, they "have in fact contracted to create additional titles and claims to the same existing quantity of property."[69] This creation is a fraud because no one can loan what she/he does not have.[70] Furthermore, the creation of additional titles and claims has brought about economic booms and recessions. Because recessions generate high costs for third parties who are innocently involved in the transaction of the bankers' money, including workers, suppliers, and consumers, the contract between bankers and depositors is a criminal act damaging the common good.[71]

The historical innovation of goldsmith banking contributed to this fraud. Earlier deposit-bankers loaned deposited funds mainly in the form of overdrafts that a depositor would use in order to settle a payment with other depositors. That is, in the system of book transfers, additional titles and claims that the bankers created were not extensively offered to third parties outside the circle of depositors and clients. In contrast, goldsmith bankers' notes payable to bearer were transferred from hand to hand between any person in a community and thus introduced a wide range of third parties. What the bankers supposedly offered to third parties was "ready cash," the present availability—ownership—of deposited cash. But due to a fractional reserve, what the bankers offered in effect was merely credit, a fraudulent creation of additional titles and claims. This credit creation exposed third parties to a new form of risk that did not exist in the traditional safekeeping business: the risk of illiquidity in the form of bank-runs and other forms of liquidity crunches.

3.4. Goldsmith Banking as a Trust

The idea of a trust in England made possible that which is logically impossible—double-ownership and the self-contradiction of deposit-taking. A trust is a double-ownership scheme and is self-contradictory by nature because it is simultaneously a loan contract and not a loan contract. These two characteristics of a trust—double-ownership and self-contradiction—enable us to think of *a trust* as the key factor underscoring goldsmith banking in particular and modern banking in general. Modern banking and the law of a trust have originated from the same historical context in the same time period and have identical mechanisms of the hybridity of property and contract.

After the Restoration of 1660, goldsmith bankers extensively started exploiting the self-contradiction of deposit-taking and the issue of negotiable paper. At the very same time, a trust became free from the legal restraints imposed by the 1535 Statute of Uses[72] and began to be transformed "from a jurisdiction based upon the personal interference of the Chancellor into a system of established rules and principles."[73]

In their origin, a trust and goldsmith banking share the same scheme. As in the case of goldsmith bankers' deposit-taking, a trust exists when the settler of a trust transfers legal ownership for safekeeping. That is, the purpose of safekeeping is satisfied by a loan transaction. As mentioned, a trust was devised to escape interference from rulers, especially the Crown, and thus avoid duties and responsibilities that were attached to property rights. A similar motive—to escape interference from rulers, especially the Crown, in order to keep safe an individual owner's interest in property—was crucial in the emergence of goldsmith banking. The historical event that allowed goldsmiths to become the biggest deposit-takers in London was Charles I's appropriation of cash deposited in the London Mint. In 1638, shortly before the outbreak of the Civil War, Charles I appropriated 200,000 pounds in coin and bullion deposited by

London merchants in the Mint. Even though the Crown returned the sum on condition that the depositors loaned him 40,000 pounds, this event destroyed the Mint's reputation as a safe depositary.[74] Many economic and legal historians, such as Richards, argue that this event "paved the way towards a system of private banking."[75] According to these historians, merchants sought places where their money could be deposited safely without interference from the Crown or Parliament. A number of London goldsmiths' establishments were chosen as safe places, and they finally developed into deposit bankers. These historians, however, do not explain *why* depositing in goldsmiths was more secure than in the Mint and other places.

No place seemed *physically* safer than the Mint. In history, the two most commonly used places for safekeeping of surplus money were temples and governmental institutions. At temples in ancient times, deposit-taking and primitive banking began.[76] A similar situation existed in England in the late medieval era. Monasteries were often used as safe depositaries.[77] They also acted as banks, providing small farmers with credit to ease their seasonal deficiencies in purchasing power.[78]

However, this form of safe-keeping and credit disappeared when Henry VIII dissolved the monasteries and subsequently when Edward VI confiscated their guild lands with the support of landowners greedy for those lands. The only remaining places for safe deposit were governmental institutions, such as the mints where money was coined.[79] These institutions acted as safe depositaries in Queen Elizabeth's time. And during the first half of the seventeenth century, the London Mint was chosen for safekeeping extensive amounts of cash.[80] However, when Charles I appropriated money deposited in the Mint, the only remaining place for a safe deposit disappeared.

Goldsmith bankers provided a safekeeping service in a non-physical way. They certainly were equipped with sturdy vaults, but there is no historical evidence to demonstrate that their vaults were safer than the vaults in the Mint. The advantage of goldsmiths was different: they safely kept money deposited by *loaning it to numerous third parties while still offering depositors the right of withdrawal on demand*, that is, by transferring the ownership of deposited money to numerous third parties while letting depositors retain the ownership. This use of loans for safekeeping was not unique in history. Around the middle of the seventeenth century, bankers in Seville loaned most deposited money to private industry and commerce to escape Charles V's attempt to confiscate funds remaining in their vaults.[81] However, goldsmith bankers were more innovative: instead of emptying their vaults, they introduced transferable bank notes. As mentioned, this introduction was very successful in "merging" the interests of numerous third parties in the same funds. Creating simultaneous ownership interests by third parties and depositors would make it harder for the Crown to appropriate the funds and would elicit greater opposition when the Crown actually did so.[82]

This innovation on the part of goldsmith bankers—loaning funds deposited with them in the form of bankers' transferable paper debts—was a trust. A trust has two essential characteristics: the *permanent indebtedness* of the trust and the *transferability* of the beneficiary's right. As described in Figure 3.4, the settlers of a trust transfer legal ownership to *a group of* replaceable trustees and in so doing solve the problem of an individual trustee whose death can terminate a trusted interest. As long as trustees are permanently replaceable, the trust can persist and can be placed in a *permanent* credit-debt relation with the settlers or beneficiaries of the trust.

This permanent indebtedness places a trusted property on the borderline between debt and property. It is a debt to the trustees insofar as they must pay a benefit to the beneficiaries. But at the same time, it is permanent capital to the trustees because they do not need to repay the principal of the debt. Here, a trust transforms debt into permanent capital or property, but with a condition to pay a benefit to the beneficiaries. The permanent indebtedness of trustees is also possible because the beneficiary's right is *transferable* between replaceable beneficiaries. These two central characteristics of a trust—permanent indebtedness and transferability—were exploited by goldsmith bankers. The permanent indebtedness of goldsmith bankers, as mentioned, allowed them to transform a portion of the bankers' debts into permanent capital and to maintain a fractional reserve. And like the transferable right of a beneficiary in a trust, the transferability of goldsmith bankers' note made it possible for goldsmith bankers to be indebted permanently. However, there is one difference between the general trust scheme described here and the specific situation of goldsmith banking. A general trust scheme does not offer liquidity—the open-endedness of a trust contract—because the termination of a trust on demand makes it impossible for a trust to be permanent. Goldsmith banking overcomes this illiquidity by pooling numerous trust contracts (Figure 3.5). By becoming a bigger debtor by taking deposits from and issuing promissory

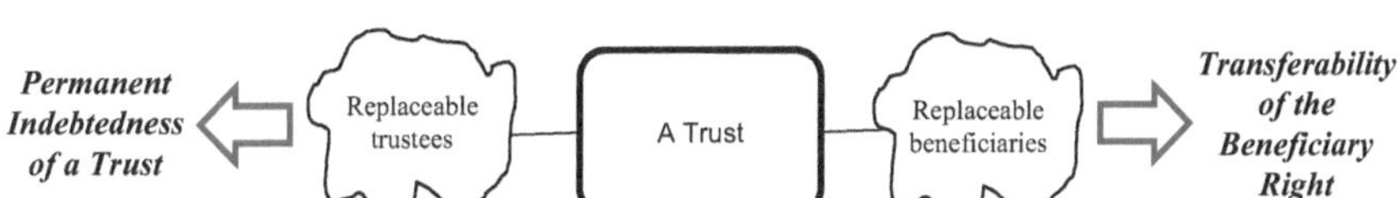

Figure 3.4 A Trust

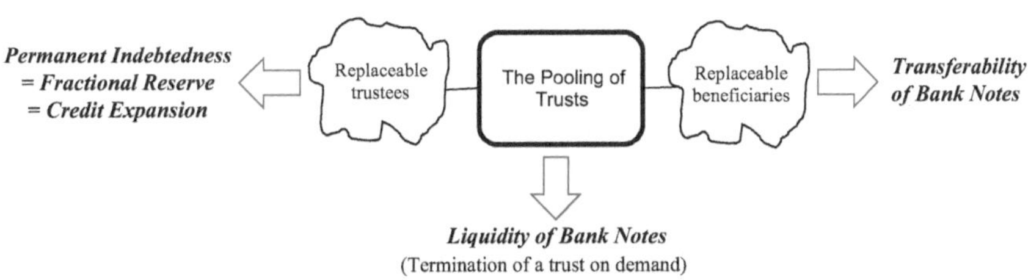

Figure 3.5 The Pooling of Trusts

notes to *numerous* individuals, goldsmith bankers could offer liquidity to a banknote holder; at the same time, goldsmith bankers could also enjoy permanent indebtedness in the aggregate because normally not all holders would demand repayment simultaneously. This method remains the foundation of modern finance: the widespread use of a trust in finance in the late twentieth century, in the form of mutual funds, pension funds, and asset-securitization schemes, among others, offers open-endedness—liquidity—by which investors can quickly exit from an investment pool by redeeming their shares or securities.[83]

This scheme that goldsmith bankers exploited fits the origin of the term *a trust*. The Statute of Uses (1535) was intended to reduce the range of the *use* extensively by returning legal ownership to equitable owners. To avoid this restriction, landowners made the double *use*: a settler of the *use* transferred legal ownership "to A to the *use* of B to the *use* of C." The settler expected that if the Statute executed the first *use*—to A to the *use* of B—and returned legal ownership to B, the second *use*, "to the use of C" still remained, that is, B still had legal ownership for the benefit of C. But this double *use* was soon nullified by the courts of equity and common law courts. In *Tyrrel's Case* (1557), for example, the Statute returned the legal interest held by A to the equitable owner B and did not allow any legal or equitable interest for C.[84] Here the Statute did not allow the equitable interest to be separated from the legal interest by executing the first and second *use* together. But beginning in the mid-1600s, courts of equity began to decide not to execute the second *use*: they began to make the double use effective by returning legal ownership to B while allowing the equitable ownership to move to C. This practice was firmly established in 1700 by *Symsom v. Turner* (1700).[85] Here in effecting this double *use*, the two transfers of legal ownership occurred: the first was made by a settler of the *use* to A, and the second was made by the Statute of Uses that returned ownership from A to B. By around 1700, the second *use* was called a trust. Goldsmith banking exploited double transfers of ownership as happened in effecting the double *use*. The first transfer of ownership was from depositors to goldsmith bankers; and the second was from the bankers to third parties. The making of loans to third parties—in the form of transferable instruments—for the purpose of safekeeping can be called the second *use*, a trust.

Like a trust,[86] goldsmith banking was a distinctively English phenomenon. This Englishness was demonstrated by the demographical distribution of bankers and customers. At this time many wealthy Dutch Calvinists and Jews immigrated to England. However, they were never conspicuous in goldsmith banking. The majority of goldsmiths and their powerful customers were Anglican rather than Calvinist or Jewish.[87]

This study does not mean that goldsmith bankers consciously thought that what they exploited was a trust scheme. There was no ready-made form of a trust that they could adopt from without. Rather, the study means that what they adopted was an ethos that had yet to be systematized but that pervaded the upper and middle classes at that time in England. The trust was at the centre of that ethos.

The law of trusts began to be systematized in the late seventeenth century and occupied the centre of English law by the end of the nineteenth century. However, modern banking has not been categorized under the law of trusts by lawyers or legal theorists. One reason for this is that the development of the law of trusts has tended to emphasize a fiduciary obligation of trustees that modern banking lacks. This trend is shown in the definition of a trust in contemporary law textbooks: for example, G. Bogert in his *Trusts* defines a trust as "a fiduciary relationship."[88] The lack of a fiduciary relationship between bankers and depositors is a central reason why the common law regarded, and continues to regard, the relationship between bankers and depositors as a creditor-debtor relationship rather than one based on a trust. When Lord Cottenham in *Foley v. Hill and Others* in 1848 finally established the legal principle that demand deposits in banks are loans to the bankers, he explained the principle as follows:

> The money placed in the custody of a banker is, to all intents and purposes, the money of the banker, to do with it as he pleases; he is guilty of no breach of trust in employing it; he is not answerable to the principal if he puts it into jeopardy, if he engages in a hazardous speculation; he is not bound to keep it or deal with it as the property of his principal; but he is, of course, answerable for the amount, because he has contracted.[89]

Lord Chancellor said the same in *Parker v. Marchant* in 1843:

> If it is merely a sum of money paid to a factor or paid to an agent, the party has a right to recall it—he has a right to deal with the factor or agent in his fiduciary character. But the banker does not hold that fiduciary character.[90]

The lack of a formal fiduciary relationship in modern banking, however, does not prevent us from considering modern banking as a trust scheme. The fiduciary duty of trustees has not been a central concern for the use of trusts in economic and financial spheres. According to Hansmann and Mattei, for recent trust funds, such as mutual funds and pension funds, "the trust form clearly is not being used . . . to take advantage of the particular fiduciary duties that are the default rule in trust law."[91] Rather, the trust form is being used to avoid a fiduciary aspect that the corporate form of business organization must impose on itself. As Hansmann and Mattei argue, the trust form

> easily permits the creation of an entity managed by persons who are not subject to direct control by the residual claimholders. . . . For example, trusts need not adopt the internal governance structures that are generally imposed on business corporations, such as the requirement that the entity be managed by a board of directors, elected annually by shareholders at a meeting held for that purpose.[92]

Here we can do what strict legal theorists cannot do because they tend to emphasize the fiduciary duty of trustees: we can categorize modern banking under the concept of a trust.

3.5. Transforming into the Capitalist Money Economy

It is important to note that the goldsmith bankers' (and the Bank of England's) practice of creating new banknotes had played a crucial role in transforming the credit economy of the Middle Ages into a capitalist money economy. The evolution of modern banking developed during the following three stages: (1) overdrafts in the system of book transfers in the Middle Ages; (2) promissory notes, particularly those issued by the goldsmith bankers in London and the Bank of England since the late seventeenth century; and (3) the current form of creating demand deposits.

In the first form of liquidity creation, deposit bankers in the Middle Ages created and loaned deposits in the form of overdrafts mainly to their clients who already had deposit accounts with them. These existing depositors used the loans to settle payments with other existing depositors. Moreover, since the bankers in this book transfer system did not use transferable banknotes, they did not loan deposits to third parties outside of their circle of depositors and clients. Thus, this old system of creating new demand deposits did not affect the credit economy of the Middle Ages where merchants used credit instruments, such as bills of exchange as the main medium of exchange, rather than money.

However, the London goldsmith bankers began replacing bills of exchange with their transferable banknotes by combining the issue of transferable banknotes with a discounting business. When bankers created their new notes and loaned them to third parties, they discounted the third parties' bills of exchange using their notes. This had two effects. First, the deposits that bankers created and offered to third parties were transferred between people in London, which introduced a large number and variety of third parties. Second, these banknotes gradually became the main medium of exchange instead of bills of exchange, thereby transforming a credit economy based on bills of exchange into a capitalist money economy where merchants and other ordinary people would use banknotes as the main medium of exchange. The goldsmith bankers' practice of loaning their promissory notes was copied by the Bank of England and other private bankers. These banknotes gradually replaced bills of exchange until Peel's Act of 1844 prevented banks (except the Bank of England) from creating *new banknotes with a demand and bearer clause* and loaning them to borrowers. Since then, however, modern banks have continued to create money by creating *new demand deposits* when making loans to borrowers. Creating new demand deposits in the current banking utilizes the same mechanism as creating new banknotes in goldsmith banking, i.e., creating liquidity.

3.6. Summary

This chapter has demonstrated the following. First, modern money cannot be considered to have evolved from bills of exchange; rather the origin of money should be found in a specific innovation of goldsmith bankers. Second, demand deposits with goldsmith bankers and bankers' notes were by nature self-contradictory: demand deposits were simultaneously loans to and deposits with bankers; banker's notes were simultaneously deposit-certificates and debts to the bankers. Third, this self-contradiction made it possible for a double-ownership title to exist in one and the same fund deposited with goldsmith bankers. This double-ownership was a fraudulent creation of additional titles and claims to the fund. The critical historical innovation of goldsmith banking—transferable paper payable to bearer—contributed to this fraud by introducing the interests of numerous third parties into the fund. Fourth, pooling demandable and transferable debts allowed bankers to enter into short-term debt relations with each creditor while simultaneously entering into permanent debt relations with the community at large. Permanent indebtedness transformed a portion of the bankers' debts into their permanent capital. Fifth, the most suitable concept to cover all these goldsmith bankers' innovative schemes—self-contradictoriness, double-ownership, transferability, and permanent indebtedness—is a trust. Finally, trusts and goldsmith banking emerged from the identical historical context and motive, i.e., from property owners' individualistic desire to keep their property interests safe from the Crown and from the intervention of the community.

Notes

1 Its religious version is the Protestant concept of inexpiable *original sin*.
2 Clark, "Restoration Goldsmith Banking," 4–5.
3 Ingham, *Money*.
4 Other types of clauses were not transferable. The bills "payable to X" were not transferable because they were payable only to a specific person "X." Also the bills "payable to X or his attorney" was very limitedly transferable because X's attorney was merely an X's representative and thus "if X died his attorney could not expect the drawer to remit" (Quinn, *Banking before the Bank*, 36).
5 The judge in the court said,

> A bill payable to J.S. or *bearer* is *not assignable* by the contract so as to enable the endorsee to bring an action, if the drawer refuses to pay because there is no such authority given to the party by the first contract. . . . But when the bill is payable to J.S. or order, there is express power given to the party to assign, and the endorsee may maintain an action.
>
> (1 Salk. 125, Italics added)

6 James Rogers properly criticises the traditional account of the English history of the laws of bills. According to the traditional account, the merchant practice of transferring bills had struggled against the common law principle that choses in action are not assignable. Criticizing this account, he demonstrates that since the early seventeenth century common law courts had accommodated the transferability of bills with relatively little difficulty (Rogers, *Early History of the Law of Bills*, 170–172).
7 Horsefield, *British Monetary*, xiii.
8 Richards, *Early History of Banking*, 237–238. Here, Richards writes, "It is a noteworthy fact that the general recognition of the assignability of bills of exchange payable to order corresponds with the development of goldsmith banking in England."
9 Horsefield, "Beginnings of Paper Money," 117; Gilbody, *UK Monetary*, 11.

10 In Proposal for Supplying the Government with Money on easie terms . . . p. 22, 1695, qtd. in Horsefield, "Beginning of Paper Money," 118.
11 Richards, *Early History of Banking*, 36.
12 Richards, *Early History of Banking*, 36; Nevin and Davis, *London Clearing Banks*, 11.
13 "Banks or other institutions carrying on a discounting business were non-existent in England prior to the reign of Charles I" (Nevin and Davis, *London Clearing Banks*, 11). His reign was between 1600 and 1644.
14 The goldsmith-bankers' notes gave way to the notes of the Bank of England, especially, after 1708 when it became illegal for any group exceeding six persons to issue note or bills "payable at demand, or at any less time than six months from the borrowing thereof" except the Bank (7 Ann., c. 7. (1708) Sect. 61.).
15 In his article, "Negotiability, Property, and Identity," James Steven Rogers expertly demonstrates this fallacy of idea of the transfer of identity that resides in the concept of negotiability of debt instruments. See Rogers, "Negotiability."
16 *Williams v. Field* (1694) 3 Salk. 68—"Every endorsement is a new bill and implies a warranty by the endorser that the money shall be paid."
17 *Starke v. Cheeseman* in 1700.
18 Holt C.J. in *Anon.* (1694) declared, "the indorsement is quasi a new bill, and a warranty by the endorser, that the bill shall be paid: and the party may bring his action against any of the endorsers, if the bill be not paid by the acceptor" (Holt, K.B. 115). In this case, the last endorsee brought an action against the first endorser. Holt C. J. gave judgment for the plaintiff, the last endorsee. Here the group of debtors was re-established by additionally including the endorser Paul and by being liable to the endorsee Martin.
19 *Bank of England v. Newman* in 1700, 1 Ld. Raym. 442.
20 "Transfer without liability, 'by bearer,' created finality for someone at the time the banknote was used" (Quinn, "Money," 154).
21 1 Salk. 127.
22 Quinn, *Banking before the Bank*, 48, "The more signatures a bill had, the more secure the bill was (Quinn, "Money," 154)."
23 Quinn, *Banking before the Bank*; Neal, *Financial Capitalism*. "Multiple assignments or endorsements therefore increased the security of this negotiable instrument [bill of exchange] and its liquidity" (Neal, "Finance of Business," 159).
24 Quinn, *Banking before the Bank*, 53.
25

> Alderman Blackwell was banker to King Charles II, the Queen Mother, the Duke of York. Sir Thomas Vyner was Lord Major in 1654 and made a baron in 1660 and was followed by his son Sir Robert Vyner. James Hoare was Comptroller of the Mint in 1661 and from 1679–1682 he was Warden of the Mint. The Martins, an established goldsmith family on Lombard Street, claimed direct ancestry to Sir Thomas Gresham, the renowned goldsmith of a century before. Sir Charles Duncombe inherited much of Blackwell's business after 1672 and became Secretary of the Treasury.
>
> (Quinn, Banking Before the Bank, 53)

26 "In no other respect were the goldsmith-bankers so attractive to the small investor than in their ability to repay on demand or at short notice" (Roseveare, *Advancement of the King's Credit*, 260).
27 Still, bills payable on demand "are rarely met with in practice" (Holden, *Negotiable Instruments*, 130).
28 *Tassell and Lee v. Lewis* (1695) I Ld. Raym. 743 at p. 744.
29 2 Ld. Raym, 928 at p. 930.
30 Cantillon, *Essai.*
31 An individual goldsmith bank maintaining a fractional reserve had very little room to expand liquidity. However, the goldsmith bankers' mutual acceptance of bankers' notes

at par allowed them, as a group, to create liquidity to the amount of the inverse of cash ratio. See Jesus Huerta de Soto's analysis of liquidity expansion in the fourth chapter of his book, *Money, Bank Credit, and Economic Cycles*. His analysis also can apply to the goldsmith bankers' liquidity expansion.

32 de Roover, *Business, Banking, and Economic Thought*, 229.

33 de Roover, *Business, Banking, and Economic Thought*, 229.

34 Richards writes, "[The discounting of a bill of exchange in England was] a rather late development: it appeared in England long before it took root on the Continent. Its originators were apparently the London goldsmiths" (de Roover, *Business, Banking, and Economic Thought*, 230) and "Banking on the European Continent, prior to 1800, was not based upon discount, but upon foreign and local exchange" (de Roover, *Business, Banking, and Economic Thought*, 236). Richards also writes, "The discounting of a bill of exchange was a form of loan, and traders in this way obtained funds from the 'exchange' goldsmiths" (Richards, *Early History of Banking*, 228).

35 de Roover, *Business, Banking, and Economic Thought*, 229.

36 "After a setback, the taking of interest had been finally legalized during the Elizabethan period, and under the Stuarts the problem of interest developed into a question of high rates and low rates" (de Roover, *Business, Banking, and Economic Thought*, 213).

37 2 Ld Raym. at 758

38 Rogers, *Law of Bills and Notes*, 170–186.

39 Holt said, "Unless some way could be found to define the limits of the law of bills, a creditor might attempt to bring an action on the custom of merchants in any case where he could find some written evidence of the debt;" and thus this attempt could be unfair to debtors (Rogers, *the Law of Bills and Notes*, 183). Rogers concludes that those decisions by Holt were "an effort, albeit unsuccessful, to deal with the inherent problem of defining the limits of commercial laws" (Rogers, *the law of bills and notes*, 186). From Holt's decision, we can infer that while the bills of exchange grew from the custom of merchants, goldsmith-bankers' promissory notes were largely an invention of the bankers.

40 Langbein, "The Secret Life of the Trust," 172–173. For example, a trust corporation that securitizes mortgage debts issues two forms of securities: Mortgage Pass-Through Securities (MPTS) and Mortgage Pay-Through Bonds (MPTB). The former are equities, and the latter are bonds. The transformation of debts into equities was not exploited by the London goldsmith bankers, but was exploited by the Bank of England at a later date, which added more overall stability to the trust mechanisms of modern banking. I will examine this in the next chapter.

41 This practice was more fully exploited by the Bank of England. As Holden writes,

> [bearer notes] were issued to depositors and may be sub-divided into two main categories: first, a promise to pay A. B. or bearer the whole of a deposit, or some irregular sum, and, secondly, a promise to pay a round sum, against a larger deposit, in connection with the discount business, or possibly as a loan. The note for a round sum soon became popular and gradually ousted that for an irregular amount.
>
> (Holden, Negotiable Instruments, 89)

Furthermore, H. Withers argues, "A trust company (still in the American sense) is to all intents and purposes a bank, without the right of note issue and is less strictly regulated by law" (Withers, *Meaning of Money*, 80 n.).

42 Horsefield, "Beginnings of Paper Money," 121.

43

> Charles II had made great use of London's goldsmith bankers in financing the Second Dutch War (1665–67) but defaulted on the eve of the Third Dutch War in 1672. Charles II's default, called the Stop of the Exchequer, left London's most prominent goldsmith bankers broken and without recourse.
>
> (Quinn, Banking before the Bank, 144)

44 Richards, *Early History of Banking*, 37.
45 Quinn, *Banking before the Bank*, 8.
46 Rothbard, *Against the Fed*, 38.
47 de Roover, *Business, Banking, and Economic Thought*, 228.
48 Huerta de Soto, *Money,* 99. However, in the 1780s the Bank began to systematically violate this principle of maintaining a full reserve ratio: During the fourth Anglo-Dutch war, it made large loans to the Dutch East India Corporation and the City of Amsterdam; hence, the reserve ratio of the Bank "had been cut from 100 percent to less than 25 percent" (Huerta de Soto, *Money*, 106; Quinn & Roberds, "Big Problem of Large Bills," 43.)
49 Nevin and Davis, *London Clearing Banks*, 11.
50 Anonymous, *Mystery of the New Fashioned Goldsmiths.*
51 Ben-Oliel makes a similar argument about the nature of modern banks' demand deposit. He argues that "A bank deposit is a deposit *strict sensu*, being neither an irregular deposit nor a loan, nor even a combination of both, but rather a contract *sui generis*" (Ben-Oliel, "Banker's Liability," 164).
52 Nevin and Davis, *London Clearing Banks*, 17; Richards, *Early History of Banking*, 223; Powell, *Evolution of the Money Market.*
53 White, "Fractional-reserve," 427.
54 Owen 86. The maxim was used also in *Higgs v. Holiday* in 1600. This Common Law Court declared: "If a man delivers money to another, the property in the money is in the bailee, because it cannot be known" (Cro. Eliz. 746 *per* Anderson C.J.C.P.).
55 2. H.L.C., pp. 36–37.
56 *Miller v. Race* (1758), 1 Burr. 457.
57 Geva, *Bank Collections*, 67.
58 Hoppe, Hülsmann, and Block, "Against Fiduciary Media," 21.
59 Huerta de Soto, *Money,* 252–253.
60 Huerta de Soto, *Money,* 253. For the details, see Huerta de Soto, *Money*, 182–231.
61 Rothbard, *Against the Fed.*
62 White, "Fractional-reserve," 425.
63 qtd. in Richards, *Early History of Banking*, 41, underlines added.
64 There is an ambiguity as to whether the term *promise*, on its own, means the credit characteristic. But because the bankers were allowed the personal use of money deposited, the term could mean the credit characteristic.
65 Feavearyear, *Pound Sterling*, 107.
66 Richards, *Early History of Banking*, 37.
67 Rothbard, *Mystery of Banking*, 88–90.
68 Richards, *Early History of Banking* 37.
69 Hoppe, Hűlsmann, and Block, "Against Fiduciary Media," 22.
70 Hoppe, Hűlsmann, and Block, "Against Fiduciary Media," 22.
71 Huerta de Soto, *Money,* 394.
72 The trust evolved from the *use* of land. The *use* dates back to at least the reign of Henry III in the early thirteenth century. And in the late fourteenth century, the Courts of Chancery began to enforce the *use*. In medieval times, if land was given to "A" to the *use* of "B," "A" owned a legal title to the land but should use the land for the benefit for "B." But the Statute of Uses 1535 restricted the *use*.
73 Martin, *Modern Equity*, 12.
74 Richards, *Early History of Banking*, 35–36.
75 Richards, *Early History of Banking*, 36.
76 Huerta de Soto, *Money,* 41.
77 Bisschop, *London Money Market*, 42.
78 Nevin and Davis, *London Clearing Banks*, 10.
79 Bisschop, *London Money Market*, 42.

80 Bisschop, *London Money Market*, 42.
81 Huerta de Soto, *Money*, 79.
82 This point is argued by Raghuram Rajan, who explains how goldsmiths offered better security than the Mint: "a hoard dispersed among many goldsmiths, and in large part further dispersed to borrowers, is both harder [for the Crown] to seize and elicits more opposition when seized" (Rajan, "Past and Future of Commercial Banking," 532).
83 Hansmann and Mattei, "Trust Law," 477.
84 73 ER 336.
85 1 Eq. Ca. Abr. 383.
86 The development of trust as an important legal system was, as F. Maitland argues, a distinctively English phenomenon (Maitland, *Collected Papers*, 272).
87 Richards, *Early History of Banking*, 212–222. As Herman Van der Wee argues, England learned and borrowed from the continent, especially from Antwerp, many financial techniques such as the assignment of bills of exchanges and the discounting of the bills and other credit instruments (Van der Wee, "Antwerp."). This fact does not contradict my argument of the English uniqueness of goldsmith-banking. Rather, the goldsmith bankers' unique combination of deposit-taking with loan-making—that is, the massive issue of unbacked deposit certificates in the form of loans to the private sector in London—developed those borrowed techniques on a different level. Discounting, in the modern sense, is to lend money on commercial paper before its due date after deducting the interest. Discounting on the Continent before goldsmith bankers was, as mentioned, not of the modern type and *not a form of a loan*, while the discounting of bills of exchange in England that the London goldsmith bankers initiated was *a form of loan* and of the modern type. Thus, it is evident that goldsmith bankers' lending on bills of exchange as a means of issuing their paper debts was an innovation that differentiated it from its parent. Furthermore, on the Continent, the assignment of bills of exchange developed away from the early use of a bearer clause to the establishment of the rule of endorsement, because bills of exchange with a bearer clause were troubled with negotiability. (The principle of negotiability is to guarantee "the new holder of a title the right to greater recourse than that to which the earlier bearer had been entitled" (Van der Wee, "Antwerp," 154–155)). But goldsmith bankers, as seen, succeeded in making the bearer type of their promissory notes prosperous without harm to negotiability.
88 Bogert, *Trusts*, 1.
89 *Foley v. Hill and Others* in 1848, 2. H.L.C., pp. 36–37.
90 *Parker v. Marchant*, 1 Phillips, p. 361.
91 Hansmann and Mattei, "Trust Law," 468.
92 Hansmann and Mattei, "Trust Law," 472–473.

Bibliography

Anonymous. *The Mystery of the New Fashioned Goldsmiths or Bankers: Their Rise, Growth, State, and Decay—Discovered in a Merchant's Letter to a Country Gent. who Desired to Bind his Son Apprentice to a Goldsmith*. London: s.n., 1676.

Ben-Oliel, R. "Banker's Liability in the Bank Deposit Relationship." *Israel Law Review* 14, no. 2 (1979): 164–183.

Bisschop, W. R. *The Rise of the London Money Market 1640–1826*. London: Frank Cass & Co. Ltd., 1968.

Bogert, G. T. *Trusts*. 6th ed. St. Paul, MN: West Publishing Co., 1987.

Cantillon, R. *Essai sur la nature du commerce en ge'ne'ral*. Edited and translated by C. Henry Higgs, 299–303. London: Frank Cass, 1755 [1559].

Clark, D. K. "A Restoration Goldsmith banking House: The Vine on Lombard Street." In *Essays in Modern English History: In Honor of Wilbur Cortez Abbott*, edited by C. Seymour. Port Washington, NY: Kennikat Press, 1941.

de Roover, R. *Business, Banking, and Economic Thought in Late Medieval and Early Modern Europe*. Chicago: University of Chicago Press, 1974.

Feavearyear, A. *The Pound Sterling—A History of English Money*. 2nd ed. Oxford: Clarendon press, 1963.

Geva, Benjamin. *Bank Collections and Payment Transactions: Comparative Study of Legal Aspects*. Oxford and New York: Oxford University Press, 2001.

Gilbody, J. *The UK Monetary and Financial System: An Introduction*. London and New York: Routledge, 1988.

Hansmann, H. and U. Mattei, "The Functions of Trust Law: A Comparative Legal and Economic Analysis." *New York University Law Review* 73 (1988): 434–479.

Holden, J. M. *The History of Negotiable Instruments in English Law*. London: University of London, The Athlone Press, 1955.

Hoppe, H.-H., J. G. Hülsmann, and W. Block, "Against Fiduciary Media." *Quarterly Journal of Austrian Economics* 1, no. 1 (1998): 19–50.

Horsefield, J. K. *British Monetary Experiments 1650–1710*. Cambridge, MA: Harvard University Press, 1960.

Horsefield, J. K. "The Beginnings of Paper Money in England." *Journal of European Economic History* 6, no. 1 (1977): 117–133.

Huerta de Soto, Jesus. *Money, Bank Credit, and Economic Cycles*. Auburn, AL: Ludwig Von Mises Institute, 2006.

Ingham, Geoffrey. *The Nature of Money*. Cambridge, UK: Polity Press, 2004.

Langbein, John. H. "The Secret Life of the Trust: the Trust as an Instrument of Commerce." *the Yale Law Journal* 107 (1997): 165–190.

Martin, Jill. E. *Modern Equity*. London: Sweet & Maxwell Ltd., 2001.

Maitland, Frederic. *The Collected Papers of Frederic William Maitland*. Edited by H. A. L. Fisher, Vol. 3. Cambridge University Press, 1911.

Neal, Larry. "The Finance of Business during the Industrial Revolution." In *The Economic History of Great Britain, Vol. 1, "1700–1860"*, edited by R. Floud and D. N. McCloskey, 2nd ed. Cambridge: Cambridge University Press, 1994.

Nevin, E. and E. W. Davis. *The London Clearing Banks*. London: ELEK Books Limited, 1970.

Powell, E. T. *The Evolution of the Money Market 1385–1915*. New York: Augustus M. Kelley, 1966.

Quinn, Stephen F. *Banking before the Bank: London Unregulated Goldsmith Bankers, 1660–1694*. Ann Arbor: University of Illinois at Urbana-Champaign, 1994.

Quinn, Stephen F. "Money, Finance and Capital Markets." In *The Cambridge Economic History of Modern Britain, Vol. 1 Industrialisation, 1700–1860*, edited by R. Floud and P. Johnson. Cambridge, UK: Cambridge University Press, 2004.

Quinn, Stephen F. and W. Roberds. "The Big Problem of Large Bills, the Bank of Amsterdam and the Origins of Central Banking." *Federal Reserve Bank of Atlanta Working Paper* (2005).

Rajan, Raghuram G. "The Past and Future of Commercial Banking Viewed through an Incomplete Contract Lens." *Journal of Money, Credit and Banking* 30, no. 3 (1998): 524–550.

Richards, R. D. *The Early History of Banking in England*. New York: Augustus M. Kelley, 1965.

Rogers, James Steven. "Negotiability, Property, and Identity." *Cardozo Law Review* 12 (1990): 471–508.

Rogers, James Steven. *The Early History of the Law of Bills and Notes: A Study of the Origins of Anglo-American Commercial Law*. Cambridge: Cambridge University Press, 1995.

Roseveare, H. G. *The Advancement of the King's Credit 1660–1672*. Unpublished Ph.D. Thesis. Cambridge University, 1962.

Rothbard, Murray N. *The Case Against the Fed*. Auburn, AL: Ludwig von Mises Institute, 1994.

Rothbard, Murray N. *The Mystery of Banking*. Auburn, AL: Ludwig von Mises Institute, 2008.

Van der Wee Herman. "Antwerp and the New Financial Methods of the 16th and 17th Centuries." In *The Low Countries in the Early Modern World*, translated by L. Fackelman, 145–166. Aldershot: Variorum, 1993.

White, L. H. "Accounting for Fractional-reserve Banknotes and Deposits—or, What's Twenty Quid to the Bloody Midland Bank?" *The Independent Review* 7, no. 3 (2003): 423–441.

Withers, H. *The Meaning of Money*. New York: E. P. Dutton and Corporation, 1919, 192

4 The Political Economy of Modern Money in Early Modern Times

Indebted Personae and the Rise of Modern Money

This chapter analyzes how the governance scheme of trusts, which creates personified groups—the modern state and business corporations—and makes them debtors, contributed to the evolution of modern bank money into de facto currency in early modern England. It examines why the concept of legal personae and trusts is critical to our understanding of modern money. Credit economies that existed before capitalism created institutions to protect debtors or often revived the social order by canceling consumer debts. By contrast, the capitalist credit economy considers strict debt obligations to be a supreme moral good and a way of maintaining the social order. It creates a political scheme to ensure that debt obligations are strictly fulfilled. This scheme is a trust. The trust turns the debts of individuals, whose death can cancel their debt obligations, into the debts of imaginary groups, such as the modern state, whose identities and obligations are permanently maintained by replaceable trustees. The section further argues that without this politics of the trust, modern banking could not have developed.

According to conventional wisdom, the modern state is the mere regulator of the market. By contrast, this book conceives of politics and the modern state as the constructors of modern banking. This book also helps to better understand the nature of bailout packages that governments provide to private banks during times of financial crisis. Through these bailout packages, governments turn the private debts of banks into the debt obligations of the state. Many scholars have regarded these bailouts as a remedy to these crises. However, to meet these debt obligations, governments must cut public spending, sell off public corporations and deepen inequality over the long term, as the financial crises in developing countries over the last three decades have demonstrated. Thus, if one regards a financial crisis not just as a relatively short-term problem characterized by bank runs and liquidity crunches, but as a long-term decline in people's well-being and equality after the resolution of the short-term problem, bailouts can be seen as important facilitators of a long-term crisis.

This chapter shows that the modern state can turn the private debts of banks into the debt obligations of the state because the state has an abstract personality distinct from that of a state's government and population. This abstraction is the most distinctive characteristic of the modern state.[1] When representative democracy arose, the abstract personality of *the* people was given to people, and the people as a whole were made liable for the obligations incurred by

DOI: 10.4324/9781003052210-5

their governments. This was a historically new phenomenon. Democracy in the ancient city-state of Athens, by contrast, began with debt cancellation, that is, when Solon, as statesman, cancelled the debts of the poor and banned debt bondage in 594 BC. However, literature on the origin of capitalism fails to analyze how the abstraction of the state or the people was decisive in the development of modern banking. This chapter argues that, had it not been possible to transform individual governments' debts into the debts of *the people*, and had the abstract identity of the state not been constructed, modern banking could not have developed in its present form. It further suggests that the vehicle of this transformation and construction is a trust.

Arguably, it is *the trust* that turns the debts of individuals into the debts of an imaginary group of the trust, whose identity and obligations are maintained permanently through the use of replaceable trustees. This is only possible because the trust is a governance mechanism in which property owners create and govern a personified group by making the group their moral debtor. I call this the politics of the trust. This chapter will analyze how these politics contributed to the construction of modern capitalism in early modern England.

4.1. Modern Banking as a Trust Scheme

Depositors in the case of demand deposits of modern banking are equitable owners because the demand deposits are repaid on demand, and thus the ownership of the deposits, in practical terms, remains in the depositors' hands. However, the demand deposits of modern banks are not regarded as equity under existing law. Instead, by treating modern demand deposits as loans, the law has legalized what was once considered illegal in traditional Roman and civil law.

Like the trust, modern banking arose out of the violation of the Roman legal principle that strictly separated rights *in rem* from rights *in personam*. As explained previously, these two inherently different rights become mixed when depositaries attempt to loan deposited funds for profit. Such an attempt—and mixture—was considered embezzlement under Roman law, where an honest depositary of fungible things, such as money or grain, had to keep 100% *tantundem* of deposits. For example, in Catalonia in 1360, a banker who failed to return deposits to depositors was beheaded in accordance with the law.[2] However, when the House of Lords in the case of *Foley v. Hill and Others* in 1848 finally declared demand deposits with banks to be loaned to the bankers, modern bankers could legally lend demand deposits to third parties in the bank's name.

When one conceptualizes modern banking as a trust, one can better understand the distinctiveness of the capitalist economy, which includes systemic vulnerability and the rise of big and powerful debtors. First, modern banking's use of the hybridity of rights *in rem* and rights *in personam* exposes a community to a new form of risk that did not exist in either the traditional safekeeping business or credit economy: the risk of illiquidity in the form of bank runs and other types of liquidity crunches. Such risk is similar to the risk in a "pass the parcel" game, in which "the loser is the one holding the parcel when the music stops."[3] When depositors suddenly realize that the banks' loans to third parties are failing and have placed the banks themselves at risk, the depositors initiate a run on the banks in order not to be left "holding the parcel." Furthermore, when modern banking creates economic recessions, it generates high costs for third parties—including workers, suppliers, consumers, and peripheral countries—who are innocently involved in the transactions of banks' money.

Second, utilizing the hybridity creates big and powerful debtors. Modern bankers can collect a large number of deposits because they can make two discrete promises. One promise is made as depositaries (payable on demand) and the other as creditors (interest payments). When modern banks issue additional deposit certificates, they do so by loaning them to third parties, who themselves become debtors to the banks. However, these banks simultaneously become the debtors of those third parties because the banks maintain only a fractional reserve. Thus, the more money is created, the more that banks and people become mutually indebted.

This was the birth of big debtors and the beginning of society's indebtedness to big debtors. A debt crisis in the capitalist economy is a crisis that affects not only individual debtors but also big and powerful institutional debtors. In traditional ancient credit economies, by contrast, a debt crisis was only a crisis for destitute peasants who were forced to sell their daughters into slavery to pay their debts, or to submit themselves or their wives to debt peonage or prostitution. Developed countries have devised various means of keeping big and powerful debtors safe from bankruptcy, such as establishing a central bank as a lender of last resort and creating deposit insurance.

4.2. Acceptance for the Payment of Tax

As mentioned earlier, goldsmith bankers were supposed to embed the interests of numerous third parties within the same fund in order to safeguard it. To this end, paper money had to circulate widely beyond the circle of the bankers' depositors. However, the goldsmith bankers ultimately failed to acquire third-party trust. They frequently suspended specie payment, and bankruptcies were relatively common. Illiquidity from bank runs and other forms of liquidity crunches were, as mentioned, easily facilitated by external agitation or defaults by goldsmith bankers' large debtors. Goldsmith bankers were therefore considered untrustworthy, and this untrustworthiness was widely perceived by the public. Furthermore, the goldsmith bankers' maintenance of a low fractional reserve—sometimes as little as 10%—also raised doubts about their trustworthiness. This raised the question: how was the unreliable goldsmith bankers' paper money able to circulate widely among a public that perceived it as untrustworthy?[4]

Here, the key to such circulation would be making the bankers' notes acceptable for tax payments. All citizens would then be able to accept even unreliable notes because the notes would allow them to finalize their tax payment obligations. However, the acceptance of goldsmith bankers' notes seems strange at first glance because the Tellers of the Exchequer, the cashiers of the English government, accepted specie for payment of taxes during the late seventeenth century.

A prominent, first-generation goldsmith banker in this period, Edward Backwell, contrived a detour. The following description of Backwell's detour is a summary of S.F. Quinn's research.[5] Backwell enabled acceptance of his notes for tax payments by making a private connection with a tax receiver, Richard Mounteney, who was the Receiver and Cashier of the Customs revenue for the Port of London. Most of the Crown's debts, known as tallies, were earmarked by specific future revenue streams that were committed to repaying the tallies. Thus, tax receivers could present paid tallies to the Treasury as proof of revenues collected. Prominent goldsmith bankers exploited this Exchequer's system, which combined sovereign debts with future revenues. First, Backwell bought the tallies that the customs duties were committed to repaying. He then assured the receiver of customs revenue, Mounteney, that he could exchange Backwell's bank notes with the tallies that Backwell held if he accepted Backwell's bank notes as payment of taxes by the public. Mounteney accepted Backwell's bank notes, checks, and bills of exchange from the public as tax payments.

This private connection between Backwell and Mounteney was doubly beneficial to Backwell's tallies investment. First, the tallies yielded very high interest, up to 10%, because the Crown was exempt from usury laws limiting the rate of interest to 6%. More importantly, the acceptance in payment of taxes solidified public acceptance of Backwell's notes and expanded their circulation. Everyone who had tax bills payable to the tax receiver would accept the notes, which could then settle tax bills. When Mounteney accepted Backwell's notes, it signaled to the public that those notes were as good as money for meeting tax obligations. Furthermore, this acceptance of a prominent goldsmith banker's notes for tax payments offered a benefit—due to the mutual acceptance of bank notes between goldsmith bankers—to other goldsmith bankers who did not hold tallies. Other goldsmith bankers' notes that Backwell received were also possibly accepted in payment of taxes to Mounteney. For example, in 1670, Mounteney presented Backwell with notes from most of the goldsmith bankers, which Backwell accepted at par with cash.[6]

The connection between Backwell and Mounteney was an early example of the late seventeenth-century arrangement between goldsmith bankers and tax receivers that enabled private bankers' notes to settle tax obligations. According to Quinn,[7]

> [s]ubsequent generations of goldsmith bankers and tax collectors continued the partnership. The team of Charles Duncombe and Richard Kent was the zenith of the late seventeenth-century alliance between goldsmith bankers and revenue offices. Charles Duncombe was following in the

> footsteps of his mentor, Edward Backwell, under whom Duncombe was apprenticed until 1671. What Duncombe learned firsthand as an apprentice . . . was Edward Backwell's purchasing of tallies secured on the Customs coupled with the goldsmith banker's extensive connections with the then Receiver and Cashier of the Customs, Richard Mounteney.

Before the goldsmith bankers' notes were accepted as payment of taxes, they were merely considered "money-like" thanks to their demand and bearer clause. However, when they were accepted as payment of tax, the notes became *de facto* money, circulating widely in the community as a means of settling debt obligations.

4.3. Modern Politics as the Constructor of Modern Banking

The Bank of England subsequently pushed goldsmith bankers' enterprise even further. However, the bank money issued by the Bank of England in early modern England were also unreliable due to the bank's series of suspensions of specie payment. For example, in May 1696, the bank suspended specie payment and only resumed it two years later. Immediately after the suspension, its notes depreciated severely: they promptly fell to a 20% discount against specie.[8] The rest of the early history of the bank was plagued by periodic specie suspensions and bank runs, such as in 1720 with the crash following the "South Sea Bubble" and in 1745 with the rise of Bonnie Prince Charlie in Scotland. This raises a question. How could have the bank's unreliable paper money circulated so widely among a public that perceived it as untrustworthy?

Simply stated, paper money could circulate widely because the English state supported modern banking in order to use it as a way of extracting war resources. War-making by sovereign kings in the seventeenth century created an urgent need for funds. Around the time of the Glorious Revolution of 1688, the English state's foreign policy was imperialist, eager to expand colonies and trade advantages. A major barrier to this imperialist policy was France. The huge accumulation of short-term debt—almost 6 million pounds—after the Glorious Revolution threatened to overwhelm the government's credit system.[9] To fund wars against France after the revolution, Parliament needed to move in the direction of long-term borrowing that did not require quick repayment. This need was satisfied by the proposal offered by some financiers and a City group in 1693 to institute permanent loans.[10] These individuals proposed to *incorporate public debt.* The Crown organized a group of its creditors into corporations—including the Bank of England (1694), the New East India Company (1698), the United East India Company (1708), and the South Sea Company (1710). The loans to the state were *securitized* into these corporations' stocks. The loans were pooled into these corporations, and, in turn, these corporations sold claims on the pool to investors in the form of shares. This securitization allowed the state to use the loans permanently without repaying the principal as long as the corporations remained incorporated. In return for permanent loans to the state, the Bank of England was granted the right to create paper money and to have this money accepted in payment of taxes. Because citizens who had tax obligations to the state could use the bank's private money in settling these obligations, they accepted the money as a means of payment. Furthermore, in 1697 forgery of the bank's notes was punishable by death. From then on, the deal between the bank and the state became the central node in the history of modern paper money. In 1833, the English state made this paper money legal tender, which forced the public to accept the private banker's money. Thus, private paper money, if it was legal tender, *had to be* accepted by a creditor when it was offered to him or her in payment of a debt. The bank's notes were not the king's money but private money, because they were a promise to pay issued by the *privately owned* Bank of England. "But they were getting near to [king's money]."[11] They were public currency.

However, this privilege of the bank's money was realized, as shall be seen, through the ongoing struggle and compromise between the Bank of England and the state. In spite of the proposal from financiers to offer a permanent loan, the government incorporated the bank initially for only eleven years and required the renewal of its charter to extend its incorporation.

Had the state not been continuously engaged in war, the Bank of England may have been abolished in its early days. Had the state not needed to collect long-term public debt, it would no longer have granted bankers and financiers the privileges of money creation and chartered incorporation. Parliament, especially MPs representing landed interests, was hostile to the moneyed interest of bankers and financiers that emerged in the latter half of the seventeenth century. MPs often depicted bankers as "upstarts who had been born in relative poverty but now flaunted their wealth" or referred to them as usurers. MPs in the late seventeenth and early eighteenth centuries reproached bankers for plunging the landed class into a permanent depression.[12] During the several decades that followed the Glorious Revolution, the tension between the two interests—the landed interests dominating Parliament and the moneyed interests as the government's major creditors—became one of the central themes of English society.[13]

The Bank of England was rechartered nine times between 1694 and 1844. Every time rechartering came up, ministers or Parliament threatened to review the statutory arrangements for the bank's operation. They threatened, for example, to dissolve the bank's incorporation or to establish other competing banks.[14] In fact, Parliament in 1696 authorized the Land Bank to serve the landed interest, hoping to create a competitor to the moneyed interest of the Bank of England. Even though the Land Bank failed instantly, this challenge prompted the Bank of England to negotiate the recharter of 1697. This negotiation extended both the fiscal capability of the state and the privilege of the Bank of England. The government was offered additional loans, and in return the 1697 Continuation Act proclaimed that "no other Bank or Constitution in the nature of a bank be erected or established, permitted or allowed by Act of Parliament during the Continuation of the Bank of England."[15] However, in spite of such a proclamation, the state remained omnipotent in constitutional theory. Another statute could have been enacted at any time to suspend what had been contracted.[16] In other words, Parliament could have set up another competing bank even after the 1697 Continuation Act. In fact, in 1800, after more than a century, the Bank of England had to negotiate an early recharter because of parliamentary pressure to establish a rival public bank.[17]

Arguably, this tension between the state and business corporations—the former being indebted to the latter—constitutes the politics of the trust. The corporate ownership of British public debt held by the Bank of England, the East India Company, and the South Sea Company rose to 80% by 1720 and then slowly declined to 20% by the late 1750s.[18] In spite of this decline, the politics of the trust, which maintained the tension between the state and business corporations, remained an important tool for restructuring public debt, because the bank's role as an administrator of public debt continued. The Bank of England has not been rechartered since the Continuation Act of 1844. As the landed class, beginning in the middle of the eighteenth century, effectively extended its investment into intangible property (such as governmental and commercial stocks and debentures, along with other forms of transposable goods), the distinction between landed and financial interests became blurred.[19] However, the politics of the trust remained an important governmental tool in nineteenth-century England.[20]

Public debt was war money. According to Michael Mann, British government expenditures between 1700 and 1815, most of which were funded by public debt, grew fifteenfold.[21] This unprecedented rate of increase was due primarily to a large increase in military expenditures. Huw V. Bowen argues that:

> [b]etween 1688 and 1815, England or Britain was involved in seven extended wars. . . . It was this continuing element more than any other single factor that defined the Bank's term of reference and the scope of its different forms of banking activity. This meant that public finance and the institutional mechanisms designed to service the spiraling national debt were forged in an atmosphere of ongoing conflict and crisis.[22]

One may speculate that, without the recurrent wars and war-related crises of the eighteenth century that generated the government's urgent need of funds, the hostility of Parliament to bankers might have led to the abolition of the Bank of England early in its existence. In 1702, a strong section of the Tory Party opposed the renewal of the bank's charter and claimed that large-scale continental campaigns only served the selfish interests of sectional groups and financiers by binding Englishmen to large and long-term debt obligations. This group of Tories insisted that England should first concentrate on naval and colonial campaigns, and that the wars could then be financed exclusively by taxes and limited short-term borrowing.[23] Without English involvement in large-scale continental wars, this Tory policy would have been realized.

The Bank of England began as a makeshift project to support the state temporarily during the war against France. So, initially few, if any, expected its huge success in mobilizing resources for large-scale wars. The financial revolution,[24] however, triggered by improved government access to credit allowed England to defeat France and to emerge as a dominant power in the West by the late eighteenth century. This unexpected success made the bank an indispensable long-term project for modern England. This explains why English banking, rather than continental public banking, became the dominant form of modern banking. Because English banking played a role as the provider and administrator of public debt, it became an effective means of supplying the state with war resources. By contrast, the continental public-deposit banks at that time were forbidden to provide loans not only to private parties but also to the public sector.[25]

4.4. Modern Politics as a Trust Scheme

This military-banking complex was possible because of politics centered on public debt. This politics can be characterized as a trust. As mentioned, the trust is a governance mechanism that creates and governs a personified group by making it a moral debtor. How does this process occur? A trust makes it possible for the individualistic purposes of property owners to endure permanently beyond a life span, and this is possible because the trust constructs a personified group independent of its constituents. The group of replaceable trustees solves, as mentioned, the problem posed by the death of an individual trustee, which can terminate a trusted interest. Here, the group personality of a trust is created by the group of replaceable trustees, who are obligated to promote the will of the settler.[26]

Similarly, the Bank of England's joint-stock banking was a governance mechanism between two personified groups—the bank and the English state—and the bank's shareholders (see (b) in Figure 4.1). As shall be seen, there are close links and the mirror image between modern banking ((a) in Figure 4.1) and modern politics ((b) in Figure 4.1), so that the governance mechanism of the trust scheme—modern politics—enabled the development of modern banking. This specific governance mechanism emerged when the relations between a community (a group) and its individual members took an entirely novel form. I specify two such novelties: (1) the personification of groups—the modern nation-state and the business corporation—independent of their constituents and (2) the establishment of these personified groups' indebtedness to their constituents. The blending of these two factors institutionalized the trust because the trust is the combination of the personification of a group and indebtedness. In the trust, an independently personified group is constructed, and this personified group becomes permanently indebted to its beneficiaries because it must be of benefit to them in perpetuity. As with the double-ownership of modern banking, in modern politics the two groups—the people and people—are exclusive owners simultaneously, as Figure 4.1 shows.

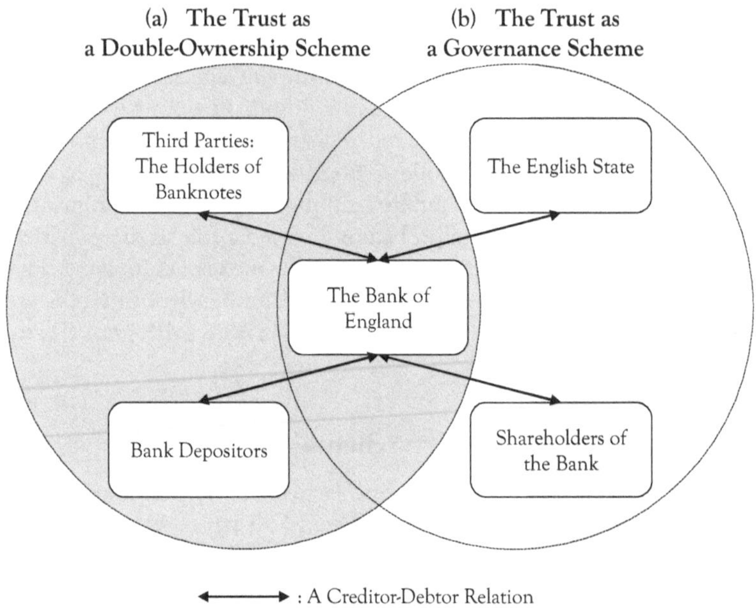

Figure 4.1 Early Modern Banking as the Combination of Two Trust Schemes

Public debt—a state's indebtedness to its citizens or groups of citizens—is a modern and Western European phenomenon. It existed neither in ancient Greece nor in Rome.[27] Traditionally, sovereign kings did not tolerate being indebted to their subjects because this indebtedness contradicted their supreme authority. Medieval English monarchs thus preferred to borrow money from foreign bankers, including Sienese and Florentine, rather than from their own subjects. The medieval monarchs of other countries in the West did the same.

Public debt does have some intrinsic problems. First, it defines the relationship between a community and its members as a creditor-debtor relationship, in that it considers a citizen's contribution to a community to be a debt that the community must repay in the future. This is an extreme case of individualism.

Second, as mentioned earlier, public debt has been seen as part of a war machine, in that it is the most efficient way of extracting war resources quickly and on a massive scale. Knowing how public debt put international peace in danger, the eighteenth-century philosopher Immanuel Kant argued that public debt allowed "the warlike inclinations of those in power" to wage war easily and was therefore "a great obstacle to be in the way of perpetual peace."[28] He therefore suggested that "no public debt shall be contracted with the external affairs of the state."[29] This state of affairs remains to this day. The U.S. military still used it to fund military expenses and wars during the twentieth century, including the Vietnam and Iraq wars. David Graeber argues that the

U.S. military expenditures "take up such a huge proportion of the budget that by many estimations, were it not for them, the United States would not run a deficit at all" and would not accumulate public debt.[30]

Third, public debt has contributed to increasing inequality. As Sandy Harger showed in Figure 4.2, the top 1% of wealth ownership decreased and increased together with the top 1% ownership of public debt in the U.S.[31] This means that inequality in the ownership of public debt has a strong correlation with inequality in the ownership of wealth. Over the past 35 years, ten-year U.S. Treasury bond yields have averaged 5.5%,[32] and in 2020, the United States paid 5.3% of the government spending (1.6% of GDP) as interest on government bonds.[33] This payment went to the rich, who own public debt, and was made at the cost of government spending on public education and public health, which have contributed greatly to reducing inequality.[34]

Fourth, public debt requires the state to be more than a simple collective. Instead, the state and its members must be treated as separate persons, since only separate persons can make debt contracts with one another. Public debt is incurred when a state becomes indebted to its subjects and when the responsibility for repaying this debt lies with the state itself rather than with each individual subject. Regarding the term "public debt," Maitland argues that "the public" is not so much a sum of individuals as a personified group that is separate from the personalities of the individual group members.[35] Here, the public becomes both *a collective person* with people as its members and *a non-collective*

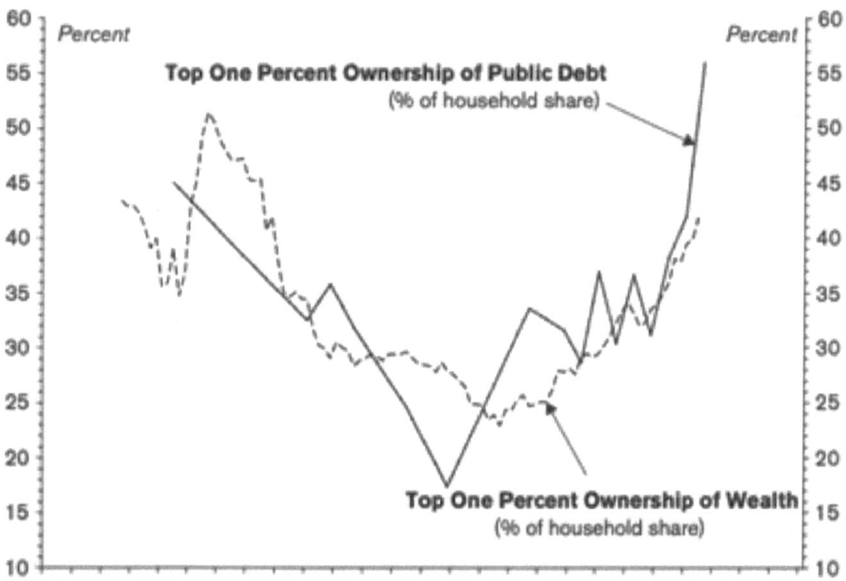

Figure 4.2 Public Debt and Wealth Inequality

Source: Harger, Public Debt, p. 41

person that has its own personality separate from the personalities of its members. This is a contradiction. As I have shown, this contradictory separation happened first in early modern England.[36]

The independent personality of the state can be regarded as growing out of the traditional body politics. The political relationship between the sovereign and its subjects in England has been instituted since medieval times as the relationship between two corporate actors—the Crown, as a corporation, and civil corporations. Since medieval times, various sectors of the population had been organized into corporations. Cities and boroughs, guilds, universities and colleges, hospitals and other charities, and bishops, deans, chapters, abbots, convents and other ecclesiastical bodies were corporate persons. In relation to these permanent corporate persons, the Crown, too, was a corporation. The king or queen in succession was a member of the Crown as a corporation. A corporation having a single member at a given time was called a corporation sole, in contrast to a corporation aggregate, which was comprised of many members. This relationship between two personified groups, the Crown as a corporation and civil corporations, was called the body politic. When the English state organized a group of its creditors into the Bank of England in 1694, it continued the traditional governing method of organizing a group of its subjects into a corporation.

The incorporation of the bank, however, had novel elements too. First, the state began to involve itself in permanent creditor-debtor relations with the corporate persons into which its subjects were incorporated. Second, the bank as a corporate person also began to involve itself in permanent creditor-debtor relations with its individual owners. I conceptualize this as the combination of the personification of a group and indebtedness—the trust.

The corporate state's permanent indebtedness to its constituents should be understood as a result of the political struggle in seventeenth-century England that revolved around the question of who was the sovereign that imposed tax and accumulated the sovereign debt? The Glorious Revolution resolved the question by creating a new personality of the state—*the* people—an entity that was sovereign over the Crown and Parliament and was responsible for public debt. Governments were no longer sovereigns but mere representatives of the interest of the people. Sovereign debt was not the debt of the Crown now, but public debt—the debt of *the* people. This innovation increased the government's credibility in regards to its debt obligations. Previously, sovereign debt had been the personal debt of kings, and thus went bad when kings died or their royal privilege allowed them to easily repudiate debt obligations. For example, Florentine bankers the Bardi and the Peruzzi went bankrupt when King Edward III repudiated his war debts in 1345. In 1672, King Charles II defaulted on the money that goldsmith bankers had loaned him. This default, called the Stop of the Exchequer, resulted in the failure of many London goldsmith bankers and made their notes unacceptable during the 1670s. However, after the revolution, the people became liable for the debt obligations of the government regardless of who the king was. This political change enhanced the government's commitment to and credibility in being able to repay its debt. This became the basis for developing the financial system in early modern England.

Public debt first appeared in the medieval Italian city-state of Venice in the twelfth century, and later in Genoa and Florence. Because public debt presupposed the corporate personality of the state, there was an important development in political theory. For the first time in history, there emerged the modern conception of the state. During the thirteenth and fourteenth centuries, commentators on Roman law in Italian city-states, especially Bartolus of Saxoferrato and Baldus de Ubaldis, regarded the state as an abstract entity, distinct from its government and its members.[37]

However, the indebtedness of Italian corporate city-states to their citizens was not public debt in the strictly modern sense, because the rights and responsibilities of a republic and its citizens were not fully separate. When a republic could not repay its debt, its creditors could claim repayment against a few of its wealthy citizens. The republic often forced its citizens to buy public debts. England was the first to fully develop the separate group personality of the state. Private property rights, which had been developed since the late Middle Ages and were settled by the Bill of Rights after the Glorious Revolution, prevented the state's creditors from claiming repayment against individual citizens and thus assigned the debt obligation to the state itself.

Modern business corporations have also become like a trust. Incorporation is generally understood to create a group identity. In traditional corporations, however, the personality of the group was not clearly separated from the identities of its constituents. As Georg Simmel writes,

> [t]he medieval guild included the entire person; a weavers' guild was not an association of individuals that only pursued the mere interests of weaving. Instead, it was a living community in occupational, social, religious, political and many other respects. . . . [I]ts members . . . were absorbed in it without rights of their own.[38]

Peculiar to the evolution of a separate group identity in England is the fact that the trust was a more popular scheme for group identity. With the Bubble Act of 1720, the English state forbade all corporate forms of joint-stock corporations that were not authorized by statute. However, until general incorporation was made possible by statute in the nineteenth century, trusts were widely used to create joint-stock companies. Corporations were *traditionally* a governing tool of the state to regulate civil activities such as trade. Thus, the group personality of corporations was granted, from the top down, by the Crown. By contrast, trusts were a tool for individual freedom to avoid the interference of the state, and they were organized autonomously, from the bottom up, by private property owners. Thus, the group personality of the Bank of England was a hybrid between a trust and a corporation. It had to be chartered by the Crown but, at the same time, depended upon the limited liability and transferability of its ownership. When the Companies Act of 1862 permitted the establishment of business corporations without a charter from the state, the traditional form of corporation was transformed into a trust scheme.

The first joint-stock corporation, the Dutch East India Company, emerged in the Netherlands in 1602. When the corporation borrowed money from its constituents—stockholders—in the name of the corporation, it could be regarded as a person possessing an identity distinct from the identities of its constituents. However, the independent personality was not fully formed in the strictly modern sense because the rights and responsibilities of the corporation and its constituents were not fully separated. The stockholders were less the owners of the corporation than its creditors. They could not control the corporation's business, because the directors of the corporation were elected by city councils, not by its shareholders. We can thus regard the separation of the rights and responsibilities of the corporation and its stockholders as the traditional separation between debtors and creditors rather than between the corporation and its constituents. By contrast, the stockholders of the Bank of England were owners and thus had the right to vote to select directors as well as decide important managerial issues. The directors, in turn, were accountable only to the stockholders. At the same time, the stockholders had limited liability. Due to this limited liability, the responsibilities of the Bank of England became separate from those of its constituents. Thus, the personality of a business group, understood in the strictly modern sense, was first formed in England.

4.5. Representative Democracy as a Trust

Representative democratic government contributed to the origins of public debt in two ways. First, it created the group personality of the state independent of the personalities of the rulers and the ruled. Second, it contributed to the conceptualization of the state as a moral debtor to its citizens. The same logic of representation applies to business corporations.

As Thomas Hobbes and John Locke argued, representation makes the impossible possible. A state cannot achieve unity or uniformity because its constituents—people—are diverse. Each citizen has its own interest, will, and desire differently from other citizens. However, representation transforms diversity into unity, and *people* into *the people*. Here, the interest of the people that representative government puts into practice is not the interest of *the majority of people*. Rather, it is the interest of the people distinct from the interests of *people*.[39]

Representation is a mythical concept. Tracing the semantic development of the term *representation* helps one understand how representation creates the myth of group personality. The verb *repraesentare* in Latin originally implied that "something absent is being re-presented to the gaze."[40] For example, representation refers to the asserted *magical* potency of aesthetic acts. A successful painting or sculpture, according to this understanding, does more than produce resemblance. It re-presents actual things or persons so that someone who sees the work of art will believe that he or she is seeing the things themselves and not merely their resemblance.[41]

From about the fourth century of the Christian era, the terms *repraesentare* and *repraesentatio* were extended to include references to speaking or acting in the name of someone else.[42] Here representation revolved around the term *persona*, from which the English term *person* originated. The public role of magistrates was to re-present or bear the personage of the city.[43] In England, Queen Elizabeth I as a public person was considered to represent the persona of the English state. This idea of representing group personality in a public person prevailed in Protestantism. "The idea that Adam and Jesus Christ are representatives of the whole of mankind was adopted by a large number of Protestants from Luther onwards, though the phrase is not Biblical in any of its variations."[44] An English innovation was to adapt this mythical idea of representation to democratic ideology. The radical propagandists of the 1640s began to claim that Parliament represented the people.

This doctrine had a serious flaw, however, and Locke and Hobbes tried to solve this problem by using the idea of the trust. As Hobbes and Locke correctly claimed, a collective consisting of the diverse interests of people cannot be considered *a* person who has one interest, and thus there is no preexisting personality or identity of the people that a parliament can represent. Hobbes and Locke thus argued that representation creates the personality of the people when each individual citizen *entrusts* his liberty and power to rule himself (by elections or through other voluntary means) to a king or parliament. By this *trust*, a unity or uniformity becomes possible in one body, whether that of the king or parliament. People are numerous and diverse, but a king or a parliament is a singular or small body that can achieve unity more easily.[45]

This trust added a new characteristic—a creditor-debtor relation—to the relationship between representatives and people and, by doing so, contributed to conceptualizing the state as a moral debtor. According to the modern doctrine of public trust, a small group of representatives *brings about* the interest of the people, and the power of trustees to govern people according to this interest is supreme. Unless this created interest betrays the good of the people, people cannot overthrow a representative government.[46] However, the power is entrusted by—or *borrowed* from—people. Public trustees have been charged with a moral and legal obligation to exclude their own interest and promote the purpose of the people. As a result, under the doctrine, the power to rule people is a hybrid, double-ownership scheme. On the one hand, it is the trustees' property because the body of the trustees brings about the united interest of the state. On the other, it is borrowed power that belongs to people.

Furthermore, the doctrine of public trust contributed to enhancing the government's commitment to the repayment of public debt. The creditors of public debtors pressed the state to honor its debt obligations, and this pressure caused the state to undertake administrative reforms in the late eighteenth century. For example, the *Reports of the Commissioners for Examining the Public Accounts (1780–7)* brought about one of the significant administrative reforms of the English government to improve the transparency and accountability of the government. In these reports, the doctrine of the trust is used as a central argument in favor of the administrative reform.[47]

In modern politics, the politics of the trust allows politicians to disguise their imperial ambitions as the universal interest of the people. The invasion of Iraq in 2003 was condemned as illegal by Kofi Annan, the Secretary General of the United Nations, but the invasion was disguised as the universal interest of United States even though American opponents to the war have outnumbered supporters since the summer of 2005. This construction of the universal interest of the people by representation has been criticized by postmodernists. Their main objections are manifold. First, the people and the interest of *the* people do not really exist because people are diverse in reality. Second, the creation of an imaginary entity of *the* people is anti-democratic. Third, representative politics comes from the desire to reduce diversity and creativity to sameness. As postmodernist Simon Tormey argues, "'[w]hat The People want,' is not what people want, but rather what it is that someone thinks the people want. It is what the 'representatives' of The People's interests want."[48] This construction of the interest of the people is a means for the representatives to project their class interest as universal interest.[49]

4.6. Socialization of Debt

Douglass North received the Nobel Prize in 1993 for his research, which demonstrates that the British government's commitment to repaying public debt after the Glorious Revolution contributed to economic growth. His historical research has often been used as a theoretical justification for advanced countries forcing the government of a low-income country to bail out its private banks and repay their debts to the banks of creditor countries, thus effectively turning private debts into the debt obligations of the people of the country. This policy was implemented by the IMF during low-income countries' debt crises in the 1980s and the Asian financial crisis in the late 1990s. The argument typically is that this commitment to repayment will improve the credibility and stability of the debtor country's national financial system and contribute to the long-term economic growth, even if this debtor country needs to adopt austerity policies in order to make the repayment. However, the long-term result of IMF policy has diminished well-being and equality for the people of many debtor countries.

This study challenges North's reasoning. It has critically discussed the nature of modern banking. What the banks from advance countries supposedly offered to private banks of low-income countries was cash. But due to the fractional-reserve system, what the banks effectively offered was only credit, a mere additional creation of titles and claims from one and the same amount of property. This created conflicts with the foundation of liberal democracy—the principle of property. According to this principle, it is deceptive for someone to create additional deposit certificates (i.e., additional titles and claims, from one and the same amount of property). Ultimately, the crises were caused when the funds that the developed countries offered were suddenly withdrawn from the developing countries both in the 1980s and (from the Asian countries) in the late 1990s. This sudden withdrawal occurred mainly because of the *vulnerable* nature of modern banking in the developed countries rather than because of the supposed corruption of developing countries.

The risk that a debtor will go bankrupt is, after all, what a creditor must endure in return for earning high interest on its loan. Nevertheless, during the crises of the 1980s and the 1990s, the IMF forced the government of developing countries to bail out their private banks and repay their debts to the banks of creditor countries. In the modern international state system, such behavior is based on the modern idea of the state, where the people of a developing country as a whole have been made liable for the obligations incurred by their often-despotic governments.

Something similar seemed to happen in the global financial crisis of 2008. This crisis began as a banking crisis in the United States. To stabilize their financial systems, governments in the European Union (EU) provided large bailout packages to their financial sectors. Due to these bailout packages and the subsequent global economic slowdown, the average fiscal deficit in the EU grew to 7% during the financial crisis, from only 0.6% in 2007, before the crisis. For example, Spain and Ireland had successfully maintained the deficit threshold of 3.0% of the GDP, as required by the EU fiscal rules, and they had usually even maintained a surplus.[50] These two countries' public debt crises resulted from their bailout programs, which turned the debts of private banks and financiers into the debt obligations of the people of Spain and Ireland.

As argued, this socialization of debt is possible because the politics of the trust creates an *immortal* debtor—*the* people. With immortality, the debt obligations of this imaginary group are maintained permanently, and creditors are strictly guaranteed that they will be paid back. This politics of the trust helps one understand how the capitalist economy differs from previous credit economies. Previous credit economies often accommodated reforms that reestablished debtors' status as equal to that of their creditors through the cyclical abolition of consumer debt, since unpaid consumer debts contributed to rising inequality in society. The hybrid, double-ownership of modern banking has led to unprecedented expansion of creditor-debtor relations. Concomitantly, the scale of debt crises has also become unparalleled. The politics of the trust has secured creditors' rights to save modern banking, but it has now increased inequality between people and between developed and developing countries. This growing inequality will destroy the social foundation of the capitalist economy because, to work, debt contracts require that they are made between equal persons. In the global financial crisis, the question is one of survival of our civilization.

Notes

1 Skinner, "Hobbes."
2 Graeber, *Debt.*
3 Horsefield "Beginnings of Paper Money," 124–125.
4 Horsefield, "Beginnings of Paper Money," 122; Holden, *History of Negotiable Instruments*, 92.
5 Quinn, *Banking before the Bank.*
6 Quinn, *Banking before the Bank*, 141.
7 Quinn, *Banking before the Bank*, 115.
8 Rothbard, *Mystery of Banking*, 180.
9 Carruthers, *City of Capital*, 73.
10 Clapham, *Bank of England*, 15.
11 Clapham, *Bank of England*, 50.
12 Jones, "Fiscal Policies," 71–72.
13 Carruthers, *City of Capital*, 202.
14 Bowen, "Bank of England," 17.
15 Clapham, *Bank of England*, 47.
16 Jones, "Fiscal Policies," 83.
17 Bowen, "Bank of England," 8–9.
18 Quinn, "Securitization of Sovereign Debt," 2–3.
19 Jones, "Fiscal Policies," 90.
20 Alborn, *Conceiving Companies.*
21 Mann, *Sources of Social Power*, 485–486.
22 Bowen, "Bank of England," 5.
23 Jones, "Fiscal Policies," 84–85.
24 Dickson has argued that improved government access to credit formed the basis of the development of financial markets, where the stocks of chartered corporations, the banknotes of the Bank of England, bills of exchange and perpetual annuities issued by the government were traded. Dickson calls this development a "financial revolution" that formed a national credit economy in late-seventeenth-century England (Dickson, *Financial Revolution*).
25 In this and subsequent sections, we discuss early modern banking, focusing on the development of the Bank of England. Even though the Bank was, until the 1826 Bank Act, the only joint-stock bank, country banks that issued their notes with a fractional reserve increased rapidly in the second half of the eighteenth century and numbered more than 780 by 1820 (Richards, *Early History of Banking*, 193). Our focus on the Bank of England is justified, however, because the development of the Bank's money served as a basis for the English national banking system at that time: those private country banks "increasingly used Bank of England notes as reserves and pyramided their own notes on top of them" (Rothbard, *Mystery of Banking*, 182).
26 In trust settlements, the group personality of the trust is not explicitly stated, but it is implicitly generated through the group of replaceable trustees and by the transferability of beneficiaries' rights.
27 Hamilton, "Origin and Growth of the National Debt," 118.
28 Kant, *Political Writing*, 95.
29 Kant, *Political Writing*, 95.
30 Graeber, *Debt*, 365.
31 Harger, *Public Debt,* 41.
32 Harger, *Public Debt,* 5.
33 www.cbo.gov/publication/56910
34 Piketty, *Capital and Ideology*. According to Piketty, a main reason why public debt has escalated since the late 1970s is that progressive income tax and progressive inheritance tax have been greatly reduced.

35 Maitland, *Collected Papers*.
36 After its creation, public debt has been often owed to foreign entities. Even in this case, the state is separated from its citizens' personality, and the responsibility for repaying the debt lies on the state itself rather than on each individual subject.
37 Canning, "Ideas of the State," 23–24.
38 Simmel, "Money," 18.
39 Runciman, *Pluralism*.
40 Skinner, "Hobbes," 160.
41 Skinner, "Hobbes," 160–161.
42 Skinner, "Hobbes," 161.
43 Skinner, "Hobbes," 162.
44 Hill, "Covenant Theology," 300.
45 Hobbes, *Leviathan*, §212.
46 Goodhart, "English Contributions," 677–678.
47 Torrance, "Social Class," 56–81.
48 Tormey, "Not in My Name," 144.
49 Moreover, as examined, representation is possible only when liberty is assumed to be a property that can be separated from a man and be transferred to someone else. Here, Locke's ontology of person-property is the philosophical basis of representative democracy. However, liberty is not such a property. You cannot separate it from yourself and sell it to another person. If so, you sell the whole of yourself and become a slave. The ideology of representative democracy as a trust is another metaphysical fiction.
50 Park, *European Fiscal Crisis*.

Bibliography

Alborn, Timothy L. *Conceiving Companies: Joint-Stock Politics in Victorian England*. London: Routledge, 1998.

Bowen, Huw V. "The Bank of England during the Long Eighteenth Century, 1694–1820." In *The Bank of England*, edited by Richard Roberts and David Kynaston, 1–18. Oxford: Clarendon Press, 1995.

Canning, Joseph P. "Ideas of the State in Thirteenth and Fourteenth-Century Commentators on the Roman Law." *Transactions of the Royal Historical Society* 33, 5th series (1983): 1–27.

Carruthers, Bruce G. *City of Capital: Politics and Markets in the English Financial Revolution*. Princeton: Princeton University Press, 1996.

Clapham, John. *The Bank of England: A History*. Cambridge: Cambridge University Press, 1958.

Dickson, Peter. *The Financial Revolution in England: A Study in the Development of Public Credit, 1688–1756*. New York: St. Martin's Press, 1967.

Economistes Atterres. *Manifesto of the Appalled Economists*. Available at http://old.atterres.org/?q=node/13&page=6. Accessed October 27, 2011.

Goodhart, A. L. "English Contributions to the Philosophy of Law." *Columbia Law Review* 48, no. 5 (1948): 671–688.

Gorton, Gary and Andrew Metrick. "Regulating the Shadow Banking System." *Brookings Papers on Economic Activity* (2010): 261–312. Available at www.brookings.edu/~/media/projects/bpea/fall%202010/2010b_bpea_gorton.pdf. Accessed July 19, 2013.

Graeber, David. *Debt: The First 5,000 Years*. Brooklyn, New York: Melville House, 2011.

Hamilton, Earl J. "Origin and Growth of the National Debt in Western Europe." *American Economic Review* 37, no. 2 (1947): 118–130.

Harger, Sandy Brian. *Public Debt, Inequality and Power: The Making of a Modern Debt State*. Oakland, CA: University of California Press, 2016.

Hill, Christopher. "Covenant Theology and the Concept of 'A Public Person'." In *The Collected Essays of Christopher Hill*, edited by Christopher Hill, Vol. 3, 300–324. Amherst: University of Massachusetts Press, 1986.

Hobbes, Thomas. *Leviathan*. London: Penguin Books, 1651.

Holden, J. M. *The History of Negotiable Instruments in English Law*. London: University of London, The Athlone Press, 1955.

Horsefield, J. Keith. "The Beginnings of Paper Money in England." *Journal of European Economic History* 6, no. 1 (1977): 124–125.

Huerta de Soto, Jesus. *Money, Bank Credit, and Economic Cycles*. Auburn, AL: Ludwig von Mises Institute, 2009.

Jones, J. R. "Fiscal Policies, Liberties, and Representative Government during the Reigns of the Last Stuarts." In *Fiscal Crises, Liberty, and Representative Government 1450–1789*, edited by Philip T. Hoffman and Kathryn Norberg, 67–95. Redwood City, CA: Stanford University Press, 2001.

Kant, Immanuel. *Kant: Political Writing*. Cambridge: Cambridge University Press, 1991.

Kim, Jongchul. "How Modern Banking Originated: The London Goldsmith Bankers' Institutionalisation of Trust." *Business History* 53, no. 6 (2011): 939–959.

Locke, John. *Two Treatises of Government*. Cambridge: Cambridge University Press, [1690] 1988.

Maitland, Frederic. *The Collected Papers of Frederic William Maitland*. Cambridge: Cambridge University Press, 1911.

Mann, Michael. *The Sources of Social Power*. Cambridge, UK: Cambridge University Press, 1986.

Martin, J. E. *Modern Equity*. London: Sweet and Maxwell, 2001.

Neal, Larry. "Venture Shares of the Dutch East India Company." In *The Origins of Value: The Financial Innovations that Created Modern Capital Markets*, edited by William N. Goetzmann and K. Geert Rouwenhorst, 165–176. Oxford: Oxford University Press, 2005.

Neale, Stanley. "The Bourgeoisie, Historically, Has Played a Most Revolutionary Part." In *Feudalism, Capitalism and Beyond*, edited by Eugene Kamenka and R. S. Neale, 84–103. London: Edward Arnold, 1975.

Park, Hyeng-Joon. *Analysis of the Causes of the European Fiscal Crisis*. GPE Research Report. Available at www.gpe.kr/100. Accessed July 4, 2013.

Piketty, Thomas. *Capital and Ideology*. Translated by Arthur Goldhammer. Cambridge, MA: Harvard University Press, 2020.

Quinn, Stephen F. *Banking before the Bank: London Unregulated Goldsmith Bankers, 1660–1694*. Ann Arbor: University of Illinois at Urbana-Champaign, 1994.

Quinn, Stephen F. "Securitization of Sovereign Debt: Corporations as a Sovereign Debt Restructuring Mechanism in Britain, 1694 to 1750." Fort Worth, TX: Texas Christian University, 2008. Available at http://ssrn.com/abstract=991941. Accessed July 19, 2013.

Richards, Richard David. *The Early History of Banking in England*. New York: Augustus M. Kelley, 1965.

Rothbard, Murray N. *The Case against the Fed*. Auburn, AL: Ludwig von Mises Institute, 1994.

Rothbard, Murray N. *The Mystery of Banking*. Auburn, AL: Ludwig von Mises Institute, 2008.

Runciman, David. *Pluralism and the Personality of the State*. Cambridge: Cambridge University Press, 1997.

Simmel, Georg. "Money in Modern Culture." *Theory, Culture & Society* 8, no. 3 ([1896] 1991): 17–31.

Skinner, Quentin. "Hobbes on Representation." *European Journal of Philosophy* 13, no. 2 (2005): 155–184.

Tormey, Simon. "'Not in My Name': Deleuze, Zapatismo and the Critique of Representation." *Parliamentary Affairs* 59, no. 1 (2006): 138–154.

Torrance, John. "Social Class and Bureaucratic Innovation: The Commissioners for Examining the Public Accounts 1780–1787." *Past and Present* 78 (1978): 56–81.

5 Shadow Banking in Neoliberalism

This chapter uses the notions of property and trusts to explain the nature of shadow banking from the twentieth century to the present day. As examined, the legal concept of property was created in the image of money in the late Roman Republic. This chapter argues that shadow banking creates money by mirroring credit in the image of property. That is, it is a social institution by which financiers obtain the privilege of enjoying both contractual rights and property rights. Moreover, it argues that the financial crisis of 2008 occurred as a result of this privilege.

Conventional wisdom has always been that the market is equivalent to capitalism. However, the historian Fernand Braudel and the anthropologist David Graeber refute this by pointing out that these two institutions are polar opposites in nature: capitalism can be viewed as a money-making system wherein money begets more money, and this occurs as a market is disturbed when capitalists ally with politicians to be grated with monopolistic power.[1] Agreeing with this view, this book is pro-market but anti-capitalism. The market has brought together groups of people not only with different commodities but also with "different modes of life, different technologies, and different ways of thought."[2] Simply put, civilizations would not have prospered without the market.

This study finds that historically there have been three forms of market: (1) markets that use credit instruments as the main medium of exchange, (2) markets that use money as the main medium of exchange, and (3) markets that use hybrids of money and credit as the main medium of exchange. This final one is the capitalist market where capitalists ally with politicians to be grated with the privilege of enjoying both contractual rights and property rights. The study has argued that capitalism is concerned with constructing both the *combination of creditor-debtor relations with personae*—the modern nation-state and business corporations—and *the combination of creditor-debtor relations with property*. The previous chapters of this book have explored how these two combinations have been realized in modern commercial banking. This chapter explores how they are realized in shadow banking—particularly money market funds and repurchase agreement—in the twenty-first century.

DOI: 10.4324/9781003052210-6

5.1. Money Market Funds and Propertization

Money Market Funds (MMFs) are a key element of shadow banking. However, MMFs have rarely been discussed in the literature surrounding the 2008 crisis because many scholars focused their attention on securitization and sub-prime mortgages. However, as a few scholars have correctly noticed, MMFs played a decisive role in creating the crisis[3] and transmitted it to Western Europe.[4] In the next chapter, I will identify that shareholders in the present form of business corporations are almost reduced to functionless debenture holders with limited responsibility. In other words, their responsibilities are those of creditors in their economic substance. Nonetheless, the law grants them the opposite: property rights. This granting can be named a "propertization of creditor's rights" In this chapter, I argue that a similar type of propertization also occurs in MMF shares and repurchase agreement (repos) and was a key cause of the financial crisis of 2008.

The concept of trusts as a hybrid between property and contract can be interchangeable with the concept of "propertization of contractual claims" because these two concepts imply the same process through which creditors are granted property rights. Recently, some scholars have used the term *propertization* to describe a social phenomenon wherein what is not originally property becomes property. This term is most often used for common natural resources or intellectual abilities such as ideas and knowledge. These resources and abilities are not originally property but should be commonly available to everybody according to the social rules of distribution. However, when someone is granted exclusive rights over the use, disposal, and transfer of these resources and abilities, they undergo propertization and become property. The term *propertization* is used in this book in a similar sense: what is not originally property becomes property. However, its use here has a difference. The propertization of contractual claims does not completely change contracts into property but makes them Janus-faced hybrids of the two legal rights (property and contractual rights) that constantly change their faces to enjoy the benefits and reduce the costs of both rights.

The law has simultaneously endowed shareholders with two disparate rights, namely property rights and contractual rights, something which will be explained in the next chapter in more detail. This situation also applies to MMF shares. The U.S. Investment Corporation Act grants MMF shareholders both creditors' rights—the right to claim dividends, limited liability, and no responsibility on corporate business—and property rights, which include voting rights at general meetings to elect and dismiss directors and to make important business decisions.[5]

However, MMF shares largely differ from ordinary shares in three respects. First, the ability of MMFs to buy other MMF shares has legal restrictions. For example, it is illegal for an MMF to acquire more than 3% of the outstanding shares of another MMF.[6] This means that the power of large shareholders to control other MMFs is legally curtailed. Second, unlike ordinary shareholders,

MMF shareholders redeem their shares on demand on the same day, by writing checks. In 1977, Merrill Lynch for the first time introduced "cash management accounts" from which their shareholders could write checks.[7] Third, and again, unlike ordinary shareholders, MMF shareholders are promised that a share maintains a net asset value of $1.

The last two aspects make MMF shares an even more contradictory combination of rights *in rem* and rights *in personam*, because they cause the ownership of the money invested in MMFs to be both *transferred* and yet *not transferred* from shareholders to the fund. On the one hand, ownership is not transferred: because MMF shareholders can withdraw the funds invested in the pool of MMFs at any time, on demand, by writing checks, they practically retain the present availability and ownership of the funds. A portion of the pool remains as the property of a shareholder, and because ownership is *not transferred* to MMFs from the shareholders, the shareholders enjoy rights *in rem*, and the relationship between the shareholders and the funds is an owner-representative relationship. On the other hand, however, ownership *is* transferred: MMFs lend the funds at their own discretion and in their own names, both attaining and retaining the ownership title of the loans. Thus, the ownership of the funds is *transferred* from the shareholders to MMFs because MMFs can lend property in their name only when they have ownership of it. As long as the ownership is transferred, the rights of MMF shareholders are rights *in personam*, and the relationship between the shareholders and MMFs is a creditor-debtor relationship. How can the ownership of a thing be *transferred* and *not transferred* simultaneously? This situation is self-contradictory, and this self-contradiction occurs because of propertization; i.e., because shareholders who are mere creditors are granted rights *in rem*, the right to use and withdraw funds at any time by writing checks.

In MMF shares, two disparate purposes coexist: interest-gaining, which characterizes a loan transaction, and the right to redeem an investment on demand, which characterizes a deposit transaction. One justification for charging interest on a loan has been what economists today call opportunity cost. Interest is considered compensation for the giving-up of the present availability and ownership of funds for a specific period. However, MMF shares do not entail an opportunity cost because they can be paid at any time on demand. Despite this lack of opportunity cost, gaining interest is one of the purposes of MMFs. This co-existence is the hybrid between rights *in rem* and rights *in personam*.

This propertized hybridity is the money-creation mechanism of modern finance. It creates a double-ownership structure in which two exclusive owners—shareholders and MMFs—enjoy the present availability of the same amount of funds. This double-ownership is a creation of an additional ownership title on one and the same amount of money.[8]

To sum up, the hybridity of shareholders' rights aims to enhance the absolute ownership of property—rights *in rem*. To express this situation in Hegelian style, shareholders enhance their property rights far beyond the limit of traditional property rights by appropriating their opposite, creditors' rights, as their element.

The enhancement can be called propertization. As mentioned before, shareholders, including MMF shareholders, are almost reduced to creditors when concerning responsibilities. Like creditors, they do not need to take any responsibility for their corporation's unethical behaviors, and they will only lose their invested money should their corporation goes bankrupt. Because the law has treated shareholders as creditors, it should have stopped granting them the opposite—property rights—if it had wanted to maintain consistency in the legal principle that separates the two legal categories: property and contract. However, the law is not showing consistency as it continues to grant property rights as well.

This propertization is a key cause of the emergence of big institutional debtors. By offering shareholders the two disparate benefits together—interest gathering and redemption rights on demand—MMFs can collect huge amounts of capital. Since their creditors (the shareholders) are very unlikely to withdraw all their money simultaneously, a portion of the debt always remains in the hands of MMFs and is transformed into permanent capital that MMFs do not need to repay and which they can use for their own gains most of the time.

Figure 5.1 shows that MMF assets have grown rapidly, from less than $2 billion in 1974 to $11 billion in 1978, $76 billion in 1980, $1 trillion in 1997, and

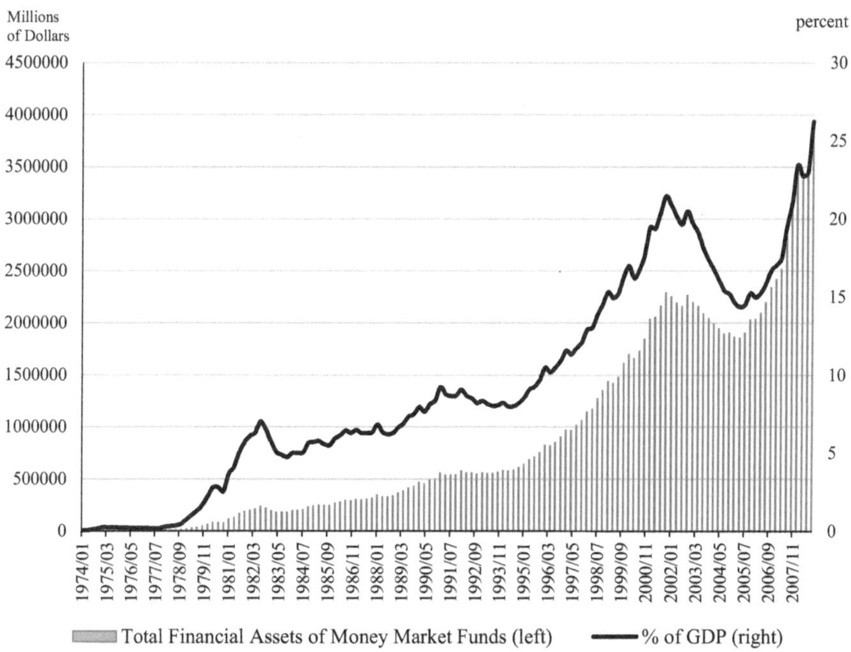

Figure 5.1 Total Financial Assets of Money Market Funds

Source: Board of Governors of the Federal Reserve System; U.S. Bureau of Economic Analysis

$3.8 trillion in 2008. This rapid growth has only been possible because MMFs have offered both the *demand*-deposit services of safekeeping *and* high interest to the large amounts of funds, often in billions of dollars, of institutional investors such as asset managers and global corporations. Commercial banks could not match these interest rates because an interest ceiling had been imposed on their demand deposits by Regulation Q, which existed from 1933 until 2011.[9]

The hybrid, double-ownership of shadow banking was enhanced when many institutional investment funds were organized as trusts rather than corporations. According to John Langbein, in 1997 half of all mutual funds were in trusts.[10] Funds choose the trust form because it offers them freedoms that are unavailable to corporations. For example, the investment trust can avoid the internal governance structure that state corporation statutes impose on corporations. Furthermore, the trust form allows MMFs to create and extinguish trust shares and thus be open-ended. By contrast, corporations need shareholder approval to increase the maximum number of shares authorized in the corporation's certificate of incorporation. Asset securitization trusts also take the trust form because it gives them the freedom to carve shares into tranches, which, again, is a freedom that corporations do not have.[11] These freedoms of the investment trust—the freedom to tailor interests flexibly, and freedom from regulatory governance mechanisms—reflect the root principle of the early trust, which was to give property owners absolute freedom over their property.[12] Investment trusts have the freedom to structure their organizational regimes in any way they wish in order to preserve and enhance private property ownership.[13]

5.2. Propertization and the Crisis of 2008

Before discussing how the propertization of MMF shares played a decisive role in the crisis, we need to understand the mechanism of "off-balance-sheet financing," where the financial crisis of 2008 occurred.

Figure 5.2 illustrates a (possibly overly) simplified mechanism of "off-balance-sheet financing." Traditional commercial banks supply "securitized financial products" to the shadow banking system, where dealer (investment) banks develop a "repo market" to broker these securitized products to MMFs and other institutional funds that either invest in these products or in the repo market.

In Chapter 3, I examined point ① of Figure 5.2—the traditional banking relationship between commercial banks, depositors, and borrowers, which establishes a hybrid, double-ownership scheme. Previously, commercial banks held within their balance sheets the portfolios of all the loans they made to borrowers. These portfolios are the banks' assets and include mortgage loans, credit-card loans, and automobile loans that the banks offer to their customers, all of which generate a stream of income over the long term. However, in the twentieth century up to the present day, in point ② of Figure 5.2, the banks sell the portfolios to a trust corporation (a special-purpose conduit, SPC), i.e., they put the portfolio out of their balance sheets. This trust corporation then slices the pool of debts into different tranches, which it then sells to investors

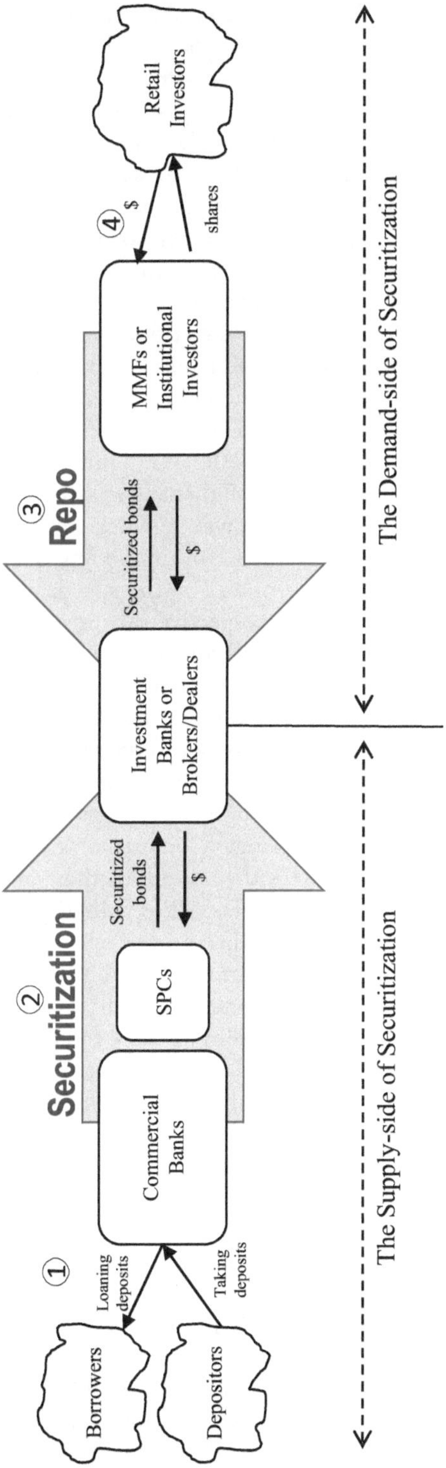

Figure 5.2 Off-balance-sheet Financing

as asset-backed securities (ABSs) and collateralized debt obligations (CDOs). To raise the funds to buy these products, those conduits sell short-term asset-backed commercial papers (ABCPs). These safe ABCPs are ensured an AAA rating and sold primarily to MMFs, with the sale of the products usually brokered by broker-dealers such as Merrill Lynch and Morgan Stanley.

This off-balance-sheet financing has become so popular, in part, because of the banks' need to avoid the capital-regulation requirement imposed by the Basel I Accord.[14] However, the main reason for its popularity is the high demand for securitized products from investment banking, particularly from MMFs, for safe, high-quality assets to invest in.[15]

Before the 2008 crisis, the off-balance-sheet financing looked safe from the standpoint of investors. For example, large banks typically promised to provide credit guarantees to their conduits if the conduits faced a default. In addition, the CDOs sold to the demand side of off-balance-sheet financing were mainly the safest tranches, while the toxic waste—the most junior tranche of sub-prime mortgage loans—was often held by the issuing bank and was thus rarely injected into the off-balance-sheet financing. However, when investors created a run on MMFs, these funds suddenly created a run on the repo market. The reason for these runs cannot be explained entirely by the sub-prime mortgage crisis because, as Ben Bernanke claimed, "prospective sub-prime losses were clearly not large enough on their own to account for the magnitude of the crisis."[16]

MMFs are the demand side of the off-balance-sheet financing. They are open-ended mutual funds that are registered under Rule 2a-7 of the Investment Corporation Act of 1940. The crisis of 2008 began within the *demand side* of the off-balance-sheet financing when investors, especially institutional investors, created a run on MMFs.[17] Unlike other mutual funds, MMFs are exempted by the Security and Exchange Commission's (SEC) "Rule 2a-7" from mark-to-market, so that MMFs do not adjust their prices per share to reflect the daily market value of their assets. Thus, MMFs can claim that their assets are always worth 100 cents on the dollar, even when they are not. MMFs are also open-ended, making it possible for their retail investors to redeem their shares on demand on the same day. Together with the open-endedness of the shares, by promising to maintain a net asset value of $1 per share, MMFs falsely lead their shareholders to believe that they have kept their cash in MMFs.[18] However, in reality, the cash that MMF shareholders invest in MMFs is loaned to third parties in the name of MMFs. When the shareholders suddenly realize that their belief is wrong and that MMFs' loans to their parties might be at risk, they create a run on them.

On September 16, 2008, when the Reserve Primary Fund—a large MMF with $65 billion in assets—announced that its shares were worth only 97 cents, it faced approximately $39.6 billion worth of redemption requests. This event triggered bank runs on other MMFs and resulted in the withdrawal of about $172 billion in a week.[19] Thus, MMFs were forced to sell their assets, such as commercial papers (CP) and certificates of deposits (CD), at fire-sale prices, creating a major liquidity crisis among the prime borrowers in the CP and

CD markets. Such runs would have been much greater, and the U.S. financial system would have probably collapsed entirely, had the U.S. Department of the Treasury not promised temporary deposit insurance covering the entire $3.45 trillion worth of MMFs on September 19.

MMFs were also responsible for transmitting the crisis to Western Europe. At the time, MMFs in the United States invested massively in European banks, especially in CDs issued by the banks. Interestingly, a large part of these purchases by MMFs started after August 2007 because they wanted to find safer investments in order to be away from the sub-prime mortgage crisis of 2007. In September 2008, when MMFs sold commercial paper and CDs at fire-sale prices, a major liquidity crisis was created among European banks.[20] This private-banking crisis of European banks then became a sovereign-debt crisis when European states provided bailout packages to the banks.

The aforementioned double-ownership scheme of MMF shares is almost the same as that of commercial banks. In commercial banking, one amount of cash deposited creates two cash balances of the same amount: one for depositors, the other for a commercial bank. This double-ownership scheme has historically created financial crises. A similar crisis happened with MMFs in 2008 because the creditor-like shareholders had a property right, namely the right to withdraw funds at any time on demand. When shareholders run on MMFs in order not to be the loser like someone holding a parcel when the music stops in a pass the parcel game, they shift the risk to others and create the risk of financial collapse. In this sense, as Gorton and Metrick argue, the crisis of 2008 is analogous to the banking panics of the nineteenth century that happened because of bank runs in the demand deposits of commercial banks.[21]

MMFs also exacerbated the crisis by contributing to the creation of another type of propertization: a repo. A repo consists of two sales transactions in which a seller (e.g., a broker-dealer) sells an asset to a buyer (e.g., MMFs) at a price lower than the market price, with a promise to repurchase the same asset at a higher price in the future. Even though a repo takes the legal form of a sale, it is not actually a sale for the following two reasons. First, a repo does not involve an equal exchange. In an ordinary sale, a seller would not intentionally sell an asset at a price lower than the market price. Second, an obligation to repurchase it at a higher price is imposed on the seller (as long as the buyer wants it), which is essentially a debt obligation. In an ordinary sale, the seller would not be obliged to repurchase an asset at a higher price than its selling price. Therefore, substantially, a repo is a secured loan: the selling price of the asset becomes the amount of the loan; the difference between the selling price and the repurchased price becomes interest; and the asset sold to the repo buyer (i.e., the creditor) functions as a collateral that the buyer would refuse to sell back to the repo seller (i.e., the debtor) if the seller fails to pay back the loaned money. In 2008, MMFs made a run on repo markets. This run and the resultant collapse of the repo markets were major events that triggered a systemic crisis.[22] MMFs could make these runs because their investment in repo markets was, as shall be seen, propertized.

Interestingly, this propertization of repos was demanded by MMFs. The Investment Corporation Act in the United States restricted mutual fund investment in entities engaged in securities-related businesses because a mutual fund can be exposed to the risks of the business. This restriction should have been applied to repos whenever a broker-dealer is a counterparty because MMFs' investment in repos is in substance a loan and MMFs are therefore exposed to the risk of the loan. However, the U.S. SEC made an exception for repos to satisfy MMFs' investment demand by regarding repos as a "purchase" of securities rather than a "debt" of the broker-dealer *when the purchase satisfies certain conditions*.[23] These conditions were that: (1) the legal ownership of the collaterals should be completely transferred to MMFs; and (2) MMFs should be excluded from the Chapter 11 bankruptcy process and be permitted to withdraw their investment when the seller of a repo goes bankrupt.[24]

As will be outlined below, if an investment satisfies these two conditions, an investor (the creditor) is granted property rights that other simple creditors will not enjoy. It is a scheme of propertization. Repos can satisfy those two conditions because they are structured as a sale, even though they are, in substance, a secured loan. However, unlike a secured loan, a repo satisfies condition (1) shown previously.

Because a repo takes the form of a sale, the ownership of collateral is *transferred* from a debtor (a seller) to a creditor (a buyer, MMFs in our case) in repo contracts. This transfer does not occur in a secure-loan contract. In a secure-loan contract, a debtor retains property rights in the collateral, while a creditor has the right to possess the collateral or to sell it only if the debtor breaches a payment obligation. By contrast, the creditor in a repo has complete power and the right to possess and sell the collateral because the ownership of collateral has been completely transferred to the creditor (in our case, an MMF). The creditor (buyer) is only obliged to replace the collateral with equivalent security by the date of the repurchase contract.

A single piece of collateral is often used to effect settlement in a number of repo contracts on the same day, a process known as rehypothecation. Through rehypothecation, for example, a broker-dealer can leverage her initial capital twenty times in the repo market.[25] Bear Stearns and Lehman Brothers had leverage ratios of over 30:1 before their bankruptcies.[26] Money is created in repos. As mentioned, the selling price of collateral is the amount of the loan that is delivered to the debtor of a repo. The debtor enjoys the ownership of the loan and uses its availability. However, its creditor simultaneously takes ownership of the collateral and uses it for other contracts. It is money creation because the creditor does not loan any money to a debtor from the perspective of the creditor, even though the debtor borrows and uses the money. This money creation happens because repos are a propertization scheme; i.e., the creditors of repos are granted property rights on collateral.

The above two conditions (1) and (2) grant a repo buyer the property right to freely withdraw their investment when the seller goes bankrupt. Because repos are loan contracts in their economic substance, they should have been subject to the Chapter 11 bankruptcy process, which is designed to distribute the assets of a bankrupt debtor as fairly as possible among the creditors. The process includes an automatic stay, which prevents creditors from collecting a debtor's assets before a court assesses both the value of the debtor's assets and the full extent of the creditors' claims. The process also voids any recent payments made by the firm, because payments made just prior to bankruptcy can favor one creditor over others. This procedure is known as avoidance. Thus, collateral posted against a derivative contract during the ninety days before declaring bankruptcy is subject to avoidance.

A repo, however, is excluded from the Chapter 11 bankruptcy process and is therefore not subject to the requirements of an automatic stay and avoidance because repos legally take the form of a sale contract. In this way, creditors can quickly withdraw the contract by selling collateral before their prices collapse, even when a debtor goes bankrupt. This advantage of repos has been criticized for giving creditors of repos an unfair privilege because other creditors cannot withdraw their loans until a court's final decision. This privilege is a property right—the right of property owners to withdraw their money and finalize a contract regardless of the agreement or consensus between parties, including other creditors and the court.

This propertization, which grants property rights to the creditors of repos, has led to a boom in the repo market over the past few decades. Even though there is no official data, the U.S. repo market exceeded $10 trillion in mid-2008.[27] The amount of money that security brokers and dealers borrowed by repos reached its highest level of $3.1 trillion in 2007, as seen in Figure 5.3. In July 2008, MMFs alone held $605 billion in repos, as seen in Figure 5.4. However, a run on repo markets occurred in 2008 because the creditors of repos, including MMFs, could enjoy the property right of rapidly withdrawing their investment.

To sum up, a repo is a propertization of contractual claims. Even though repo buyers are substantially creditors having rights *in personam*, they can also enjoy rights *in rem* because the repo is disguisedly structured as a sale. By doing so, the law considers a buyer of a repo (the creditor) to have rights *in rem* on collateral. This propertization grants the privileged finality of money to a creditor-debtor contract, and by doing so the creditors of repos are free to finalize their creditor-debtor contracts without the aforementioned intervention of bankruptcy courts.

Propertization in repos would not have been possible without political support from Congress. In 1982, a U.S. bankruptcy court in *In re Lombard-Wall* ruled that a repo is a secured loan and ordered the buyer (creditor) of a repo to turn over the collateral to the seller. This court decision made the collateral posted for a repo subject to the requirement of an automatic stay during the bankruptcy process. This decision aimed to defeat the artful self-serving attempts by lawyers and financiers to make loan transactions look like sale transactions in order to avoid the bankruptcy process.[28] However, this court decision so distressed the government, the Federal Reserve,

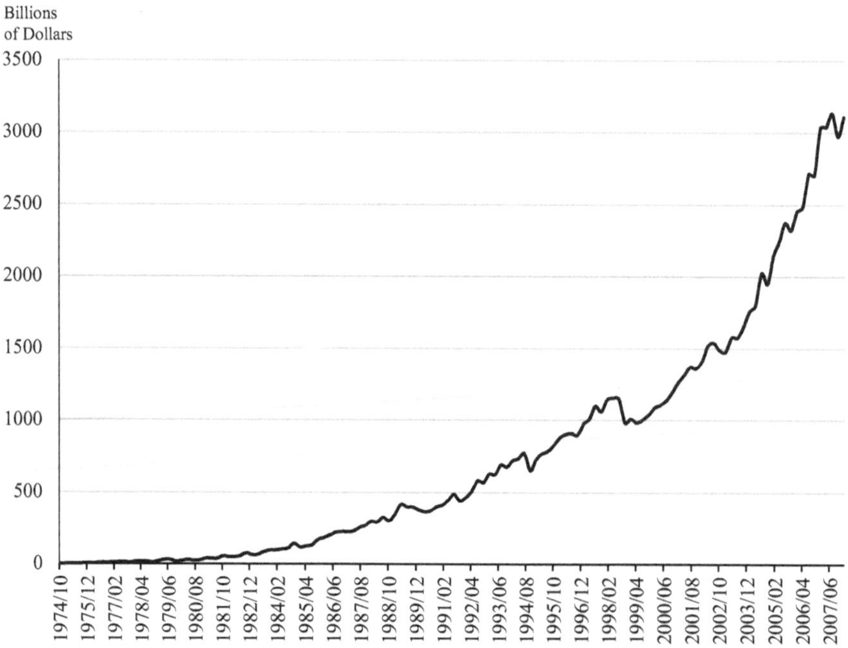

Figure 5.3 Security Brokers and Dealers' Liability of Repurchase Agreements in the U.S.

Source: Board of Governors of the Federal Reserve System

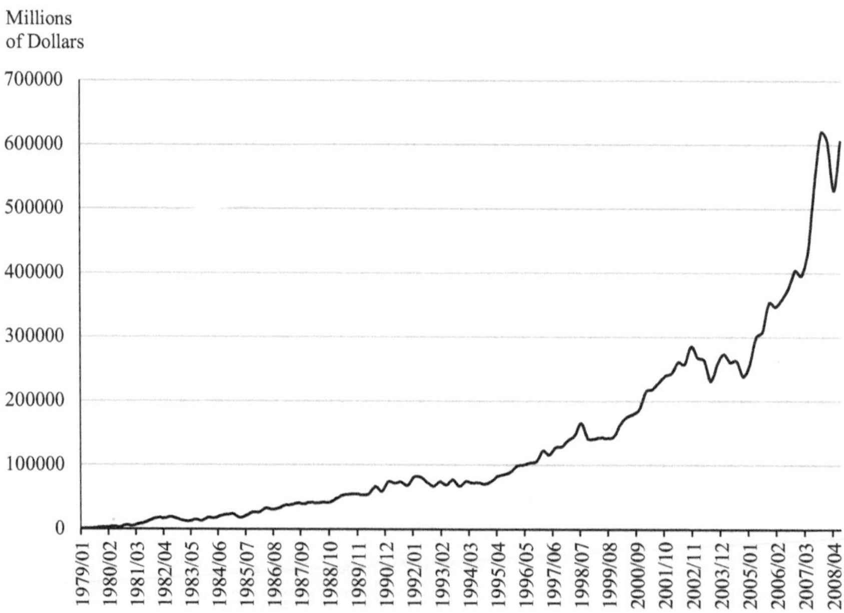

Figure 5.4 Repurchase Agreements held by Money Market Funds in the U.S.

Source: Board of Governors of the Federal Reserve System

and the financial community, which feared that it would impair repo markets, that Congress overrode it in 1984 by amending the Bankruptcy Code and exempting repos from the bankruptcy process.[29] Since then, when the courts have considered the nature of repos for bankruptcy purposes, they have determined them to be sales and prioritized the form of the contracts over their substance to support this decision.[30] This prioritization differs from the early decisions of the courts in *United States v. Drickson* (1979) and *SEC v. Miller* (1980), which considered the economic substance of the contract when they addressed the nature of repos. However, U.S. courts still consider the economic substance of the contract when they have to deal with the issue of the taxability of the interest income received by the creditors of repos. For example, in *Nebraska Department of Revenue v. Loewenstein* (1994), the Supreme Court of the United States justified government taxation of interest income by declaring that:

> It does not matter that the Trusts and Seller-Borrower characterize the repos as sales and repurchases since the substance and economic realities of the transactions show that the trusts receive interest on the cash they have lent to the Seller-Borrower.

It would be interesting to research what happened when Congress attempted to override the legal reasoning made in *In re Lombard-Wall*. A detailed study of the relationship between MMFs, the SEC, the Federal Reserve, the government, and other institutional investors at that time would improve our understanding of the political economy of finance and law and will be the next topic for my future research.

In fact, the military-banking-public debt complex that existed in early modern England still holds for shadow banking in twenty-first-century America. Since the 1970s, the U.S. government has had to continue increasing its public debt in order to wage wars, including in Vietnam, the Persian Gulf, and Iraq. Before the 1970s, commercial banks were the main purchasers of U.S. public debt, but they could not extend the purchase after the 1970s because they were still restricted by the banking regulations set after the Great Depression. For example, Regulation Q had restricted commercial banks to interest rate ceilings for demand deposits from 1933 until 2011 and thus constrained the banks' ability to create the money required to purchase U.S. public debt.[31] The government therefore sought alternative purchasers and allowed them to avoid the regulations imposed on commercial banks. This alternative has been shadow banking. Shadow banking has also needed the government's legal and political support to ensure that its money-like credit instruments are treated differently from other simple credit instruments.[32] Thanks to the government's legal and political support, since the late 1970s, shadow banking has increasingly supported the growth of U.S. public debt. For example, mutual funds and MMFs have invested heavily in public debt. Prime dealers in public debt finance their activities by using repurchase agreements that amounted to $4.2 trillion in early 2008. In repurchase agreements, treasury bills and bonds are used as the main collateral.

Notes

1 Graeber, *Debt*, 260.
2 Whitehead, *Adventures*, 84.
3 Gorton and Metrick, "Shadow Banking."
4 Baba, Robert, and Ramaswamy, "Money Market Funds."
5 Kaplowitz, "Money Market Mutual Funds."
6 Kaplowitz, "Money Market Mutual Funds," 121.
7 Financial Crisis Inquiry Commission, *Report, 30,*
8 This double-ownership differs from fragmented or shared ownership, as explained in the Chapter 3.
9 Fink, "Historical Rationale," 86.
10 Langbein, "The Secret Life of the Trust."
11 Langbein, "The Secret Life of the Trust," 183.
12 Langbein, "The Secret Life of the Trust," 184.
13 Langbein, "The Secret Life of the Trust," 184.
14 Brunnermeier, "Credit Crunch 2007–2008," 80–81.
15 Financial Crisis Inquiry Commission, *Report*, 30.
16 qtd. in Financial Crisis Inquiry Commission, *Report*, 27.
17 Brunnermeier, "Credit Crunch 2007–2008"; Gorton and Metrick, "Shadow Banking."
18 In the UK, this false belief is written into English law, which regards money market deposits as "cash," differentiated from financial instruments that include shares in companies or bonds. According to the Financial Collateral Arrangements (No. 2) Regulations 2003, Article 3, " 'cash' means money in any currency, credited to an account, or a similar claim for repayment of money and includes money market deposits."
19 Kacperczyk and Schnabl, "When Safe Proved Risky," 41.
20 Baba, Robert, and Ramaswamy, "Money Market Funds."
21 Gorton and Metrick, "Securitized Banking," 2.
22 Gorton and Metrick, "Shadow Banking."
23 Kaplowitz, "Money Market Mutual Funds," 122–123.
24 Kaplowitz, "Money Market Mutual Funds," 122–123.
25 Gorton and Metrick, "Shadow Banking"; Singh and Aitken, "Role of Rehypothecation."
26 Duffie, "Failure Mechanics of Dealer Banks," 61.
27 Gorton and Metrick, "Shadow Banking"
28 Schroeder, "Repo Madness."
29 Schroeder, "Repo Madness," 1011.
30 For example, see *Cohen v. Army Moral Support Fund*, 67 B.R. at 598.
31 Fink, "Historical Rationale," 86.
32 Kim, "Identity and the Hybridity of Modern Finance," 444.

Bibliography

Baba, N., M. N. Robert, and S. Ramaswamy. 2009. "U.S. Dollar Money Market Funds and Non-U.S. Banks." *BIS Quarterly Review* (2009): 65–81.

Brunnermeier, M. K. "Deciphering the Liquidity and Credit Crunch 2007–2008." *Journal of Economic Perspectives* 23, no. 1 (2009): 77–100.

Duffie, D. "The Failure Mechanics of Dealer Banks." *Journal of Economic Perspectives* 24, no. 1 (2010): 51–72.

Financial Crisis Inquiry Commission (FCIC). *The Financial Crisis Inquiry Report*. 2011. Available at http://fcic.law.stanford.edu/report.

Fink, M. P. "The Historical Rationale for U.S. Money Market Funds." In *Money Market Funds in the EU and the U.S.: Regulation and Practice*, edited by Viktoria Baklanova and Joseph Tanega. Oxford: Oxford University Press, 2014.

Gorton, G. and A. Metrick. "Regulating the Shadow Banking System." *Brookings Papers on Economic Activity* 2 (2010): 261–312.

Gorton, G. and A. Metrick. "Securitized Banking and the Run on Repo." *Journal of Financial Economics* 104, no. 3 (2011): 425–451.

Graeber, David. *Debt: The First 5,000 Years*. Brooklyn, NY: Melville House Publishing, 2011.

Kacperczyk, M. and P. Schnabl. "When Safe Proved Risky: Commercial Paper during the Financial Crisis of 2007–2009." *Journal of Economic Perspectives* 24, no. 1 (2010): 29–50.

Kaplowitz, B. "Regulation of U.S. Money Market Mutual Funds." In *Money Market Funds in the EU and the U.S.: Regulation and Practice*, edited by Viktoria Baklanova and Joseph Tanega. Oxford: Oxford University Press, 2014.

Kim, Jongchul. "How Modern Banking Originated: The London Goldsmith Bankers' Institutionalisation of Trust." *Business History* 53, no. 6 (2011): 939–959.

Kim, Jongchul." Identity and the Hybridity of Modern Finance: How a Specifically Modern Concept of the Self Underlies the Modern Ownership of Property, Trusts and Finance." *The Cambridge Journal of Economics* 38, no. 2 (2014): 425–446.

Langbein, John. H. "The Secret Life of the Trust: The Trust as an Instrument of Commerce." *the Yale Law Journal* 107 (1997): 165–190.

Schroeder, J. L. "Repo Madness: The Characterization of Repurchase Agreements under the Bankruptcy Code and the U.C.C." *Syracuse Law Review* 46 (1996): 999–1050.

Singh, M. and J. Aitken. "The (Sizable) Role of Rehypothecation in the Shadow Banking System." *Working Paper WP/10/172*. International Monetary Fund, 2010.

Whitehead, Afred North. *Adventures of Ideas*. New York: The Free Press, 1933.

6 Person, Property, and Trusts

Revisited

This chapter discusses two cases of combining creditor-debtor relations with a social institution of persons: limited liability joint-stock corporations and quantitative easing. It argues that this combination can be considered a trust and a capitalist method to enjoy property rights but avoid responsibilities.

6.1. Trusts and the Person-Property Formula

As mentioned earlier, a trust allows the individualist purposes of property owners to endure beyond a natural lifespan. The trust can also overcome the limited life span of property. Because things can decay or be destroyed, the endurance of the Lockean person-property relationship that was discussed in Chapter 2 is limited. However, the trust fund "makes possible the creation of enduring objects of property . . . in the form of funds which can be invested in various ways to preserve and enhance their value."[1] In the trust fund, therefore, the particular assets that are owned at any given time merely represent the *abstract value* that the trust intends to preserve and enhance. To sum up, in the trust fund, the formula of person-property becomes more abstract: it becomes the relationship between the "person in the abstract," established in the form of replaceable trustees who promote the will of the settler, and "things in the abstract," where investments in particular assets are intended to promote the abstract value of the fund (Figure 6.1).

This formula explains the co-existence of the two seemingly contradictory forms of property in capitalism: absolute private property and divisible property rights to future income. Macpherson interpreted Locke's labor theory of property as an ideological justification for the exclusive, alienable form of property: absolute private property.[2] He and other classical writers, including Marx and Weber, argued that the nature of the transition from feudalism to capitalism can be understood as *the rise of absolute private property*. Challenging this classical argument, revisionists such as Gerry Rubin, David Sugarman, and Ronald S. Neale argued that the classical argument tends to de-emphasize the other capitalist form of property.[3] They demonstrated that during the transition to capitalism in England, the divisibility of property titles and legal titles to present and future income—such as shares, mortgages, and pensions—were treated

DOI: 10.4324/9781003052210-7

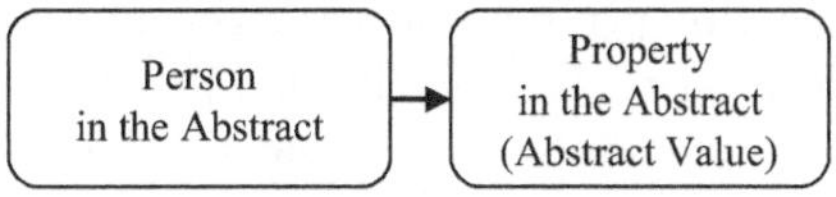

Figure 6.1 The Person-Property Formula in the Trust

as property by the law of trusts. They pointed out that without this form of property, absolute private property alone could not have made the transition possible. Responding to this challenge, Macpherson mistakenly argued that this form of property developed later, in the welfare capitalism of the twentieth century, and replaced the absolute private property system developed in early laissez-faire capitalism.[4] For Macpherson and the other classical writers, these two forms of property are considered to be fundamentally different and perhaps even contradictory.

However, my formula demonstrates that the Lockean formula of person-property that was discussed in Chapter 2 can be included and extended in the person-property formula of the trust. The Lockean formula justifies the principle of absolute private property. Likewise, the trust originated from the same principle that individuals have the absolute freedom to transfer their property as they please without consideration of the will of their family or inheritors.[5] To allow their absolute property ownership to endure permanently—i.e., to make the Lockean person-property formula endure permanently—property owners devised the concept of the trust, in which the relationship between the owners and the group of replaceable trustees is a hybrid between an owner-representative relationship and a creditor-debtor relationship. Investors *transfer* their legal ownership of funds to the trust corporation in order to secure the funds from their creditors or government taxation or to maintain the value of the funds. Without this transfer of legal ownership, the corporation cannot invest the investors' money in its own name. In return for the investors' transfer of legal ownership to the corporation, the trust corporation pays an interest-like benefit (dividends) to the investors. Thus far, because legal ownership has been *transferred* from the investors to the corporation, the relationship between the investors and the corporation is a creditor-debtor relationship. However, at the same time, the investors retain equitable ownership, due to which the corporation is obliged to work for the best interest of the investors, meaning that ownership is *not transferred* to the corporation. Here, the relationship between the investors and the trust corporation is an owner-representative relationship. The two disparate relationships—an owner-representative relationship and a creditor-debtor relationship—which had been clearly distinguished before modern times in Roman law become mixed in the trust. The shareholders of the trust are no longer the owners of the *specific* funds they invested, but instead own part of the corporation's pool of funds, and they have a right to share in the expected future earnings of the trust. When the value of their shares drops, the shareholders can withdraw quickly from the trust by selling their shares to third parties or by liquidating them on demand. Here, the motive of securing private property rights in the Lockean formula is enhanced, and the two property forms—absolute private property and divisible property rights to future income—are combined. Additionally, because the trust played a central role in bringing about the transition from feudalism to capitalism,[6] contrary to Macpherson's argument, there has been no historical transition between the two property forms.

6.2. Modern Business Corporations as a Trust

The Nature of Shares

In Chapter 4, I argued that the traditional type of corporation that developed in Medieval Europe had transformed into a trust, probably from the time when the Company Act of 1862 permitted the establishment of business corporations without a charter from the state.[7] I suggested two aspects of this transformation.[8] First, the group personality of the corporation should be established autonomously, from the bottom up, by private property owners. This is in contrasts to the traditional corporation, which was a governing tool of the state to regulate a group of individuals, and whose legal personality was granted, from the top down, by the Crown. Second, the individual members of a corporation should be established as the creditors of the corporation as well as co-owners. This sets up a contradiction because creditors have been considered the outsiders of a group while the owners have been considered insiders, and an individual cannot be an insider and an outsider in a group simultaneously. Furthermore, a modern business corporation is legally defined as *a collective person*, having shareholders as its members, but at the same time, it is legally treated as *a non-collective person*, having its own personality separate from the personalities of its members. This is another contradiction.

How do these contradictions happen? They occur because the legal status of shareholders combines two disparate legal categories: partnership and loans. Under Roman law, partners in a partnership were differentiated from creditors. As shown in Table 6.1, a partner is an insider and a member-owner who shares assets, duties, responsibilities, and risks with other partners. Partners are the joint owners of the assets of a partnership and thus take joint responsibility for any wrongful use of the assets. By contrast, a creditor is an outsider who has limited liability when a debtor goes bankrupt, and who has no responsibility

Table 6.1 Partnership versus Loan in Roman Law

	Legal Category	*Ownership*	*Assets, Duties, Responsibilities*	*Liability*
Partnership	Rights *in rem*	Not transferred	Shared	Unlimited
Loan	Rights *in personam*	Transferred	Not shared	Limited

for the debtor's wrongful behavior. This differentiation of partnerships and loans was inherited by canon law in Medieval Europe and was received into both civil law and English partnership law.[9] English partnership law "presumed that each partner was an active trader in a joint concern [with] full power to act as agent of his fellow partners."[10]

However, in a modern business corporation, the members are owners as well as creditors, insiders as well as outsiders. They also enjoy property rights, such as voting rights at general meetings to elect and dismiss directors. However, and at the same time, in terms of responsibilities, they are creditors who have limited liabilities and do not take any responsibility for the business of a corporation. This is a clear example of a hybrid of property and contract, of rights *in rem* and rights *in personam*. In other words, it is a trust.

From a modern viewpoint, the absolute power of property owners under Roman law was still limited due to its strict division of rights *in rem* and rights *in personam*. Shareholders in limited liability joint-stock corporations are likely to think that they deserve what they now enjoy: voting rights at general meetings to elect and dismiss directors and to make important business decisions, the right to claim dividends, limited liability, and no responsibility for corporate business. However, from a historical legal perspective, what they enjoy is simply undeserved privileges that other simple creditors or property owners cannot enjoy. By cleverly mixing rights *in rem* and rights *in personam*, shareholders are able to enjoy the benefits and reduce the costs of both property rights and creditors' rights. The historical process of creating this privilege is the historical process that transforms the traditional corporation as a governing tool of the state that regulates a group of individuals into a trust where property owners extend their individualistic property rights while avoiding the responsibilities entailed in these rights.

Despite this hybrid and contradictory nature of shareholders' rights, legal scholars have defined the rights using only one of the two legal categories of rights *in rem* or rights *in personam*. One group of the scholars only emphasized the contractual characteristics of shareholders' rights. The most popular example of such a definition was provided by J. Farwell in *Borland's Trustee v. Steel Bros & Co. Ltd.*, in 1901:

> A share is the interest of a shareholder in the corporation measured by a sum of money, for the purpose of liability in the first place, and of interest in the second, but also consisting of a series of mutual covenants entered into by all the shareholders *inter se* in accordance with s 16 of the Corporations Act 1862. The contract contained in the articles of association is one of the original incidents of the share. A share is . . . an interest measured by a sum of money and made up of various rights contained in the contract, including the right to a sum of money of a more or less amount.[11]

Here, Farwell argued that shareholders are able to enjoy the privileged rights thanks to a contract made between contractual parties including creditors and shareholders; i.e., because other contractual parties allow the shareholders to enjoy the rights through a contract. The theory of "the nexus of contract" also argues that a corporation is a voluntary association created by contractual parties including shareholders, directors, creditors, and others without the intervention of the state. This implies that shareholders can enjoy their privileged rights because the other contracting parties are in agreement.

Contradicting these groups of scholars, however, other legal theorists and courts have emphasized property rights. For example, the legal theorist L. C. B. Gower explains that the above definition by Farwell is trying

> to equate shares with right under a contract. . . . [But] a share is something far more than mere contractual rights *in personam*. . . . [T]he share itself is an object of dominion, i.e., of rights *in rem*.[12]

Also, Paddy Ireland argues that shareholders' rights have been transformed from contractual rights in early modern times into property rights in the present day.[13] Additionally, in *Her Majesty's Commissioners of Inland Revenue v. Laird Group PLC* in 2003, Lord Millet emphasized the property rights of shares:

> It is customary to describe [a share] as a "bundle of rights and liabilities," and this is probably the nearest that one can get to its character, provided that it is appreciated that it is more than a bundle of contractual rights. . . . These rights, however, are not purely personal rights. They confer proprietary rights in the corporation though not on its property.[14]

This struggle by legal theorists to fit shareholders' rights into one of the existing legal categories is bound to fail because the law has granted shareholders something that it is unable to conceptualize. There are only two categories available to legal theorists and courts—property (rights *in rem*) and contract (rights *in personam*)—and these two categories of law are too distinct to allow for any middle ground. Despite the exclusivity of the two rights, the law has historically granted both of them to shareholders. Nonetheless, legal theorists have vainly attempted to fit this hybrid complex of shareholders' rights into one of the two existing legal categories.

The contractual theory such as the theory of nexus of contract cannot explain the reality. Contrary to the contractual theory of business corporations, the other contractual parties including creditors would not enter into a contract that agrees to endow shareholders with such combined privileges as voting rights at general meetings to elect and dismiss directors and to make important business decisions, the right to claim dividends, limited liability, and no responsibility to corporate business. Such a contract would be unfair. Rather, a corporation is a legal construct: the privileged rights of shareholders' rights cannot be made by a voluntary contract but have been created by the law that favors one contractual side over another. For example, as Ireland argues, politicians have historically enacted the law of limited liability because they wanted to accommodate and protect the interests of rentier investors.[15]

The property theory propounded by Gower, Ireland, and Millet cannot capture both characteristics of shareholders' rights (property and contract) together. For example, Ireland correctly determines that the law of joint-stock corporation began as part of the law of partnership. But he mistakenly argues that partnership is a part of contract law and that shareholders' rights at that time are contractual.[16] He further argues, wrongly, that shareholders' rights have metamorphosed from contractual rights in early modern times into property rights in the present day. However, what actually happened, as will be discussed later, is that shareholders' rights have transformed from property rights into hybrid of property and contractual rights.

Social Irresponsibility and Inequality

Conventional wisdom states that shareholders' limited liability is justifiable because it will encourage risk-averse investors to make investments and thus enable large sums to be pooled and directed toward economically beneficial purposes. In reality, however, the opposite has been true: since the early 1980s, the ideologies and institutions of shareholders' primacy have drained large sums of money away from companies so that these companies lose the chance to use their money for economically beneficial purposes such as research and development. Figure 6.2 shows how much companies in the U.S. have paid out to their shareholders since the early 1970s. Share buybacks are an indirect form of shareholder payment because it raises share prices. Normally, dividends and buybacks are paid from the net income of a company, and the average

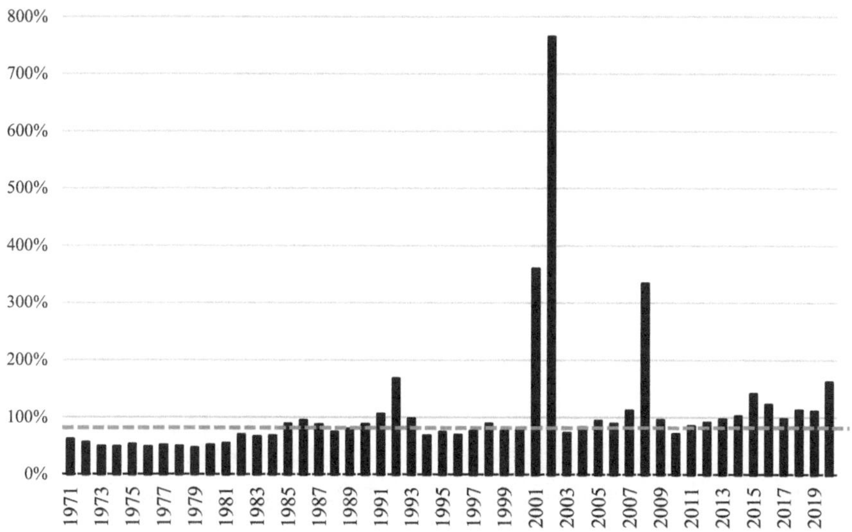

Figure 6.2 Ratio of the Sum of Dividends and Buyback to Net Income in the U.S. Companies

Source: Compustat

ratio of the sum of dividends and buybacks to the net income in the 1970s was 50%. However, since the early 1980s, the ratio has worsened, reaching 123% between 1982 and 2020, meaning that companies have paid out more in dividends and buybacks than they made in net income. Worse still, this ratio skyrockets during times of economic crisis. When every stakeholder, including both employees and customers, is experiencing hardship due to economic crises, company shareholders are the only ones filling their pockets with money. Moreover, as shown in Figure 6.3, the ratio of the sum of dividends and buyback to R&D has also worsened since 2004. The ratio between 1971 and 2003 was 221%, rising to 338% between 2004 and 2020. Companies are now using a greater proportion of their income to pay their shareholders rather than channel it into their productive business purposes.

In the U.S., these trends only worsen inequality. As seen in Figure 6.4, the massive amounts of dividends and buyback, $2.5 trillion in 2019 alone, closely parallel the share of the total wealth of the top 1%. A Pearson's correlation coefficient between the two is 0.85. When its absolute value is larger than 0.7, the relationship between two variables is generally considered strong. The correlation can be easily understood, as the top 1% have a large part of their wealth in the form of shares: a total of 53.8% of the shares issued in the United States in the second quarter of 2021.

How a company is put under the substantial control of, or in the possession of dominant shareholders, depends on the concrete methods of corporate

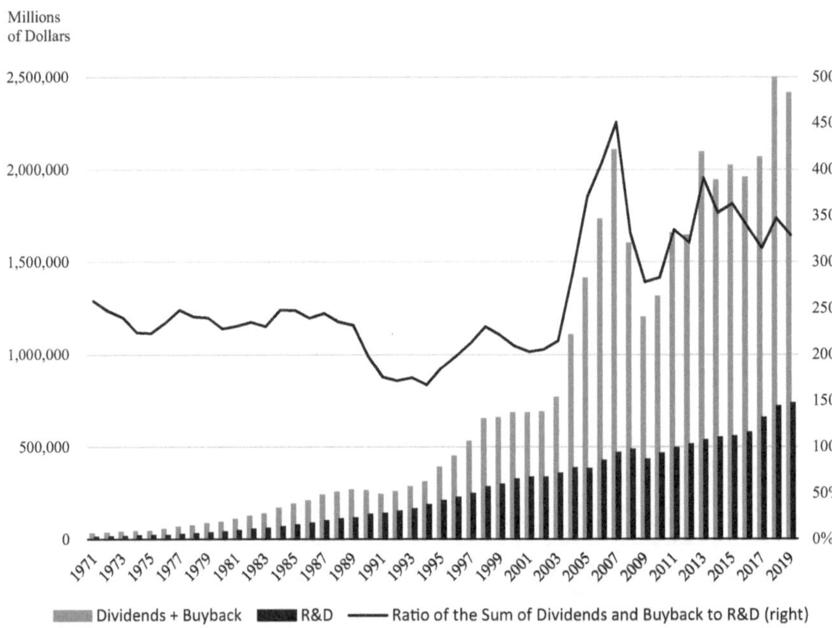

Figure 6.3 Ratio of the Sum of Dividends and Buyback to R&D in the U.S. Companies

Source: Compustat

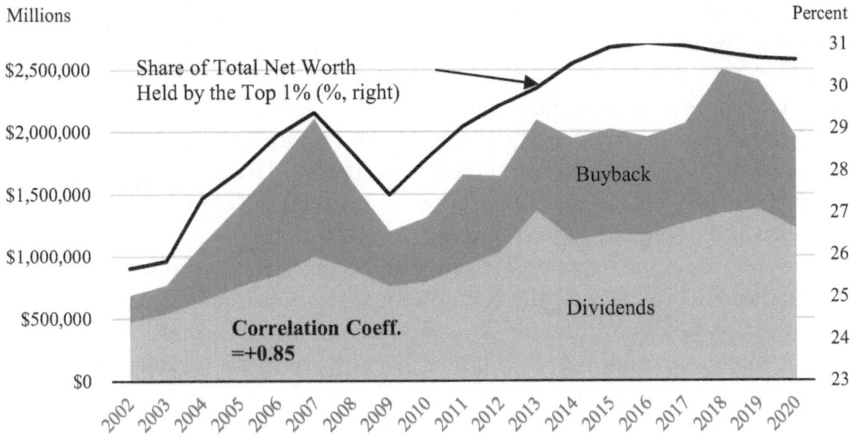

Figure 6.4 Wealth Inequality, Dividends, and Buyback in the U.S. Companies

Source: Compustat, Board of Governors of the Federal Reserve System

governance and the political and legal environment. The current corporate governance mechanism in the United States seems to allow the largest shareholder to substantially make the company under his or her possession. This substantial power is visible in the comparison of corporate governance with political governance. Unlike the political representation under the slogan "one person, one vote," corporate governance follows the rule of "one share, one vote." This rule allows the largest shareholder, who is also likely to be very wealthy, to have a large share of the voting rights and perhaps even to control the company. Unlike the political system of representation in the U.S., which does not allow the members of the House of Representatives to be recalled, the dominant shareholder can not only elect the board of directors but also dismiss them. As a result, the turnover rate of corporate CEOs is much higher than that of the members of the House. In the U.S., almost no members of the House of Representatives are removed from office involuntarily, and House reelection rates have been between 87% and 98% between 1950 and 2016.[17] By contrast, "CEOs are as likely to leave prematurely as to retire normally" in the U.S., according to an observation made around 2005.[18] The high reelection rate of House members, however, does not imply that the members of the House perform much better than CEOs. Instead, the right of the largest shareholder to dismiss a CEO is effective, while voters' rights to dismiss their representatives are less so. In other words, the shareholders' control of a company is more substantial than voters' control of their political representatives.

The substantial property rights of the largest shareholder also depend on the political and legal environment. Before the 1970s, managerialism predominated, and the political and legal environment emphasized the social roles of the corporation CEOs in achieving full employment and welfare policy. In this political environment, the power of the largest shareholder was relatively reduced compared with the managers, and legal decisions made in courts were also more favorable to the managers than to the largest shareholder. However, once Neoliberalism became predominant since the late 1970s, the political and legal environment became more favorable to the shareholders. This period is called the era of shareholder primacy in which the power of the largest shareholder to control a corporation increased markedly. Thus, it appears that the largest shareholder can control a corporation through the exercise of their voting rights and essentially have property rights over it.

However, property rights enjoyed by shareholders are not property rights in the traditional sense because the law no longer treats shareholders as the owners of the *assets* of a corporation since the case of *Bligh v. Brent* in 1837 in the United Kingdom. Although shareholders cannot use assets, cannot lend them out to others, and cannot use them as collateral, legal scholars cannot help treating shareholders as the owners of *the corporation*, though not of its property, as seen before.[19] Shareholders surrender their immediate controlling rights over the assets but instead exert controlling power against the corporation.

Some scholars might disagree with my argument that shareholders enjoy property rights. And they might also argue that a corporation cannot be owned because it is not a thing that can be owned. Against this counterargument, I present two facts that should be considered. First, property is a tendency to transform what is essentially *not* an object of exclusive possession into property. As mentioned, slaves and land are essentially not property, but the law of property in Ancient Rome and modern times *forcibly* made them into property. This propertization was, as explained earlier, a process of making human beings into "*rem*." Here, *rem* was a slave who are removed from their social relations with their family and community and put under the absolute control of the slave-owners. Similarly, a corporation is not a property because it is a group of "persons," and persons cannot be owned by other persons. If so, a corporation—a group of persons—would be treated as slaves. This may be a major reason why the law has never said explicitly that shareholders own their corporation.

On the other hand, the law is increasingly treating shareholders as creditors. For example, ever since *Bligh v. Brent* in 1837 the law in modern Western societies has considered the legal and equitable ownership of capital to have completely transferred from the shareholders to the company. This legal decision implies that shareholders are no longer the owners of the company's "property" and thus no longer take any responsibility if the property is used unethically. Furthermore, under the 1855–62 Companies Acts in the United Kingdom, the law grants them limited liability.

Bligh v. Brent and limited liability together have destroyed the principles of partnership. As mentioned earlier, a partnership has two principles. The first principle is that when partners invest in a partnership, the property rights of the invested assets remain in the hands of the partners and that partners as joint owners of the invested assets take responsibility for their use. The second principle is that partners share a duty to repay all the debts incurred from the use of the assets. *Bligh v. Brent* broke the first principle when the court declared that the shareholders are not the legal property owners of their invested assets and that the property rights of the invested assets are transferred to their corporation. Limited liability broke the second principle. When a corporation goes bankrupt, its shareholders are only liable for the amount of the money they invested. By breaking these two principles, shareholders are relegated to creditors, who are outsiders in a corporation.

Because of the hybridity described above, the legal relationship between shareholders, their company, and its assets have lost all logical coherence. If the shareholders have property rights over their corporation, and if this corporation has property rights over the assets that shareholders invest in the corporation, then according to the syllogism the shareholders must have property rights over the corporation's assets. However, because of *Bligh v. Brent*, the law denies this legitimate logic. There is also a contradiction in the relationship between shareholders and their corporations. On the one hand, the law defines that shareholders are members of their corporation, meaning that they cannot be separated from each other. On the other hand, the law presupposes, simultaneously, that a corporation has an independent personhood separate from its members. This is because the law stipulates that the corporation, rather than shareholders, is the property owner of the assets that shareholders invest in. The law of business corporations suffers from these inconsistencies.

According to Ireland, this creditor's right of limited liability and no responsibility regarding corporate business was granted to shareholders not because of advanced technology and economic efficiency, but rather because of political demands to accommodate and protect the interests of rentier investors.[20] Ireland argues that during the United Kingdom's Industrial Revolution, limited liability was unnecessary because manufacturing was predominantly carried out in ordinary partnerships.[21] Industrialists generally opposed limited liability, and there was popular critical sentiment against it as well. The following writings by Edward Cox, editor of the *Law Times* in 1856 took such a stand:

> The basis of the law of partnership was that there is a moral obligation, which is the duty of the laws of a civilized nation to enforce, pay debts, perform contracts, and make reparation for wrongs. . . . Limited liability was founded on the opposite principle . . . permit[ting] a man to avail himself of his agents' acts if advantageous to him, and not to be responsible for them if they should be disadvantageous; to speculate for profits without being liable for losses; to make a contract, incur debts, and commit wrongs, the law depriving the creditor, the contract, and the injured, of remedy against the property or the person of the wrongdoer, beyond the limit, however small, at which it may please him to determine his own liability.[22]

Most British industrial companies were in the form of partnerships and did not become limited liability companies for a long period of time, even after company laws were passed in 1855–62 and limited liability became freely available.[23]

According to Ireland, the number of limited liability joint-stock companies increased rapidly at the end of the nineteenth century. However, this increase was not caused by technological advances or increased demand for capital, but rather because capitalists wanted to avoid competition and establishing monopolies via mergers and acquisitions.[24]

To sum up, a business corporation, by law, is both a property and not a property. On the one hand, a business corporation is legally a collection of shareholders and thus cannot be owned. On the other hand, the law has allowed shareholders to have voting rights in general meetings, i.e., to have a property right on their corporation. Therefore, a corporation becomes an object of ownership.

Furthermore, as explained earlier, a business corporation, by law, is both a collection of shareholders and not a collection of shareholders. In reality, however, and contrary to the legal definition, the members of a business corporation are not shareholders because shareholders have become mere outsiders in terms of their responsibilities, as examined earlier. Rather, the members of a business corporation are managers and employees who engage in the business of the corporation. Property rights—shareholders' voting rights in general meetings—go against managers and other employees. If a person or a group of persons becomes a property, the person or the group is treated as a thing. Persons who are treated as things are known as slaves. Therefore, a modern business corporation is a modern form of slavery.

Harry Glasbeek stated that "corporate shareholders have little financial or other incentives to ensure that managers behave legally, ethically or decently. . . . Because in law they are personally untouchable."[25] The reason why business corporations are the main drivers of environmental destruction and the exploitation of workers is that the shareholders hide themselves behind anonymity and thus do not feel any moral sentiment. Sitting safely behind computer screens, they pay attention only to fluctuations in stock prices and their eventual dividends. Shareholders use economic organizations as a tool to maximize profits without taking any legal responsibility. Economic organizations must pursue various values in a balanced way: contributing to consumers by producing cheap, high-quality products, ensuring stability for the members of the organization by making sufficient profits, establishing a democratic workplace, preventing workers from being turned into tools for the maximization of profits, protecting the environment, and paying taxes to contribute to the community. However, these values are frequently ignored when shareholders control the economic organizations to maximize profits.

6.3. Quantitative Easing as a Trust

A recent unconventional monetary policy known as quantitative easing is another instance of combining personae and creditor-debtor relations. It is a metaphysical trick that uses separate personhood between a central bank (for example, the Federal Reserve) and a government (for example, the U.S.

Treasury) to transform "debt" into "free money." Quantitative easing outwardly takes the form of a creditor-debtor relation between two separate persons—i.e., between the Federal Reserve and the U.S. Treasury—in which the former lends money to the latter on a large scale. Since the financial crisis of 2008, the Federal Reserve has increasingly lent more money to the Treasury, reaching up to 22.3% of the GDP in April 2021. To prevent a misunderstanding, I do not argue that the Federal Reserve has purchased Treasury securities directly from the Treasury. The U.S. Congress has prohibited this direct purchase since 1981. Instead, the Federal Reserve's purchases are conducted in the secondary market for Treasury securities, and, by this purchase, the Federal Reserve lends money to the Treasury.

In substance, however, the Federal Reserve does not lend money; it gives it to the U.S. Treasury for free. The reasons are as follows. First, the Federal Reserve must, by law, transfer to the Treasury its interest income earned from the lending of Federal Reserve notes. This means that any interest payment made by the Treasury to the Federal Reserve is a part of this interest income and must be returned to the Treasury. For example, in 2020, the Treasury paid $67.5 billion to the Federal Reserve in interest and was repaid $86.8 billion from the Federal Reserve. In 2015, the Treasury paid $63.3 billion to the Federal Reserve in interest and was repaid $117 billion. As shown in Figure 6.5, the Treasury was repaid 1.6 times more money from the Federal Reserve than it paid in interest from 2008 to 2020. Why does the creditor (the Federal Reserve) return its interest gains (or more than its interest gain) to the debtor (the Treasury)? This would not happen in an ordinary creditor-debtor relationship.

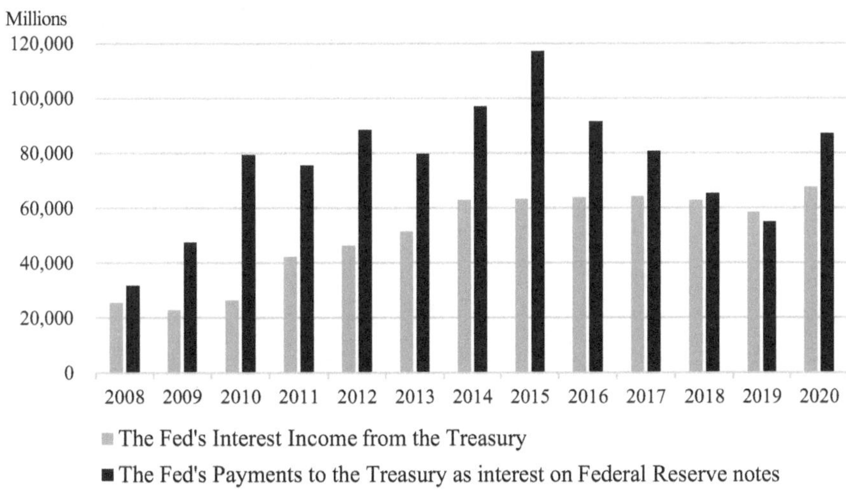

Figure 6.5 The Treasury's Earnings from the Federal Reserve

Source: Federal Reserve Annual Financial Statements

Second, the U.S. government seemed to have no intention of repaying the principal to the Federal Reserve when it began quantitative easing in 2020. Paul Krugman, who won the 2008 Nobel Memorial Prize in Economics, seems to represent this attitude of the U.S. policymakers. Before the Federal Reserve began another round of quantitative easing due to the Covid-19 pandemic, he wrote in the *New York Times* in March 2020 that the U.S. government should borrow 2% of the GDP from the Federal Reserve every year to spend on public investment, and *should not repay* it.[26] President Biden's advisers embrace the so-called *Modern Money Theory*, which argues that the Federal Government does not need to raise taxes for public investment because it can borrow money from the Federal Reserve without repayment. Moreover, regardless of its intention, U.S. public debt has already surged to such a high level (127% of GDP in 2021)[27] that the government would be unable to repay all the money even if it wanted to. The congressional budget office expects that the U.S. public debt will increase to 202% of GDP by 2051.[28] Even if the U.S. government attempts to repay its debts in part, it will be difficult to repay the debt owed to the Federal Reserve in full because the debts owed to the Federal Reserve comprise a major means for the U.S. government to reduce the overall burden of interest payment. As Figure 6.6 shows, the more the U.S. government is indebted to the Federal Reserve, the less interest it is able to pay on its overall debt. Any attempt to repay a significant part of its debt to the Federal Reserve will destabilize government finance. It will increase the interest rate of Treasury

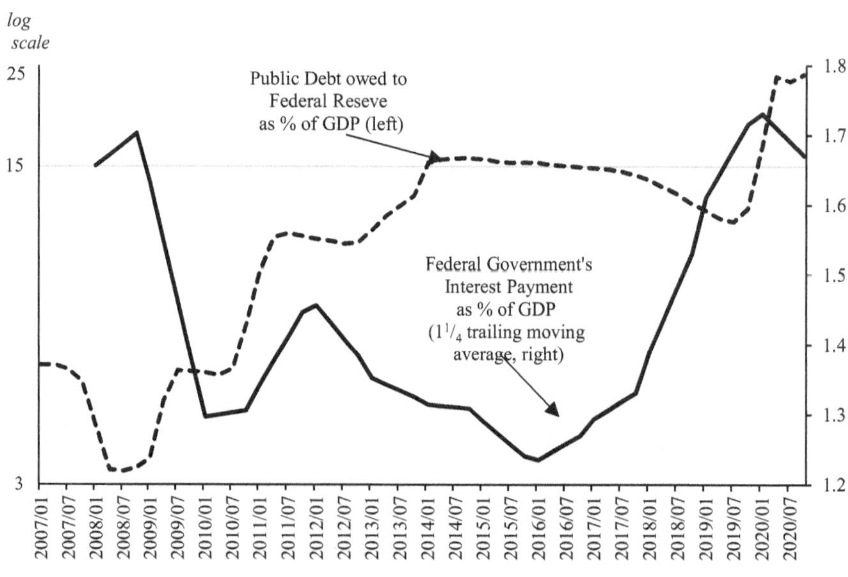

Figure 6.6 Federal Government's Interest Payment and Public Debt owed to the Federal Reserve

Source: U.S. Bureau of Economic Analysis

securities and reduce the income from the Federal Reserve, as happened in 2018 and 2019 (see Figure 6.5). It will also decrease tax revenue because it will drop the prices and transactions of assets such as shares and houses, from which a significant source of tax revenue has been made.

This is the same reason why the U.S. government and the Federal Reserve maintained low federal fund rates during the 1940s. From the twentieth century onwards, federal fund rates have trended in the opposite direction to public debt, as shown in Figure 6.7. The Pearson's correlation coefficient between the two is -0.73.

The reason why federal fund rates were low when public debt was high is easily understandable. As public debt and the federal deficit have increased, the Federal Government had to keep federal fund rates artificially low because of its increasing interest payment burden and to make it easier to refinance its debt. In fact, in 1942, the U.S. Treasury and the Federal Reserve agreed to maintain the interest rate of long-term bonds at below 2.5%, an agreement that lasted until 1951.[29] The Board of Governors at that time explained the reason for this interest control as:

> [a] major consequence . . . of . . . increasing the general level of interest rates would be a fall in the market values of outstanding government securities. These price declines would create difficult market problems for the Treasury in refunding its maturing and called securities.[30]

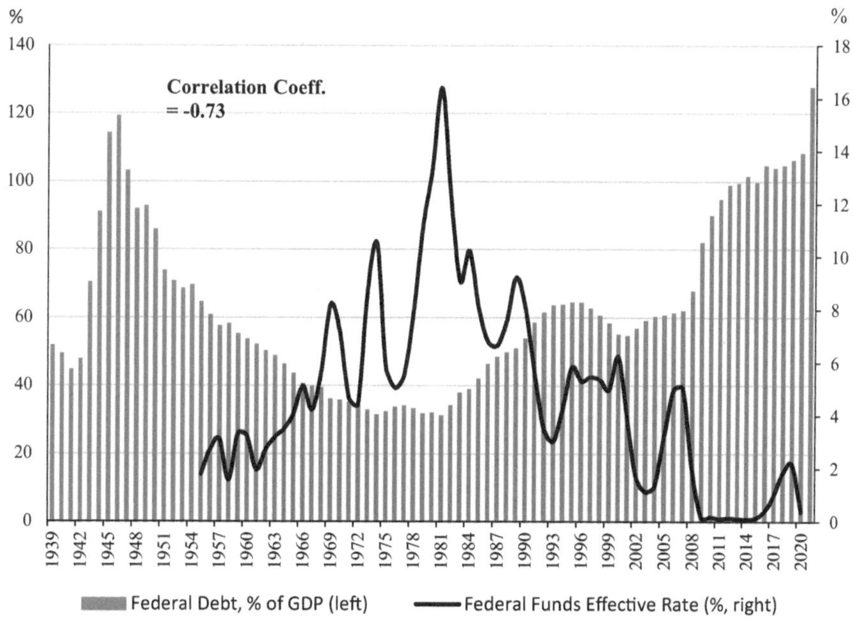

Figure 6.7 Public Debt and Federal Fund Rate

Source: Board of Governors of the Federal Reserve System; U.S. Office of Management and Budget

Likewise, there has been a similar motive in the Federal Reserve's purchase of Treasury securities since 2008. As seen in Figure 6.8, long-term securities whose maturities are more than one year amount to 96.1% of all purchases. This purchase of long-term Treasury securities has lowered the interest rate of these securities, aiming to reduce the Treasury's increasing interest payment burden and refinance its debt. Moreover, a large amount of liquidity provided by the Federal Reserve's purchase of Treasury securities to the economy has created high demand for secure investments, i.e., Treasury securities, by allowing federal fund rates to remain low.

During the 1970s, the inflationary period raised the federal fund rate to 16.38% in 1981 in an attempt to curb high inflation. This marks a significant difference between the 1970s and the present day because using the federal fund rate in this way as the main means of fighting growing inflation is not available today. In the 1970s the government could utilize this because the Federal Government's debt was relatively low. If the U.S. government would raise federal fund rates as significantly as it did in the 1970s, it could put overburdening costs of interest payments on the government and non-financial corporations because of the unprecedentedly high level of their debts, thereby creating an economic recession. As of April 2020, Federal Government debt has reached 135.9% of GDP, and the debt level of non-financial corporations has increased to 57%. In 2020, the United States paid 5.3% of government spending (1.6% of GDP) as interest on government bonds.[31] Because the Congressional Budget Office expects that U.S. public debt will increase to 202% of

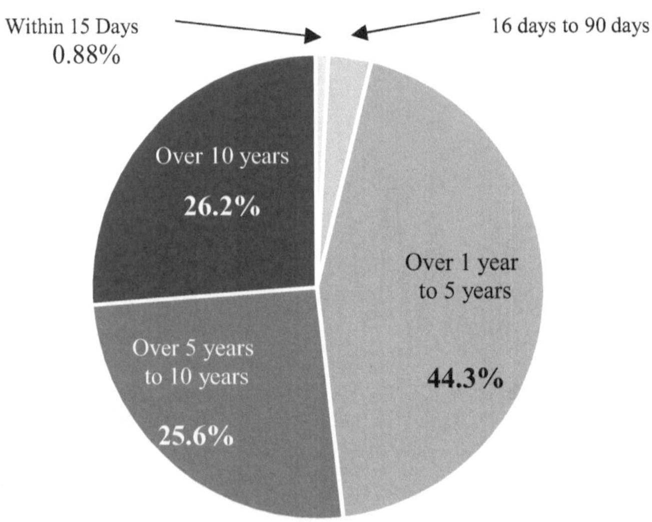

Figure 6.8 Total Treasury Securities purchased by the Federal Reserve between Sep. 2008 and Jul. 2021

Source: Board of Governors of the Federal Reserve System (US)

GDP by 2051,[32] a significant increase in the federal fund rate will cause fragility in the government's finances.

The annual growth rate of U.S. GDP, as shown in Figures 6.9 and 6.10, has gradually decreased and is expected to reduce further in the future. Furthermore, the average annual growth rate of labor productivity also portrays a decreasing trend, declining from 2.3% between 1982 and 2007 to 1.6% between 2008 and 2021, as shown in Figure 6.11. To make matters worse, the marginal revenue productivity of nonfinancial debt has decreased from an average of 0.57 between 1982 and 2000 to 0.48 between 2001 and 2008, and 0.4 after 2008, as seen in Figure 6.12. That is, as the U.S. nonfinancial sector has increasingly borrowed money, the revenue of the debt has decreased in productivity. All these facts imply that if the U.S. economy wants to match the previous GDP growth rate, the public sector must provide money in the form of debt on an increasing scale by becoming more indebted. Thus, because of the growing indebtedness of the Federal Government, the Federal Reserve cannot currently raise federal fund rates to the same levels as it did in the 1970s.

In fact, the Federal Reserve's raising of federal fund rates contributed to creating the 2020 recession. The current post-2020 crisis was not just created by Covid-19. It was another of the financial and economic crises cyclically created due to the intrinsic nature of the current capitalist financial system. The pandemic just worsened it. As seen in Figure 6.13, the spread between the yields on ten-year and two-year U.S. Treasury securities has been a powerful predictor of future recessions because this spread has reflected changing

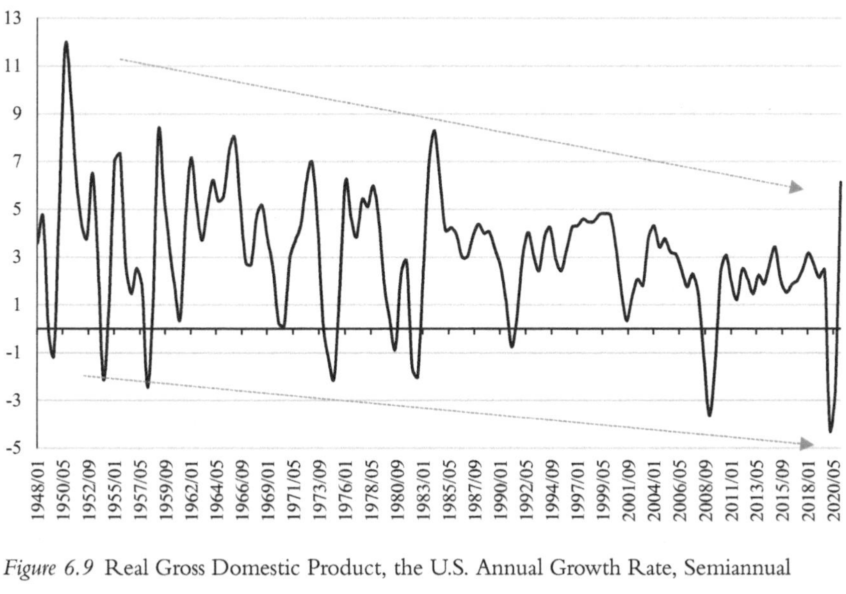

Figure 6.9 Real Gross Domestic Product, the U.S. Annual Growth Rate, Semiannual

Source: U.S. Bureau of Economic Analysis

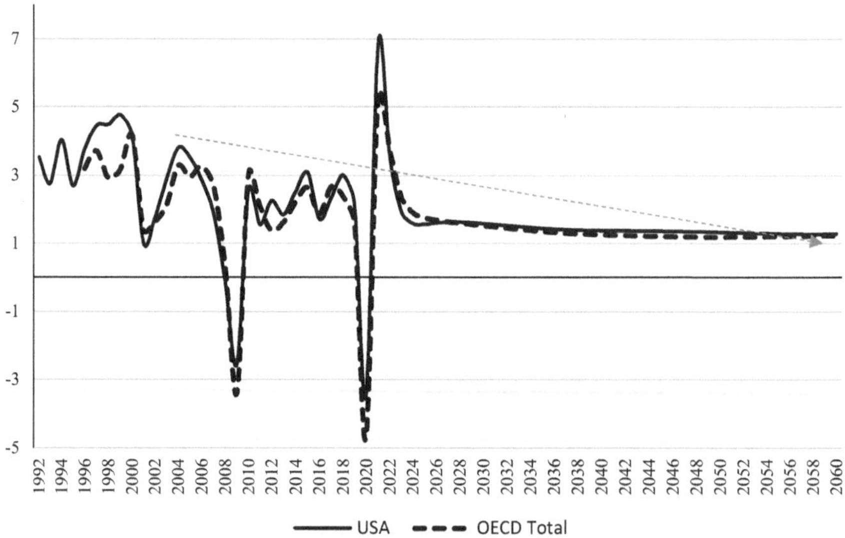

Figure 6.10 Real GDP Long-Term Forecast Annual Growth Rate, %

Source: OECD Data

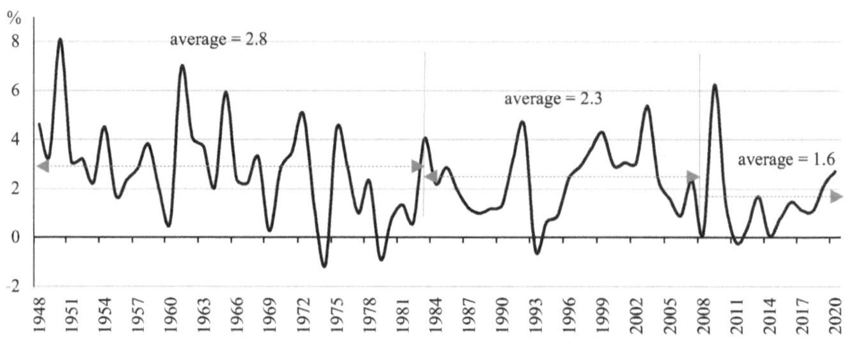

Figure 6.11 Labor Productivity (Output per Hour) for All Employed Persons in the U.S. Business Sector, Annual Change

Source: U.S. Bureau of Labor Statistics

expectations about the economy. Whenever the spread has gone below zero, a financial crisis has happened later. The crisis of 1980 occurred after the spread was down to -1.34 in October 1979. Another crisis happened in 1981 after it was down to -1.70 in December 1980. The crisis of 1990 occurred after it was down to -0.45 in March 1989. The crisis of 2001 took place a few months

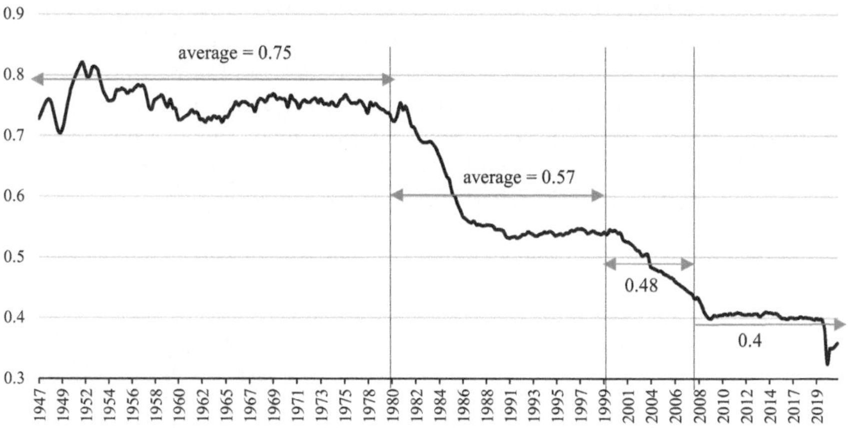

Figure 6.12 Marginal Revenue Productivity of U.S. Nonfinancial Debt (GDP per Dollar of Total Nonfinancial Debt)

Source: U.S. Bureau of Economic Analysis; Board of Governors of the Federal Reserve System (US)

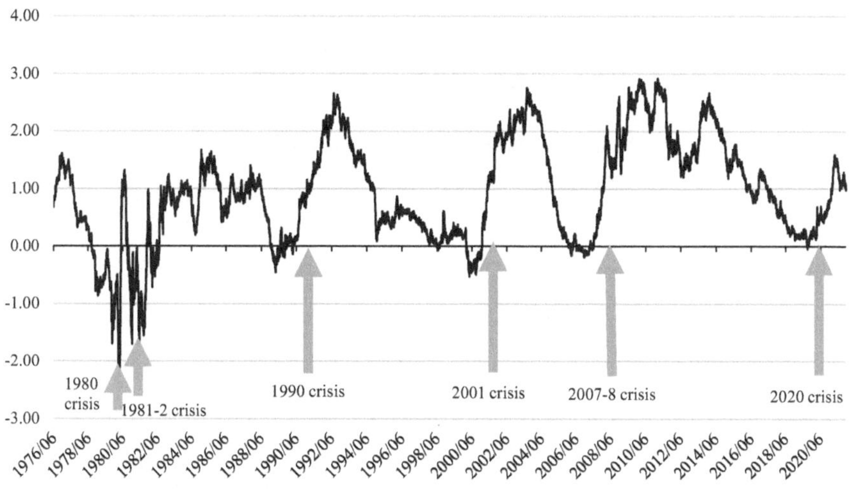

Figure 6.13 Financial Crises and the Spread between 10-Year and 2-Year Treasury Securities

Source: Federal Reserve Bank of St. Louis

after it was down to -0.52 in April 2000. The crisis of 2007–8 happened after it was down to -0.19 in November 2006. The current turmoil occurred after it was down to -0.04 in August 2019. In fact, this down occurred after the Federal Reserve raised the federal fund rate to 2.16 in January 2019.

Furthermore, after this rise in the federal fund rate, the Purchasing Managers Index (PMI)—a leading indicator of overall economic activity in the U.S.—had also fallen to 47.2 in December 2019, as seen in Figure 6.14. A PMI under 50 represents a recession in manufacturing.[33] Moreover, another economic performance—manufacturers' new orders for durable goods—had been already downturned before the beginning of the pandemic. Their annual growth rate in January 2020 had already plummeted to -9.3% as seen in Figure 6.15. These two indicators—PMI and manufacturers' new orders for durable goods—seemed to

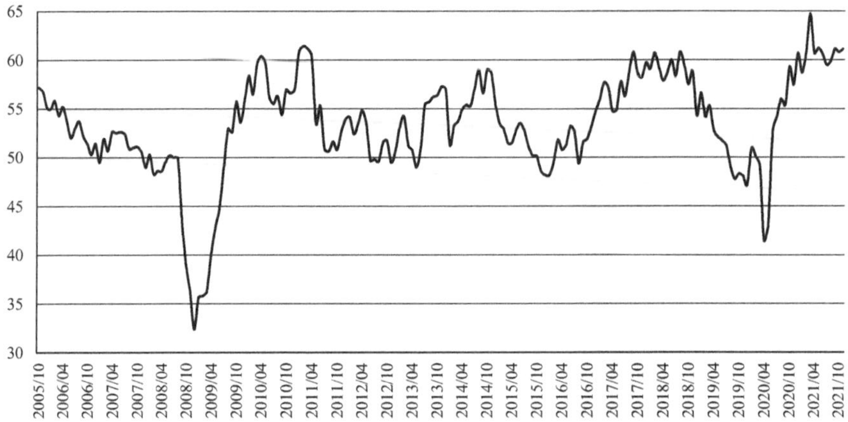

Figure 6.14 Purchasing Managers' Index in the United States

Source: Institute for Supply Managment

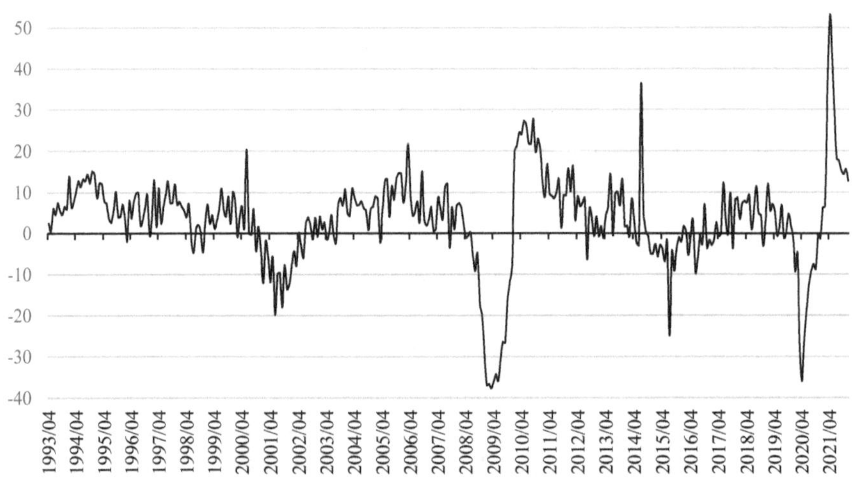

Figure 6.15 Manufacturers' New Orders: Durable Goods

Source: U.S. Census Bureau

show that the Federal Reserve's raising of federal fund rates contributed to damaging the performance of the U.S. nonfinancial sector whose debt level had already skyrocketed to 50% of GDP in January 2020.

From this fact, we can conclude that over the long term the U.S. government would increase (or at least maintain) its debts to the Federal Reserve in order to maintain or reduce its increasing overall burden of interest payment. Consequently, the government's debt borrowed from the Federal Reserve has been transformed into "gifts" that the government would not repay.[34] In this respect, separate personhoods between the two are misleading, giving us a false impression that the U.S. government borrows money from the Federal Reserve and repays the debt with interest.

However, in June 2022, when I delivered this this book to the publisher, the Federal Reserve began to raise federal fund rates and started *quantitative tightening*, by which it reduces the financial assets, including treasury securities and mortgage-backed-securities that it holds on its balance sheet by rolling them off. This will result in the amount of rolled-off treasury securities no longer being a gift to the U.S. government.

The Federal Reserve and the U.S. government seem to be in a contradictory position that will be further examined in the next chapter. On the one hand, the U.S. government's capability of repaying its debt to the Federal Reserve is limited, as previously explained. Quantitative easing is addictive and is difficult to forgo after initiation. The US's addiction to it was proven by the financial crisis of 2020. When this crisis happened, mutual funds, the household sector, and foreigners made a run on the U.S. treasury market in March 2020.[35] The sales were large in historical terms, amounting to $266 billion, $196 billion, and $287 billion dollars, respectively, for the three groups in the first quarter of 2020.[36] This run was unusual because in previous crises, investors had fled to the treasury market to buy treasury securities, which were considered the world's safest and most liquid securities. As shall be seen in the next chapter, the crisis of 2008 was overcome when the public took on the debt burden of the private, and since then, the public has played a central role in providing money to the economy. However, this excessive reliance on the role of the public, that is, on treasury securities, has increased the possibility of investors in urgent need of liquidity making a run on the treasury market. This happened in March 2020, and in response to this illiquidity in the treasury market, the Federal Reserve initiated another round of quantitative easing on a larger scale than that implemented after 2008. This means that the treasury market's role of providing the world's safest and most liquid assets to the economy has been seriously damaged. In the long term, the United States would have difficulty managing this damaged treasury market if the Federal Reserve does not purchase Treasury securities additionally. Thus, if quantitative tightening creates another illiquidity in the treasury market, the Federal Reserve will implement quantitative easing again.

On the other hand, due to high inflation caused by quantitative easing, the U.S. government begin to perform quantitative tightening. As explained, this quantitative tightening and the rapid and significant rise of federal fund rates will likely contribute to creating an economic recession. In fact, Federal Reserve chairman Powell admitted on June 22, 2022 before a Senate committee that recession is certainly a possibility.

In this contradictory position, the U.S. government may go back and forth between quantitative easing and quantitative tightening and between raising and lowering federal fund rates quickly. This back and forth will have a damaging effect on low-income countries. One the one hand, quantitative easing contributes to creating global inflation, which generates food crises and hunger in low-income countries, as shall be discussed in detail in the next chapter. On the other hand, quantitative tightening contributes to creating worldwide economic recessions. Both make the lives of people in low-income countries difficult.

The rich and powerful have used the combined scheme of persons and credit to enhance their power while simultaneously avoiding their responsibilities. For example, in the above case, when the Federal Government asks the Federal Reserve to transfer the interest income earned from the lending of Federal Reserve notes back to the government, the government uses the fact that the Federal Reserve is *a part of the Federal Government.* The Federal Reserve exists because of an act of Congress, and its Board of Governors is a *presidentially* appointed agency of the Federal Government that must report to and is directly accountable to the U.S. Congress. However, when the Federal Government wants to simultaneously create a false impression that the government borrows money from the Federal Reserve and repays the debt with interest, it emphasizes the fact that the Federal Reserve is set up like a private corporation and is therefore *not a part of the Federal Government.* Also, in other social areas, the social institution of a person has been enthusiastically used as a way to enjoy rights but avoid responsibilities. For example, in order to avoid paying taxes, the rich set up corporate persons in tax havens and hide their personalities behind them. Furthermore, the securitization of consumer loans, which was one of the causes of the financial crisis of 2007, utilizes an ambiguous relationship between two separate persons—a parent corporation and its subsidiary corporation (known as a special-purpose conduit). This relationship is almost the same as the relationship between the Federal Reserve and the Treasury. Likewise, outsourcing, which has been popular since the 1990s, is also a metaphysical trick for avoiding responsibilities or saving labor costs. Since the law treats an outsourcing corporation and an outsourced corporation as separate entities, even if a loss of life occurs in the latter, the former can be immune from any responsibilities for the loss. All the above cases can happen because the modern concept of a person is a metaphysical, ethical, and legal framework that attributes all rights and responsibilities entirely to a certain person. Even if the concept originally aims to enhance the responsibilities of a person, it has been used to avoid responsibilities in reality. Currently, if someone wants to avoid responsibility, she can set up a vacuous "legal person" and shift their responsibilities onto them.

Notes

1 Cotterrell, "Power," 85.
2 Macpherson, "Capitalism."
3 Rubin and Sugarman, "Introduction," 34–35; Neale, "The Bourgeoisie," 95–101.
4 Macpherson, "Capitalism," 114.
5 Langbein, "The Secret Life of the Trust," 184.
6 Neale, "The Bourgeoisie."
7 Kim, "Modern Politics," 821.
8 Kim, "Modern Politics," 818 & 821.
9 Ireland, "Company Law," 35–36.
10 Lobban, "Corporate Identity," 397 & 399.
11 [1901] I Ch 279, 288.
12 Davies, *Modern Company Law*, 144.
13 Ireland, "Company Law."
14 UKHL 54 at para 35.
15 Ireland, "Limited Liability."
16 Ireland, "Company Law," 459.
17 Murse, "Members of Congress."
18 Boaz, "Political Governance."
19 *Her Majesty's Commissioners of Inland Revenue v. Laird Group PLC* (2003), UKHL 54 at para 35.
20 Ireland, "Limited Liability."
21 Ireland, "Limited Liability," 839.
22 qtd. in Ireland, "Limited Liability."
23 Ireland, "Limited Liability," 839–840.
24 Ireland, "Limited Liability," 839; Jeans, *Trusts.*; Macrosty, *Trust Movement*; Utton, "Early Merger Movements."
25 Glasbeek, *Wealth by Stealth*, 129.
26 www.nytimes.com/2020/03/07/opinion/the-case-for-permanent-stimulus-wonkish.html
27 https://fred.stlouisfed.org/series/GFDEGDQ188S
28 www.cbo.gov/publication/57038
29 Toma, "Interest Rate Controls," 631.
30 Board of Governors, *Annual Report 1945*, 7.
31 www.cbo.gov/publication/56910
32 www.cbo.gov/publication/57038
33 PMI is a measure of the prevailing direction of economic trends in manufacturing and is measured based on a monthly survey of supply chain managers across 19 industries.
34 Consequently, the Federal Reserve printing money and lending it to the Federal Government in quantitative easing is, in essence, the same as when the Weimar Republic printed money during the 1920s. Why did the latter cause hyperinflation while the former does not? This question must be explored. The U.S. dollar system has two main ways of maintaining its international demand—and thus its value—in spite of too large an injection of dollars in a short time. One way is to increase the price of petroleum and thus create additional demand for dollars internationally. The other reason is the recurrent crises of foreign exchange that have happened in developing countries for the last three decades. Developing countries, fearing a sudden exit of dollars, are demanding more dollars. My next research paper will explore this matter.
35 Cheng, Wessel, and Younger, "US Treasury Debt"; Vissing-Jorgensen, "Treasury Market in Spring 2020."
36 Vissing-Jorgensen, "Treasury Market in Spring 2020," 21.

Bibliography

Boaz, D. "Political Governance vs. Corporate Governance." *Cato Institute*, 2006. Available at www.cato.org/blog/political-governance-vs-corporate-governance. Accessed October 19, 2021.

Cheng, Jeffrey, David Wessel, and Joshua Younger. "How Did COVID-19 Disrupt the Market for U.S. Treasury Debt?" Hutchins Center, *Brookings Institution*, 2020. Available at https://www.brookings.edu/blog/up-front/2020/05/01/how-did-covid-19-disrupt-the-market-for-u-s-treasury-debt/. Accessed October 19, 2021.

Cotterrell, Roger. "Power, Property and the Law of Trusts." *Journal of Law and Society* 14, no. 1 (1987): 77–90.

Davies, Paul. *Gower's Principles of Modern Company Law*. 6th ed. London: Sweet & Maxwell, 1997.

Glasbeek, Harry. *Wealth by Stealth*. Toronto: Between the Lines, 2002.

Ireland, Paddy. "Company Law and the Myth of Shareholder Ownership." *Modern Law Review* 62, no. 1 (1999): 32–57.

Ireland, Paddy. "Limited Liability, Shareholder Rights and the Problem of Corporate Irresponsibility." *Cambridge Journal of Economics* 34, no. 5 (2010): 837–856.

Jeans, J. S. *Trusts, Pools and Corners*. London: Methuen, 1894.

Kim, Jongchul. "Modern Politics as a Trust Scheme and its Relevance to Modern Banking." *Journal of Economic Issues* 47, no. 4 (2013): 807–826.

Langbein, J. H. "The Secret Life of the Trust." *The Yale Law Journal* 107 (1997): 165–189.

Lobban, Michael. "Corporate Identity and Limited Liability in France and England 1825–67." *Anglo-American Law Review* 25 (1996): 287–334.

Macpherson, C. B. "Capitalism and the Changing Concept of Property." In *Feudalism, Capitalism and beyond*, 104–125. London: Edward Arnold, 1975.

Macrosty, H. W. *The Trust Movement in British Industry*. London: Longmans, 1907.

Murse, T. "Do Members of Congress Ever Lose Re-election? Why Incumbent Members of the House of Representatives Almost Always Win." *ToughtCo.*, 2018. Available at www.thoughtco.com/do-congressmen-ever-lose-re-election-3367511. Accessed July 22, 2018.

Neale, Ronald. S. "The Bourgeoisie, Historically, Has Played a Most Revolutionary Part." In *Feudalism, Capitalism and beyond*, 84–103. London: Edward Arnold, 1975.

Rubin, Gerry R. and David Sugarman, "Introduction." In *Law, Economy and Society, 1750–1914*. London: Professional Books Limited, 1984.

Toma, Mark. "Interest Rate Controls: The United States in the 1940s." *The Journal of Economic History* 52, no. 3 (1992): 631–650.

Utton, M. A. "Some Features of the Early Merger Movements in British Manufacturing Industry." *Business History* 14 (1972): 51–60.

Vissing-Jorgensen, Annette. "The Treasury Market in Spring 2020 and the Response of the Federal Reserve." *Journal of Monetary Economics* 124 (2021): 19–47.

7 The Fall of the Neoliberal Form of Finance and Its Predicaments

The neoliberal form of finance started to fail after the financial crisis of 2008. What would a post-neoliberal economy look like? Finding an answer to this question now revolves around the debate on the nature of current high inflation rates. In the twentieth century, inflation skyrocketed when the capitalist economy was in crisis and experienced a qualitative change. If we examine the nature of current inflation, we can better understand the economic contradictions that the post-neoliberal form of finance creates. Recently, political struggle has occurred between two opposing ideologies: "sound finance" and "fiscal and monetary expansionism." Expansionists now appear to have almost won this ideological struggle. However, this chapter demonstrates that expansionism has also worsened inequality both within and between countries as shall be seen in the case of quantitative easing.

The neoliberal form of finance started to fall after the financial crisis of 2008. Since the crisis, the role of private banking and finance in creating money has been scaled back. Instead, central banks and the state have had a central role in creating money and pouring it into the economy. This chapter identifies these facts.

What would a post-neoliberal form of the economy look like? An answer to this question now revolves around the debate on the nature of current global inflation. The gradual reduction of the annual growth rate of the consumer price index (CPI) was a significant characteristic of the neoliberal period. However, growing inflation has emerged as a major economic feature after the global financial crisis of 2008 in the case of low-income countries and after 2020 in the case of the United States and other high-income countries. Some economists argue that current inflation will be transitory. For example, the White House's Council of Economic Advisors in July 2021 argued that the current economic situation is parallel to the inflationary period of the 1940s when inflation was transitory.[1] Taking the same view as these advisers, economist Paul Krugman argues that current inflation will quickly decline once supply chains fully recover and pent-up demand levels off.[2] Against this transitory view of inflation, other economists argue that current inflation will be persistent, as happened in the 1970s, unless the Federal Reserve decisively fights it.[3] Inflation became a serious phenomenon only after World War I. Before the war, "inflation was zero or close to it."[4] In the twentieth century, inflation

DOI: 10.4324/9781003052210-8

skyrocketed when the capitalist economy was in crisis and changed qualitatively. For example, the inflation between 1913 and 1950 occurred when the capitalist economy almost collapsed due to the two world wars and only recovered when the Bretton Woods system was agreed upon. In this system the U.S. dollar emerged as the world's reserve currency. 1970s' inflation occurred when the U.S. dollar was in crisis and at risk of losing its status as the world's reserve currency. Thus, if we examine the nature of current inflation, we can better understand the economic contradictions that the post-neoliberal form of finance creates.

The socioeconomic implications of inflation have been a forgotten theme among scholars. One main reason would be that high inflation in the U.S. and other high-income countries is a fairly recent phenomenon that has not occurred between the early 1980s and 2020, even though it has already occurred in low-income countries after 2008. One exception would be Jonathan Nitzan and Shimshon Bichler's article of 2016 that analyzed the social implications of high oil prices, especially their correlation with conflicts in the Middle East and beyond.[5] As shall be seen later, the prices of commodities, especially oil prices, are a major determinant of inflation. Thus, Nitzan and Bichler's article can be considered to analyze some social implications of inflation. They identify that oil prices have often risen sharply even when the production or inventory capacity of oil is high. They argue that the reasons for the sharp rises should thus be found elsewhere, especially in growing conflicts in the Middle East and beyond. They anticipate that this nexus of high oil prices and conflicts will reoccur in the near future. Their anticipation seems to be realized nowadays after 2020. However, the limitation of their theory is that they attribute the rise of the nexus only to the emergence of a global alliance among parties who get a great benefit from high oil prices, including the integrated oil companies, the large armament contractors, leading Western governments, and key oil-producing countries. This chapter argues that this is important but only a part of the whole story. To fully understand the upswing and downswing of the nexus of high inflation and conflicts since the early 1970s, we need to also consider other phenomena including the retreat of globalization, the large inequality of wealth and income, demographic change, quantitative easing, the U.S. government's high level of debt and deficit, the U.S. dollar's privilege as the world's reserve currency, and the breakdown of the Bretton Woods system. This chapter aims to fill this gap.

Charles Goodhart and Manoj Pradhan recently argued that a massively increased workforce and globalization had been the main causes of the low level of inflation during the neoliberal period. They further argue that this demographic trend is now reversing and that this reversed trend will push up both inflation and the bargaining power of scarce labor, thereby contributing to mitigating inequality.[6] This chapter argues that Goodhart and Pradhan do not recognize that the inflationary effects of the U.S. monetary and fiscal expansionist policies may actually worsen inequality.

In summary, the current debate on inflation is proceeding on the following three topics: first, whether the current inflation is transitory or persistent; second, whether the current inflation is caused by international conflicts such as Russia's invasion of Ukraine; and third, whether inflation will mitigate wealth inequality or increase it. Regarding these debates, this chapter argues the following. First, global inflation may repeatedly surge at various intervals as long as advanced countries continuously use monetary and fiscal expansionist policies and as long as the world fails to recover the globalization of trade. Second, even though international conflicts have worsened inflation, there have been some cases in which global inflation occurred before or even without international conflict. For example, the surge in oil prices—a main determinant of inflation—had already begun in early 2020, long before Russia invaded Ukraine, and there were no international conflicts when oil prices spiked in 2008. Arguably, global inflation should be understood, basically, as a monetary phenomenon that occurs as a result of a loss in purchasing power of the world's reserve currency—the U.S. dollar—for commodities. This loss has been accelerating since the gold standard of the Bretton Wood system was abolished and the U.S. monetary and fiscal expansionist policies have been actively implemented. Third, even though the growing bargaining power of labor could, as argued by Goodhart and Pradhan, contribute to mitigating inequality, inflationary policies—i.e., the monetary and fiscal expansionist policies of developed countries—have worsened, and will worsen, both domestic and global inequality.

Recently, political struggles have occurred between two opposing ideologies: "sound finance" and "fiscal and monetary expansionism." Expansionists have argued that sound finance should give way to unbalanced budgets and that the injection of money on a large scale by central banks is indispensable in saving the financial system. At present, the expansionists appear to have almost won this ideological struggle. However, this chapter demonstrates that expansionism has also worsened inequality both within and between countries as shall be seen in the case of quantitative easing. This implies that this political struggle should be changed from a struggle between "sound finance" and "fiscal and monetary expansionism" into a struggle between "expansionism" and "direct wealth redistribution." What we are currently lacking are the radical reforms that were implemented in the 1940s, which decreased wealth and income inequality by redistributing wealth.

This chapter begins by identifying that the neoliberal form of finance has withered since the financial crisis of 2008. The second and third sections of the chapter will then identify that even though the breakdown of the Bretton Woods system has exposed the world to the possibility of the highest inflation since the 1970s, globalization and demography during the neoliberal period led the world's working class to bear the brunt of the hardship caused by high commodity prices and allowed Western rich countries to remain immune to high inflation. However, this immunity has been gradually eroded since the middle of the 2010s. The fourth section discusses the main reason for the declining value of the dollar and the resultant high inflation, namely the United States' federal deficit and trade deficit. The fifth section shows that the United States is able to maintain such a high level of federal and trade deficits and implement quantitative easing because the U.S. dollar is the world's reserve currency. The chapter argues that U.S. political and military power—i.e., the nexus of petroleum and the U.S. dollar—has been a crucial factor in cementing the U.S. dollar's privilege as the world's reserve currency. The chapter also shows that the U.S.'s response to the Chinese yuan's challenge against the dollar's privilege has been to escalate the trade war against China that has been ongoing since 2019 and thus to retreat from the globalization that had contributed to the low level of inflation during the neoliberal period. The sixth section of this chapter examines the effects of quantitative easing, which is the main means of financing the U.S. federal deficit and trade deficit. Quantitative easing is a peculiar monetary expansionist policy that responded to the failure of the neoliberal form of finance and has been the primary reason for the high level of government debt. This section also shows that quantitative easing has reciprocal effects at a national level by having contributed to worsening inequality in some aspects but having mitigated it in others. The seventh section identifies that quantitative easing is a beggar-thy-neighbor policy that grants the United States free wealth by which it can use resources produced by people outside the United States for free. It also demonstrates that quantitative easing is an inflationary policy.

7.1. The Withering of Private Banking and Finance

The neoliberal form of finance is often called shadow banking, which refers to bank-like financial activities conducted by unregulated or lightly regulated institutions outside the traditional banking system. It includes money market funds (MMFs), repurchase agreements, and asset securitization trusts. In the United States, MMF assets snowballed during the neoliberal period from less than \$2 billion in 1974 to \$11 billion in 1978, \$76 billion in 1980, \$1 trillion in 1997, and \$3.8 trillion in 2008, as seen in Figure 7.1. Likewise, before 2008, the U.S. repurchase agreement market had also grown rapidly: security brokers and dealers' borrowing money through repurchase agreements reached its highest level, \$3.1 trillion, in 2007, as seen in Figure 7.2. The rapid growth of MMFs and repurchase agreements meant the rapid growth of debt in financial sectors, reaching its highest level of 105.9% of the U.S. gross domestic product (GDP) in October 2008, as seen in Figure 7.3. This overburden of debt impaired the trustworthiness of financial corporations and contributed to creating the global financial crisis of 2008.

Since this crisis, which represented the failure of neoliberal forms of finance, shadow banking has shrunk significantly. As Figure 7.2 shows, security brokers and dealers' liability for repurchase agreements in the U.S. has decreased by almost half from its highest level of \$3.1 trillion in 2008 to \$1.55 trillion in 2020. This liability is the amount of money created by repurchase agreements,

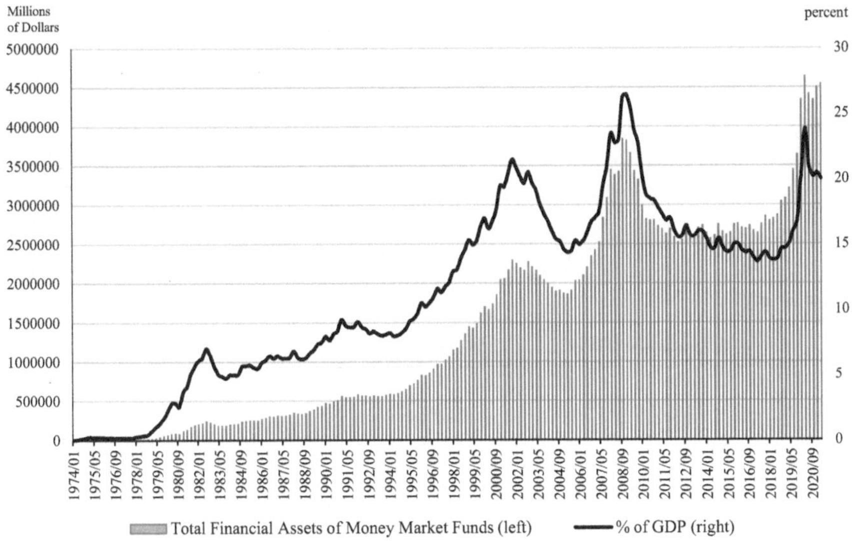

Figure 7.1 Total Financial Assets of Money Market Funds

Source: Board of Governors of the Federal Reserve System; U.S. Bureau of Economic Analysis

Figure 7.2 Security Brokers and Dealers' Liability of Repurchase Agreements in the United States

Source: Board of Governors of the Federal Reserve System

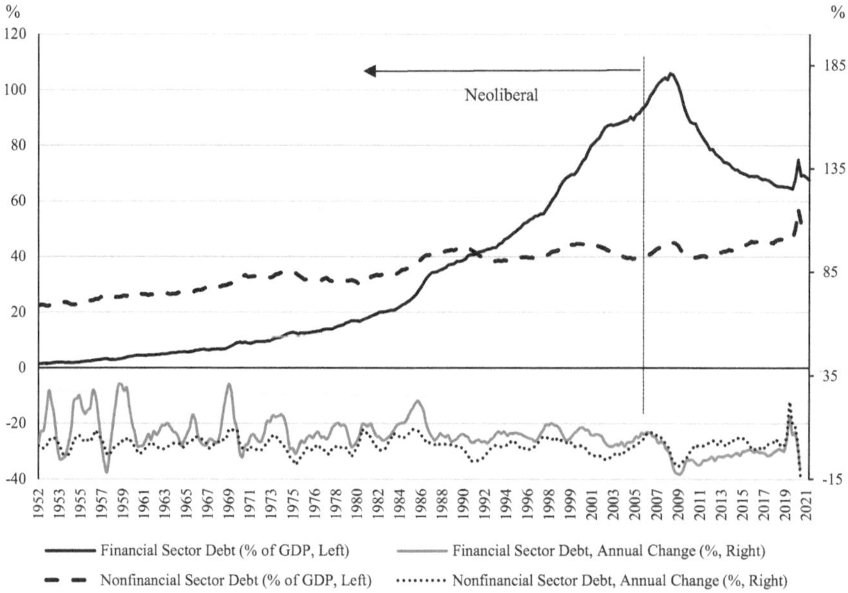

Figure 7.3 Debt Level, Financial vs. Nonfinancial Sectors in the United States

Source: Board of Governors of the Federal Reserve System

and the significant reduction in this liability implies that repurchase agreements' role in creating money has been significantly reduced. Money market funds' U.S. financial assets have also shrunk by almost half from their highest level of 26.4% of GDP in 2009 to 13.6% of GDP in 2017. Even though their level rebounded to 19.9% of GDP in 2021, the portfolio of the assets has significantly changed, as seen in Figure 7.4. During the neoliberal period, the portion of treasury securities decreased from 14.8% of the total financial assets of MMFs in 1992 to 3.6% in 2007. The remainder were financial assets issued by the private sector. However, the treasury securities portion skyrocketed to 52.5% in 2021. This significant change in the portfolio implies that the role of the private banking and finance in providing financial securities to MMFs (that is, to the economy) has withered significantly since the 2008 financial crisis.

As a result, the overall liability level of financial sectors in the U.S. has also collapsed, as seen in Figure 7.3, from 106% of GDP in October 2008 to 68% of GDP in April 2021, thus returning to the 1999 level. This liability can be an approximate proxy for how much financial sectors contribute to creating money. Before 2008, the growth rate of financial sectors was always higher than nonfinancial ones. However, since 2008, this situation has reversed, as seen in Figure 7.3.

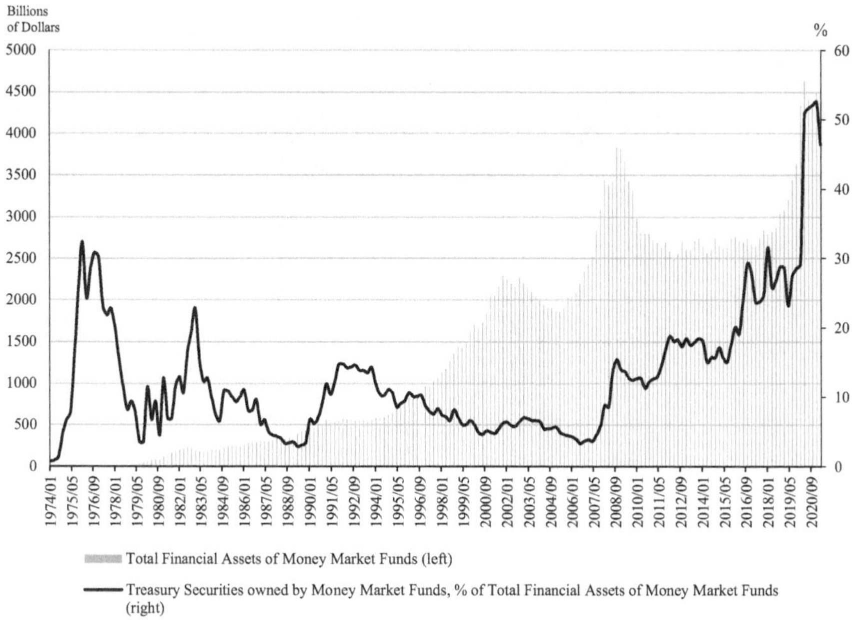

Figure 7.4 Treasury Securities owned by Money Market Funds in the United States

Source: Board of Governors of the Federal Reserve System

This withering role of private banking and finance in supplying money has caused a significant reduction in the ratio of M2 to the monetary base. The monetary base is central bank money that the Federal Reserve pours into the economy. M2 includes central bank money and the money that private banking and finance create by leveraging central bank money. It includes currency, demand deposits of commercial banks, balances in retail MMFs, and other elements. Thus, the ratio is an approximate proxy that can measure the role of private banking and finance in creating money. As seen in Figure 7.5, the ratio has collapsed from an average of 9.4 in the neoliberal period between 1982 and 2008 to an average of 3.8 after the 2008 financial crisis.

With the fall of private banking and finance, the Federal Reserve has instead taken the central role in creating and pouring money into the economy, and the U.S. government has assumed the burden of debt instead of the private sector since 2008. The Federal Reserve directly injects a large amount of money by purchasing treasury securities, mortgage-backed securities, and other securities, including junk bonds, as seen in Figure 7.6. This unconventional monetary policy is called quantitative easing. The Federal Reserve's purchase of treasury securities, that is, the public debt owed to the Federal Reserve, has

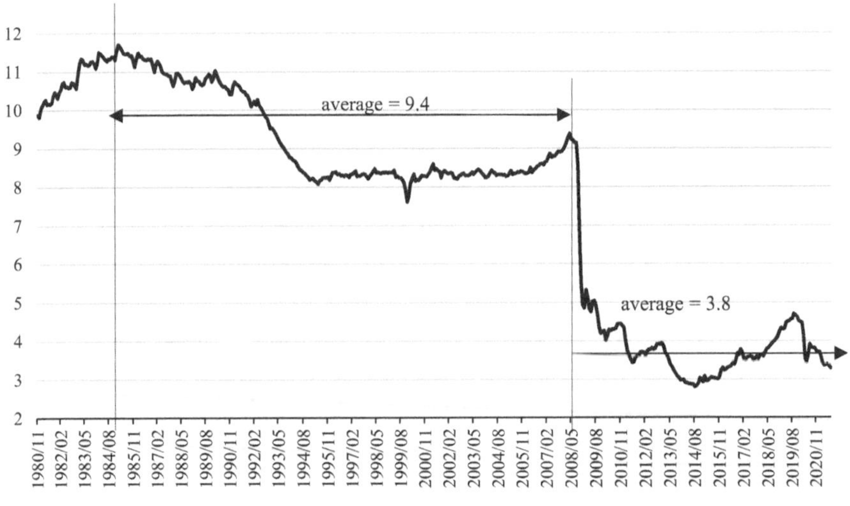

Figure 7.5 Money Multiplier (M2/Monetary Base)

Source: Board of Governors of the Federal Reserve System

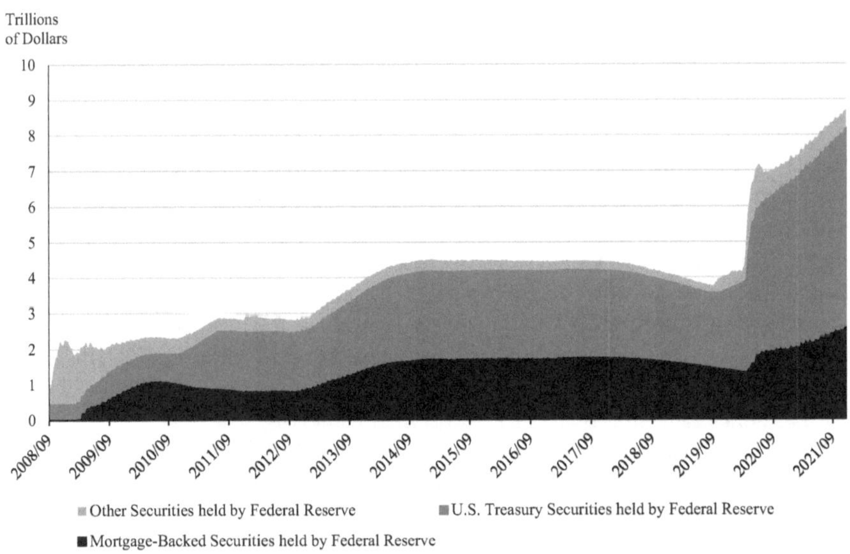

Figure 7.6 Mortgage-Backed Securities and Treasury Securities held by the Federal Reserve

Source: Board of Governors of the Federal Reserve System

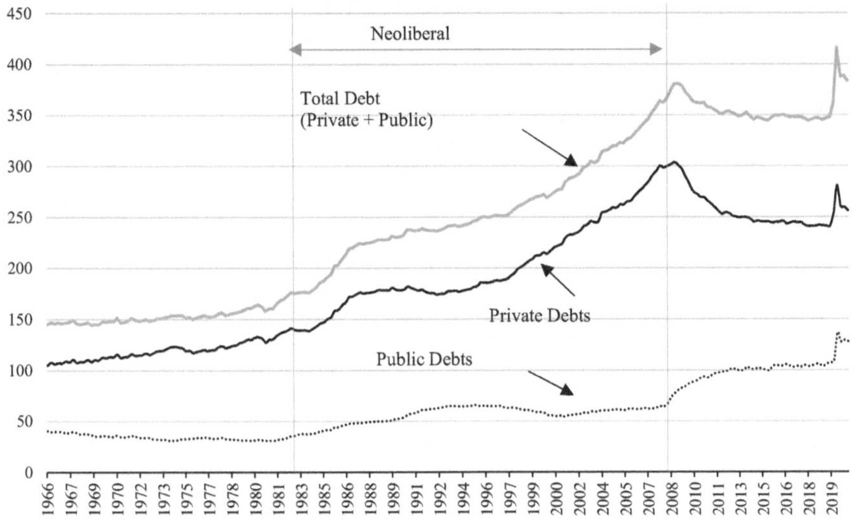

Figure 7.7 All Private and Public Debt in the United States, as % of GDP

Source: Board of Governors of the Federal Reserve System

increased to 22.3% of GDP and 17.8% of total public debt in April 2021. As Figure 7.7 depicts, all private and public U.S. debt decreased after 2008 but rebounded to its highest level, 384% of GDP, in 2021. This rebound is due to the increase of nonfinancial sector debt, especially public debt, despite the reduction of financial sector debt.

7.2. The Inflationary Period

As seen in Figure 7.8, for the last 250 years since 1774 it is not until the breakdown of the gold standard system in the early 1970s that consumer price index in the United States has skyrocketed. This stable CPI was largely due to the stable prices of major commodities including oil, wheat, and corn. The prices of commodities are a major determinant of consumer price index in the U.S., as seen in Figure 7.9. The Pearson's correlation coefficient between the two is 0.8 since 1993. In the Bretton Woods system where the value of the U.S. dollar was anchored to 35 ounces of gold, the global price of commodities was maintained stably. This stability seemed to be mainly due to two reasons. One reason is that the prices of various commodities including gold, petroleum, and wheat have a tendency to move together. As seen in Figure 7.10 and 7.11, the long-term movement of the prices of wheat and crude oil and of the prices of gold and crude oil in the U.S. since 1947 has a very strong correlation (Pearson's correlation coefficient of 0.93 and 0.87, respectively). By anchoring the

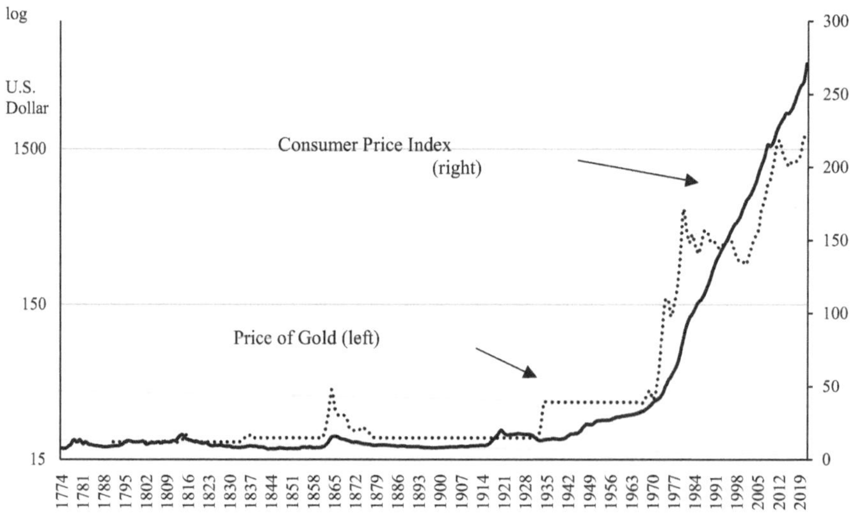

Figure 7.8 Consumer Price Index and the Price of Gold in the United States

Source: Measuring Worth, https://measuringworth.com

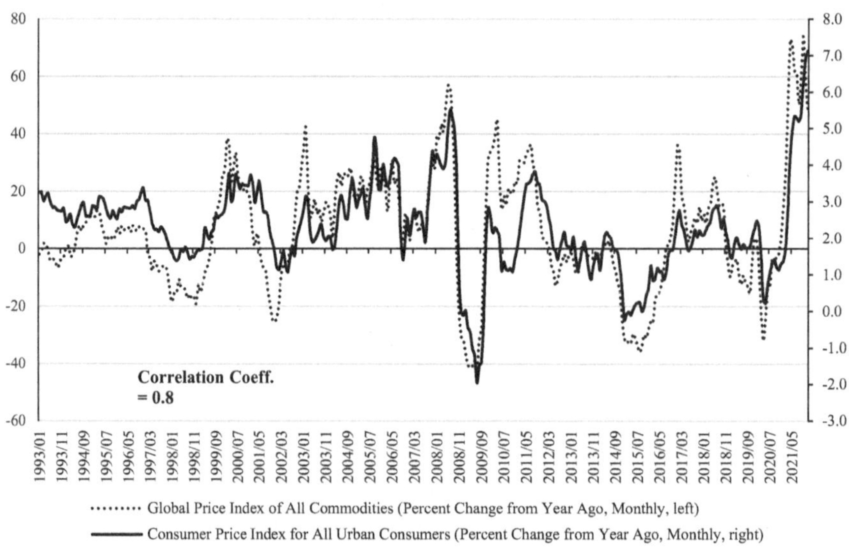

Figure 7.9 Inflation and Global Prices of Commodities

Source: U.S. Bureau of Labor Statistics, International Monetary Fund

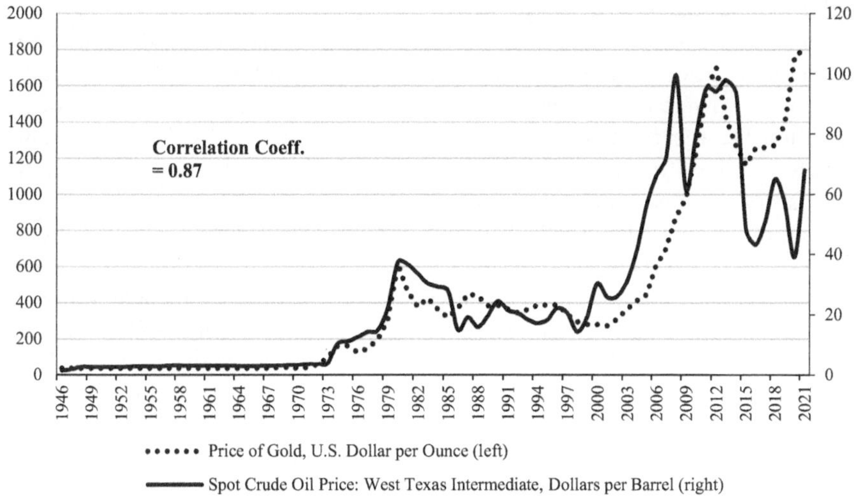

Figure 7.10 Prices of Gold and Crude Oil in the United States

Source: Federal Reserve Bank of St. Louis, Measuring Worth, https://measuringworth.com

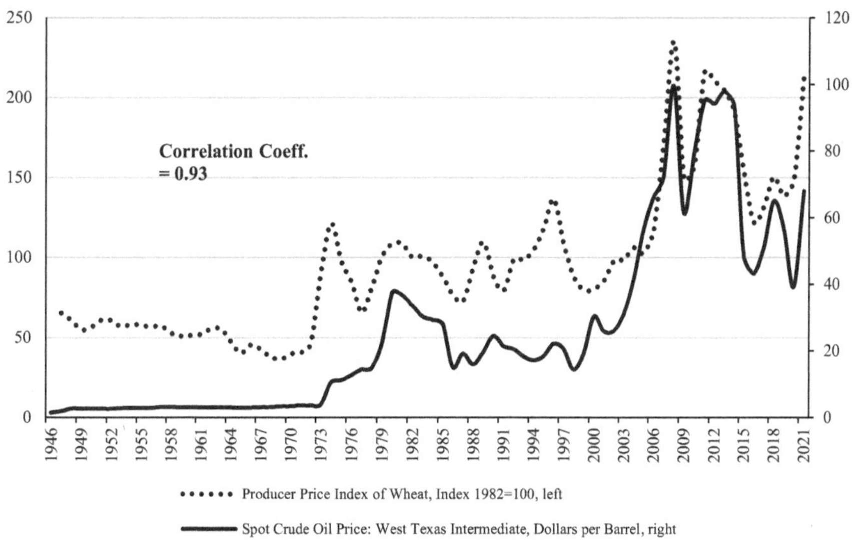

Figure 7.11 Prices of Wheat and Crude Oil in the United States

Source: Federal Reserve Bank of St. Louis, U.S. Bureau of Labor Statistics

U.S. dollar to gold, the purchasing power of the dollar for other commodities had been also maintained stably.

The other reason was that the U.S. government implemented the policy to maintain the price stability of major commodities including petroleum, wheat, and corn by maintaining a high level of the government storage for these commodities. During the two decades between 1950 and 1969 the government storage had held over two-thirds of the total U.S. wheat stocks and almost one half of the corn stock,[7] and the government implemented the regulatory policies of the Texas Railroad Commission regime, by which the government maintained an excess capacity of petroleum production.[8] By using large storage or capacity, if the prices increased excessively, the government flooded those commodities to market and thus cooled down the surge of the prices. Resultantly, as seen in Figure 7.10 and 7.11, prices of crude oil and wheat had been stable between the two decades (1949–1969): wheat price was decreased by 44%, and crude oil price was increased only by 80%. However, after the breakdown of the Bretton Woods system, that is, when the purchasing power of the dollar was no longer anchored to gold (and resultantly no longer to other commodities), the prices of commodities became extremely volatile.

Thus, global inflation since 1970s can be understood, in part, as a loss of the purchasing power of the world's reserve currency for commodities, occurring due to the change of the international financial system and to the devaluation of the U.S. dollar. However, the correlation between the global price of commodities and U.S. inflation has not been constant in the twentieth century. Figure 7.12 shows how the correlation has been changed since 1948. Even though this figure uses oil prices rather than the total prices of commodities, it can be

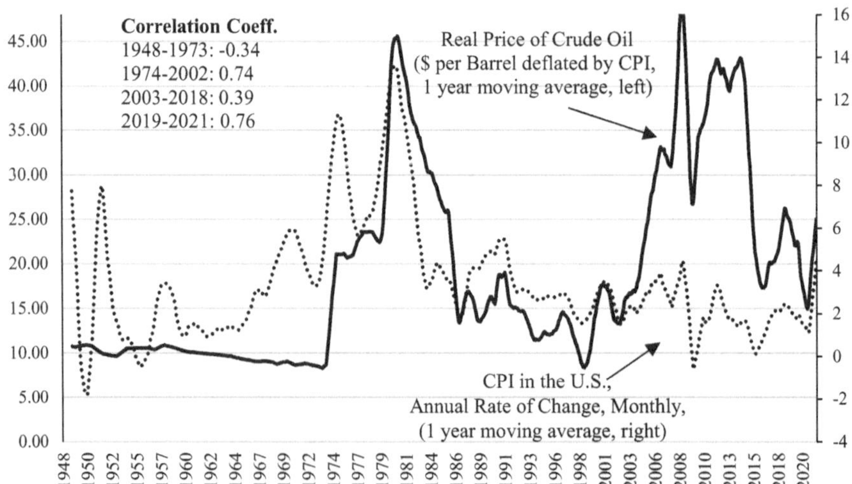

Figure 7.12 Real Oil Prices and Inflation in the United States

Source: Federal Reserve Bank of St. Louis, U.S. Bureau of Labor Statistics

a good proxy for the correlation because crude oil price accounts for over a half of the general commodity index[9] and has tended to move together with the prices of other commodities. This figure reproduces Nitzan and Bichler's insightful chart but with some revisions.[10] As seen in the figure, before 1974, the correlation between real oil price and CPI in the United States was negative (-0.34). That is, even though high inflation happened in the late 1940s, early 1950s, and early 1970s, they were caused by something other than the real oil prices that had been stable. Between 1974 and 2002, the correlation became tight (Pearson coefficient of 0.74). This means that inflation in the U.S. during this period was affected largely by global commodity prices. Between 2003 and 2018, the correlation became loose again (Pearson coefficient of 0.39). In spite of high volatility of global commodity prices during this period, inflation in the U.S. was relatively low and less affected by the commodity prices. However, since 2019, the correlation has been tight again (Pearson coefficient of 0.76).

7.3. Demography and Globalization

The abnormal period is between 2003 and 2018 in which the correlation between commodity prices and inflation was loose. To understand the current inflation, we need first examine why this abnormality occurred.

The gradual reduction of inflation rates in the neoliberal period was created by various factors, including demography, globalization, the reduction of military expenses, and many others. These factors contributed to allocating more resources and labor to productive industries, thus contributing to creating a long-term deflationary trend. Due to the combined effects of demography and globalization, a record-breaking increase in the labor force was achieved in this period. The annual growth of the world population between 1990 and 2012 was extremely high, amounting to 1.3%, as shown in Figure 7.13. Moreover, the share of the working-age population in the total worldwide population has skyrocketed, as seen in Figure 7.14.

Furthermore, after China became a member of the World Trade Organization in December 2001, the labor supply available to the capitalist economy *doubled*.[11] All these steep increases in labor supply, combined with the threat of offshoring and immigration, have led labor to increasingly lose its bargaining power and have allowed capitalists to save wage costs and increase labor intensity. This loss of labor's bargaining power has affected decreasing trade union density, as Figure 7.15 depicts.

However, these trends have been (and will increasingly be) reversed. According to a U.N. forecast, the annual growth of the world population will fall to 0.4% by the 2030s and to around 0.1% in the 2070s, as evidenced in Figure 7.13.[12] The share of the working-age population in the total world population has collapsed since 2015, as seen in Figure 7.14. The working-age population of China has also shrunk since 2015.[13] Moreover, the old-age dependency ratio—the ratio of population aged 65+ per 100 population aged 15–64—in the world has suddenly risen since 2010, as seen in Figure 7.16. As

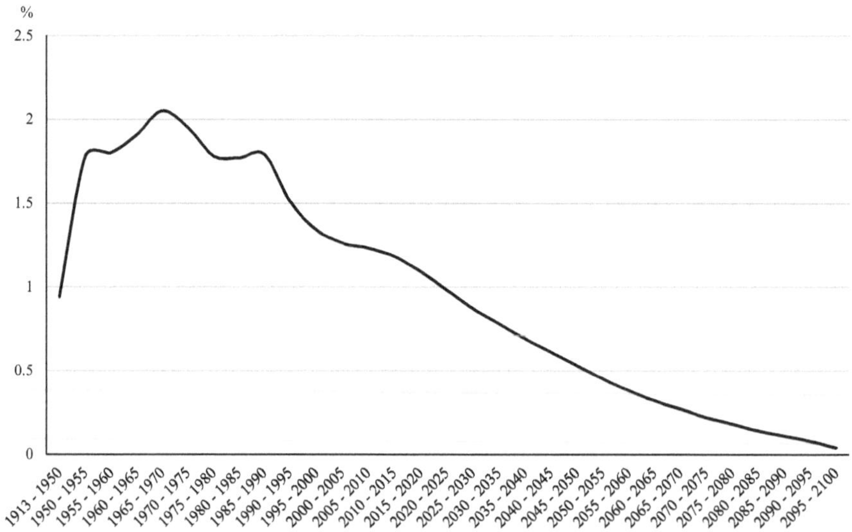

Figure 7.13 Average Annual Rate of World Population Change

Source: U.N. Population Projects; http://piketty.pse.ens.fr/fr/capital21c

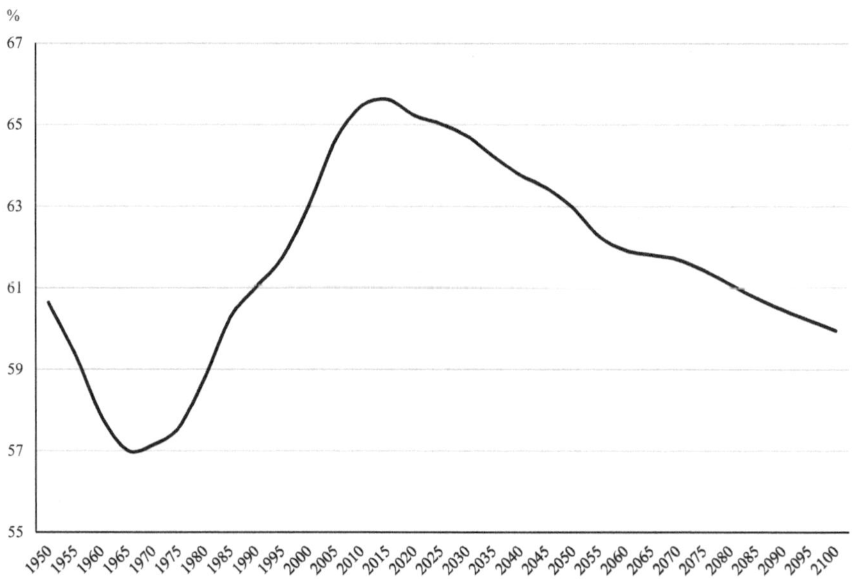

Figure 7.14 World Working Age Population (% of Total Population)

Source: U.N. Population Prospects

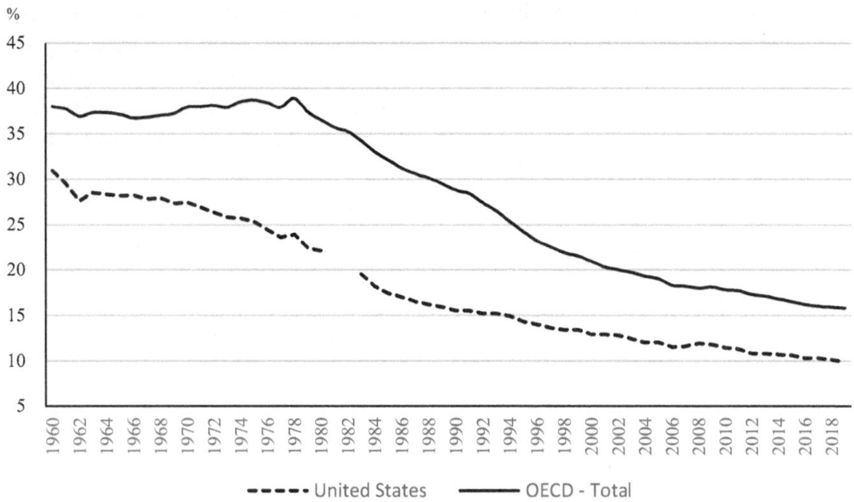

Figure 7.15 Trade Union Density (% of Total Employees)

Source: OEDC Data

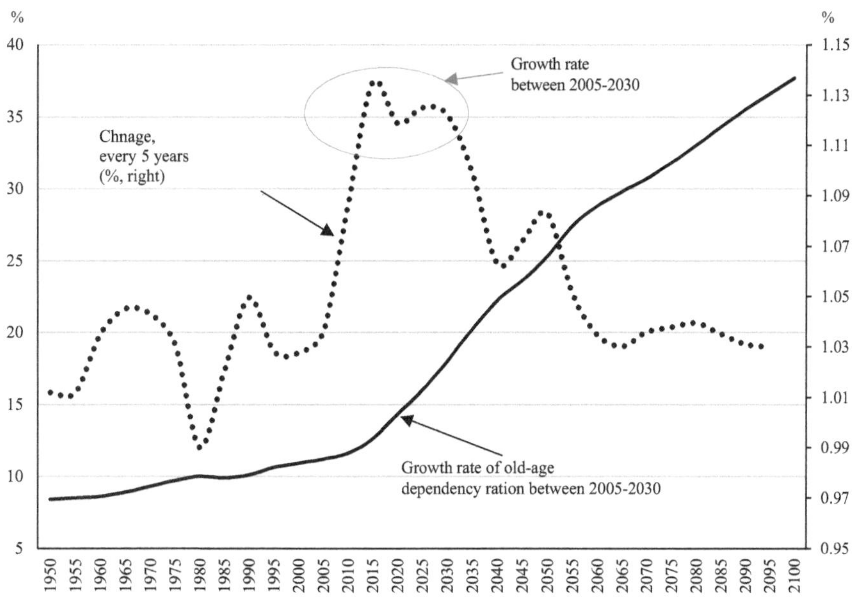

Figure 7.16 Old-age Dependency Ratio in the World (ratio of population aged 65+ per 100 population 15–64)

Source: UN Population Prospects

Goodhart and Pradhan argue, this skyrocketing ratio will have an inflationary effect because it will significantly increase the cost of pensions and medical care and allocate more labor and resources from productive industries into medical services.[14] Furthermore, as the trade war between the United States and China intensifies, and as the working-age population of China has shrunk since 2015, the Chinese role of supplying cheap goods to the capitalist economy will become increasingly restricted.

7.4. Global Inflation

Commodity prices are, as mentioned, affected significantly by the instability of the purchasing power of the world's reserve currency. This fact can be easily identified by the strong (inverse) correlation between crude oil price and the value of the U.S. dollar that has happened since 2000, as seen in Figure 7.17. A *slight* change of the relative value the U.S. dollar against other countries' currencies has been strongly correlated with the *great* volatility of crude oil price. Macroeconomists have been intrigued by this correlation and have tried to explain why this has happened. The dominant view among them is that the declining value of the dollar gave OPEC an incentive to make up for the loss caused by the declining value and strengthened the cartel.[15] Scholars have also identified that even though the U.S. government is officially and outwardly in favor of low oil prices, in reality it has preferred high oil prices when the value

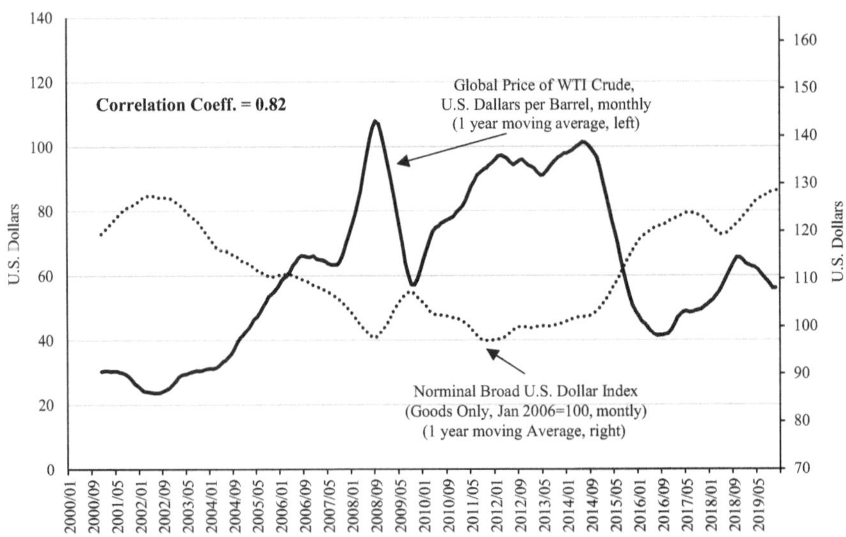

Figure 7.17 Crude Oil Price and the Fluctuation of the Value of U.S. Dollar

Source: Board of Governors of the Federal Reserve System, International Monetary Fund

of the dollar declines, that is, when the dollar's status of being the world's reserve currency is being threatened.[16] When the declining value of the dollar leads other countries to attempt to forgo the dollar and thus weakens the international demand of the dollar, rising oil prices can reverse this trend because it leads every country to need more dollars to buy expensive oil from OPEC. Furthermore, as Nitzan and Bichler point out, "rising oil prices were . . . expected to skew the geopolitical balance in favor of the United States and Britain, which had their own oil resources, and against Japan and Continental Europe, which did not."[17] Rising oil prices also pacify the complaint of its ally in Middle East—Saudi Arabia—about the loss of its oil revenue due to the declining dollar and prevent this country from accepting Euro or the Chinese yuan for oil sales. In fact, Saudi Arabia has considered to price oil trades in Euro several times, even though these have not been realized yet.[18]

Figure 7.18 describes a main reason for the declining value of the dollar: the federal deficit and trade deficit of the United States. The federal deficit in 2020 is -15% of GDP, at its worst level since 1943 when the federal deficit was -26.9% of GDP. As the sum of U.S. federal deficit and trade deficit as a percent of the U.S. GDP has increased, the value of the U.S. dollar against other countries' currencies has declined. That is, as the U.S. people "live profligately beyond their means" in Maynard Keynes' terminology, its currency's value declines. This declining value of the dollar has been a main cause for the high volatility of global commodity prices that have created food crises, serious hungers, and various forms of conflicts including protests and uprisings in low-income countries around 2006–2007 and 2010–2012. The Arab Spring of 2010–2012 is an example: it

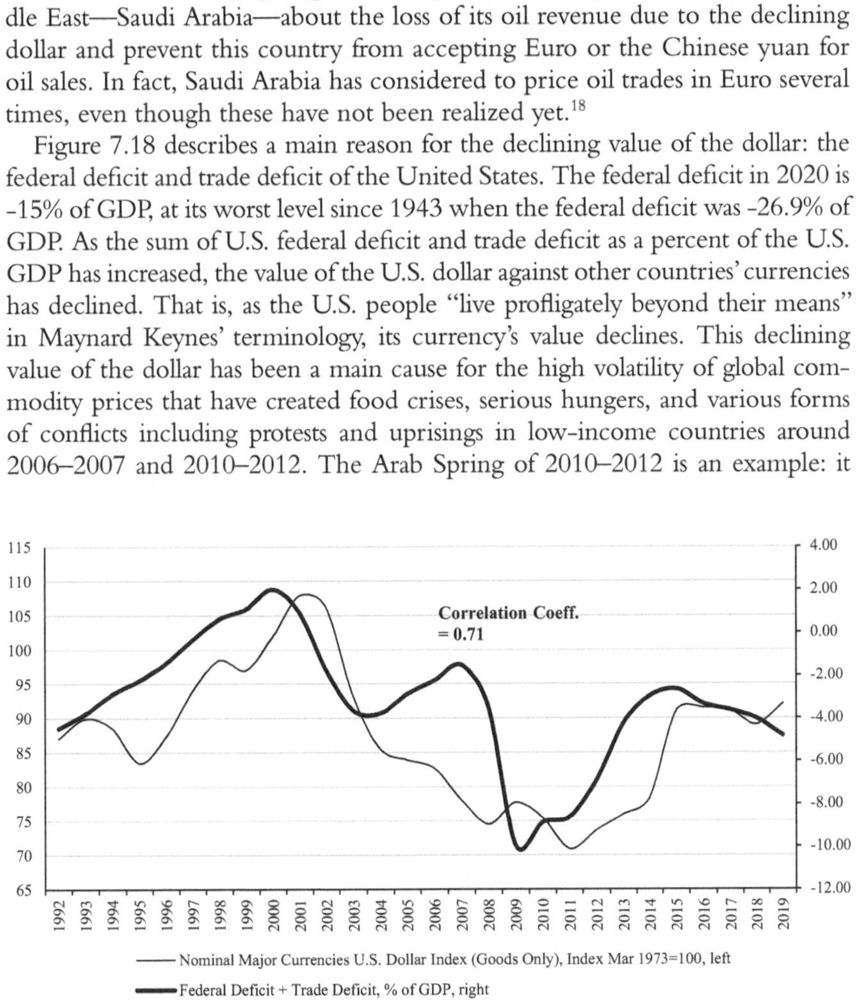

Figure 7.18 The Sum of U.S. Federal Deficit and Trade Deficit vs. Dollar Index

Source: U.S. Census Bureau, U.S. Bureau of Economic Analysis, U.S. Office of Management and Budget, Board of Governors of the Federal Reserve System

was triggered by the skyrocketing rise in the price of wheat and resultant hunger that occurred between 2007 and 2008 and between 2010–2011.[19] These price surges happened even though the 2006–2009 period had an unprecedented crop harvest in the world.[20] This creates a significant contrast with the previously-examined stability of commodity prices during the Bretton Woods system. This stability was a great achievement because the stable prices of commodities are a crucial basis for a stable life for ordinary people and for the industrialization of developing countries. Based on the gold standard of the Bretton Woods system the U.S. government used its large governmental food storage to relieve global hunger, that is, for "a food aid program, authorized by the 1954 Public Law 480, which disbursed vast quantities of grain and other agricultural commodities to Third World nations at the frontier of the Cold War."[21]

7.5. The Privilege of Being the World's Reserve Currency

How has the United States maintained such a high level of federal deficit and trade deficit? If emerging market maintain such a high level of the deficits, the increasing risk of their default will lead their currencies to decline sharply, resulting in an economic downturn. The United States is an exception. It has no risk of default as long as its currency is the world's reserve currency, which creates a strong international demand for U.S. dollars, which prevents a sharp decline in their value.

The question of how the U.S. dollar has maintained this privilege so far has been an enigma for economists. As seen in Figure 7.19, in 1960, the U.S. was a dominant economy whose GDP occupied 39% of the world's GDP, and thus the U.S. dollar could play a role as the world's reserve currency. However, its GDP continuously declined by almost half to 21% in 2011. Even though it has rebounded, it was still 24.7% in 2020. At the same time, the value of the U.S. dollar sharply declined to the index of 70 in 2011; although it rebounded, the figure was still less than 100, i.e., 92 in 2019. Why have the world's people accepted a continuously declining value of the world's reserve currency and held on to it? That is, why have the people of the world borne the loss? How has a declining economy enjoyed the privilege of holding the world's reserve currency? Some economists have argued that the size of the U.S. securities market, financial innovation by Wall Street, and the Eurodollar Market have caused the demand for the U.S. dollar to remain high.[22] However, this competitiveness of the dollar-denominated financial markets is possible because the dollar has been the world reserve currency. That is, the competitiveness is the result rather than the cause.

Instead, U.S. political and military power—that is, the nexus of petroleum and the U.S. dollar—has been a crucial factor, as some political economists have argued.[23] Petroleum has been the essential natural resource for every industrialized nation since the early twentieth century. When U.S. dollars are the only currency with which petroleum can be bought from OPEC (Organization of the Petroleum Exporting Countries) countries, dollars become the world's

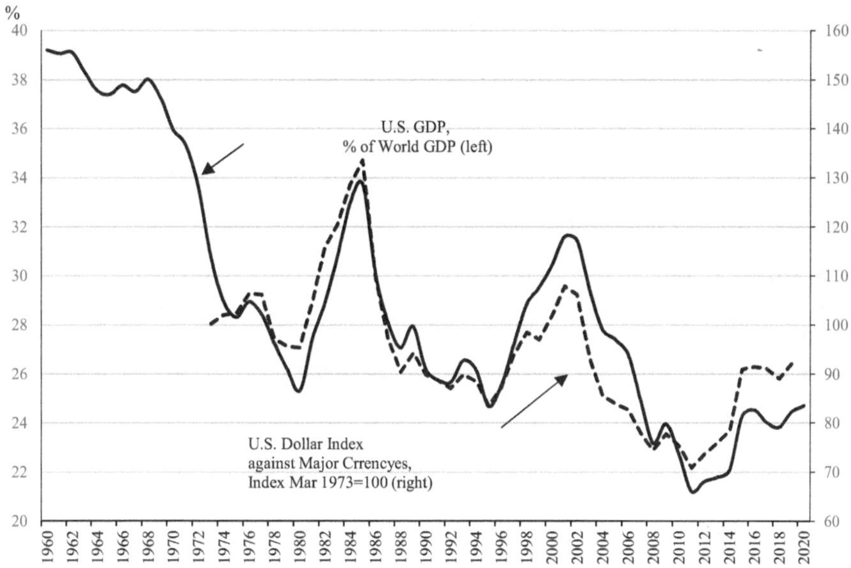

Figure 7.19 U.S. GDP, as % of World GDP & Dollar Index

Source: World Bank, U.S. Bureau of Economic Analysis, Board of Governors of the Federal Reserve System

only money. This occurred when Western countries settled on the Bretton Woods international system that existed between 1944 and 1972. When this system broke down, the dollar's privilege should have been deprived as well. However, the U.S. maintained its privilege by allying with Saudi Arabia, the dominant power among OPEC countries: Saudi Arabia agreed to accept only U.S. dollars when it sells its petroleum in return for U.S. military protection.[24] Since then, all attempts of other OPEC members to accept other currencies such as the Euro for the sale of petroleum have been severely punished by the United States. For example, when Saddam Hussein in 2000 announced that Iraq would accept Euros for the sale of petroleum, the United States invaded it and removed him.[25] The logic behind how dollars whose value has continuously declined have maintained their international demand is that every nation that needs petroleum to develop industry must acquire U.S. dollars to purchase it. The declining value of dollars has been a kind of tax that every nation has paid to the United States since 1944.

However, the privilege is now threatened by a challenge from the Chinese yuan as China's economy has grown: its GDP reaches to 17.4% of world GDP in 2020. No one knows whether the challenge will be successful or not. However, we can expect some results that the current response of the United States to the challenge would create. China, the world's largest petroleum importer, opened the Shanghai International Energy Exchange on March 26, 2018. This event can be considered the official beginning of China's challenge of the nexus of petroleum and U.S. dollars because petroleum began to be bought and sold in yuan rather than in the U.S. dollars there. The launching of the Shanghai International Exchange was likely one of main factors that provoked U.S. trade measures against China. The United States responded to this by escalating the trade war against China on September 17, 2018, when it announced it would impose tariffs of 10% on a list of Chinese imports totaling $200 billion. These tariffs increased to 25% in January 2019. The trade war is now worsening, and this would certainly worsen inflation and escalate the international conflict between them. In fact, the United States began to increase its military expenses as a percentage of GDP in 2018. On December 28, 2021, the U.S. Senate decided on an annual defense budget that costs $778 billion. This amount was $37 billion more than President Trump's last defense budget and $25 billion more than President Biden requested.

7.6. Effects of Quantitative Easing

The federal deficit and trade deficit of the United States were −9.98% of GDP in 2009, −8.8% in 2010, −8.63% in 2011, and −15.26% in 2020. The main method of financing this increasing federal deficit and trade deficit after the global financial crisis of 2008 has been quantitative easing. We now need to conduct a proper evaluation of this expansionary policy.

Quantitative easing has reciprocal effects at a national level. It has contributed to worsening inequality in some aspects but has mitigated it in other aspects. Let us look at the former negative effects. As seen in Figure 7.20, inequality—represented by the share of total net worth held by the top 1%—has increased as quantitative easing has increased (Pearson's correlation coefficient of 0.83). There are several reasons for this strong correlation between inequality and quantitative easing. First, a large part of the money provided by the Federal Reserve to the economy has been directly used to allow creditors immunity from any loss incurred from financial crises. All financial crises are the crisis of creditors who would lose money due to debtor default. The riskier this default is, the more interest these creditors receive. In return for this interest payment, it is economic ethics that creditors and debtors should share the loss caused by debtor default. However, the government's 2008 bailout program protected creditors but let individual debtors—for example, home mortgagors—lose their homes. This has resulted in the foreclosure of 5.3 million U.S. homes since the beginning of the crisis of 2008.[26]

Second, increasing inequality is also because quantitative easing has caused soaring prices of assets, including shares and real estate. As Figure 7.21 demonstrates, the total sum of quantitative easing implemented by three central banks, including that of the U.S., Britain, and Japan, have almost paralleled U.S. share prices between 2008 and the present. A large part of the liquidity created by these banks has been invested in the U.S. stock market and raised share prices. This pattern of soaring U.S. share prices was quite different from those in the

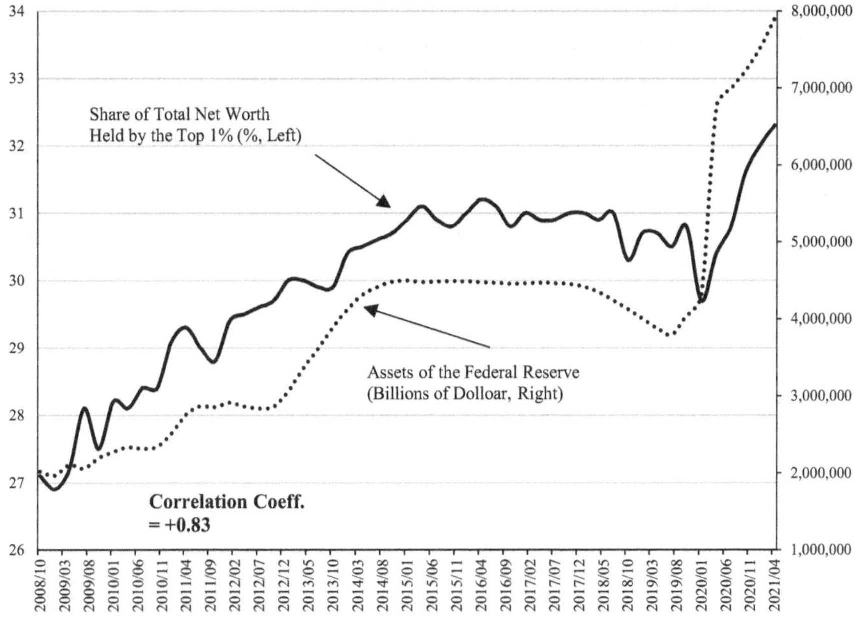

Figure 7.20 Quantitative Easing and Wealth Inequality in the United States

Source: Board of Governors of the Federal Reserve System

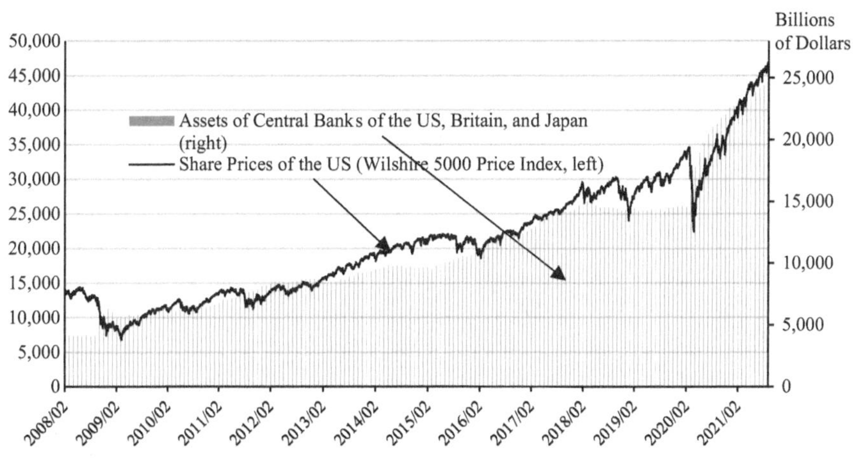

Figure 7.21 Shares Prices and Assets of Central Banks of the United States, Britain, and Japan

Source: Board of Governors of the Federal Reserve System, European Central Bank, Bank of Japan, Wilshire Associates

previous decade when the share prices of the U.S. were cyclical: the peak price of August 2000 was not recovered until January 2007. The different patterns between these two periods occur largely because cyclical industries have been offshored and because quantitative easing has been implemented since 2008. These post-2008 soaring share prices have been the main cause of wealth inequality. As seen in Figure 7.22, since 1989, the share of corporate equities and mutual fund shares held by the top 1% has paralleled the total net worth of the top 1%. As share prices have soared since 2008 and the top 1% have responded by increasing their possession of corporate shares, wealth inequality has also soared.

Quantitative easing, by which the Federal Reserve has purchased a large number of mortgage-backed securities and lowered long-term interest rates, has contributed to boosting housing prices. As seen in Figure 7.23, the amount of liquidity that commercial banks and the Federal Reserve have provided to home buyers—that is, the amount of mortgage-backed securities purchased by the Federal Reserve and commercial banks—has a strong correlation with housing prices in the United States (Pearson's correlation coefficient of 0.96). Housing prices have various causes, including the supply of and demand for housing. However, as seen in Figure 7.24, the large money supply provided by quantitative easing can be regarded as a main cause of increasing housing prices (Pearson's correlation coefficient of 0.92). These escalating housing prices have also contributed to worsening inequality because the share of the top 1% in real estate has increased for the last three decades from 12.4% in 2008 to 14.6% in 2021. The rise in housing prices has had an inflationary effect because it

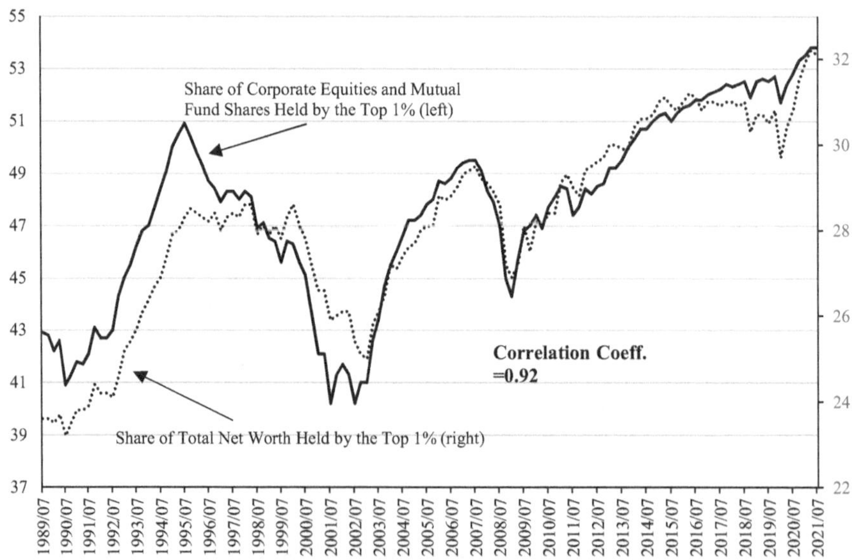

Figure 7.22 Share Ownership and Inequality in the United States

Source: Board of Governors of the Federal Reserve System

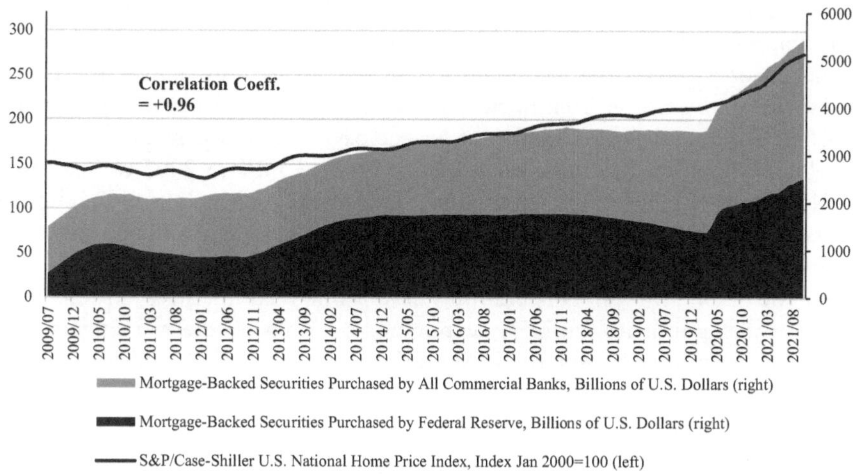

Figure 7.23 Home Prices and Federal Reserve's Purchase of Mortgage-Backed Securities
Source: Board of Governors of the Federal Reserve System, S&P Dow Jones Indices LLC

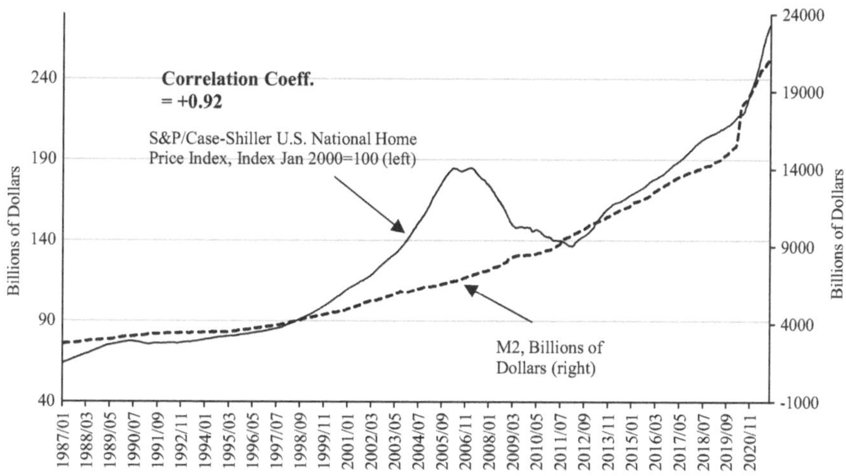

Figure 7.24 Home Prices and Money Supply in the United States
Source: Board of Governors of the Federal Reserve System, S&P Dow Jones Indices LLC

has contributed to rent raises and other housing costs, the most significant consumer price index component. The annual growth rate of housing costs in the consumer price index of December 2021 has risen to 6.8, the highest since 1982.[27]

Despite these negative effects, quantitative easing clearly aided economic recovery. Injecting considerable money and reducing interest rates allowed corporations and households to refinance their debts. For example, if a house owner's mortgage is larger than the price of their house, they cannot refinance it. However, the rise in house prices shown in Figure 7.24 made refinancing possible. Resultantly, household debt service payments as a percentage of disposable personal income have been reduced from 13.2% in 2007 to 9.2% in 2021, as seen in Figure 7.25. Thus, quantitative easing has reduced household debts by replacing them with public debt after the 2008 financial crisis, as shown in Figure 7.26.

As the U.S. business corporations have gained competitive advantages against other countries' business corporations, thanks to the refinancing of their debts at reduced costs, the U.S. GDP has also increased more than that of other countries. Since 2013, the share of the U.S. GDP proportionate to world GDP has grown, as seen in Figure 7.19. Moreover, thanks to quantitative easing, the U.S. government could spend more money for "transfer payments" to mitigate inequality. Transfer payments include social security and unemployment insurance, by which the government redistributes money to those in need. Figure 7.27 illustrates that during the neoliberal period, transfer payments were an average of 10.5% of GDP but increased by an average of 14.2% of GDP between 2008 and 2019, and an average 23.5% of GDP after 2020.

Figure 7.25 Household Debt Service Payments as a Percent of Disposable Personal Income (%)

Source: Board of Governors of the Federal Reserve System

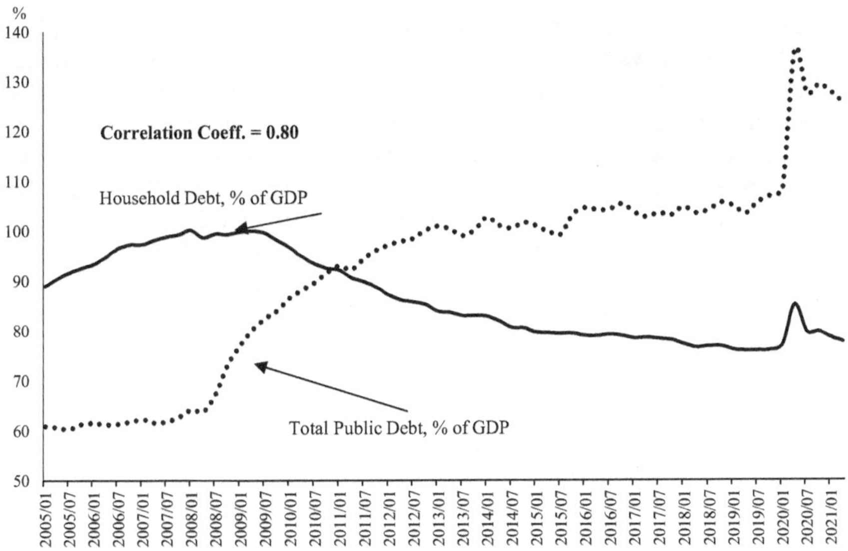

Figure 7.26 Household Debt vs. Public Debt in the United States

Source: International Monetary Fund, U.S. Office of Management and Budget, Federal Reserve Bank of St. Louis

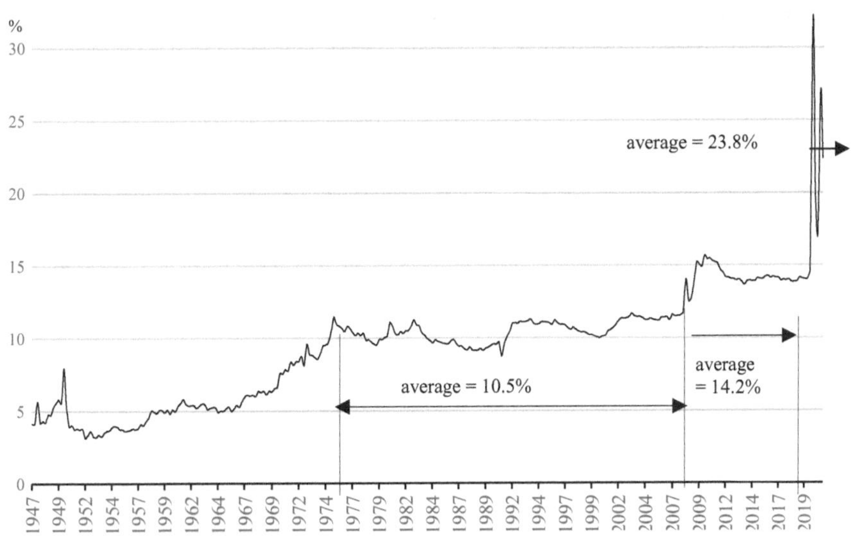

Figure 7.27 The U.S. Federal Government Current Transfer Payment (% of GDP)

Source: U.S. Bureau of Economic Analysis

7.7. Beggar-Thy-Neighbor and Global Inflation

Federal Reserve chairman, Ben Shalom Bernanke on March 25, 2013, emphasized that quantitative easing is not a "beggar-thy-neighbor" policy. However, the reality has been the opposite. Quantitative easing is deceitful and, thus, in the future, could incite anger in low-income countries affected negatively by it. Quantitative easing grants the United States free money by which it can use resources produced by the people outside the United States "for free," and this free transfer of wealth impoverishes the rest of the world by that amount of the free money. This amounts roughly to 8.96 trillion dollars (the amount of the Federal Reserve' asset purchase) as of March 23, 2022. For sure, the real value of this amount depends on the exchange rate of the dollars. If the U.S. dollars significantly depreciate, the growth of M2 (money supply) caused by quantitative easing redistributes wealth among different social groups only inside the United States. If not, the United States can earn that free money by which it can use resources produced by the people outside the United States "for free." Moreover, a slight depreciation of the dollar could help give a competitive advantage to the U.S. production industries. Figure 7.28 describes the correlation between the value of the dollar and the U.S. industrial production index that measures real output in the U.S. production industries including manufacturing, mining, electric, and gas utilities. This index has had an inverse relationship with dollar index that measures the relative value of the dollar against foreign currencies. That is, when the dollar depreciates, real output of those U.S. industries increases. Thus, when quantitative easing contributed to slightly depreciating the value of the dollar between 2008 and 2015 and after

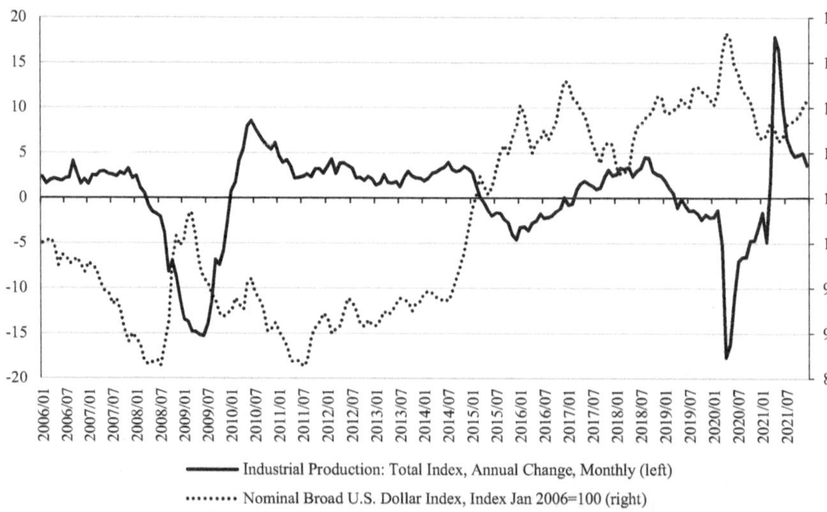

Figure 7.28 Industrial Production Index of the United States and Dollar Index

Source: Board of Governors of the Federal Reserve System

March 2020, this slight depreciation helped increase real output in those U.S. industries.

The wealth that quantitative easing transfers to the U.S. from the rest of world for free has increased an excessive demand for some goods. Due to this increase, some countries that export these goods to the U.S., such as South Korea, Taiwan, and China, have benefitted. However, other countries, especially, low-income countries, have been negatively affected. As seen in Figure 7.29, low-income countries have experienced high inflation and low GDP growth already since 2008, when the United States and other wealthy western countries began to implement quantitative easing. In this sense, quantitative easing can be seen as a beggar-thy-neighbor policy.

The way by which the free transfer of wealth impoverishes the rest of the world takes the form of global inflation of commodity prices. Here, commodities include energy commodities (coal, natural gas, crude oil, etc.) and non-fuel commodities (agricultural raw materials, metals, wheat, corn, fertilizer, etc.). Federal Reserve chairman Jerome Hayden Powell stressed on August 26, 2021 that quantitative easing is not an inflationary policy. However, the reality has been the opposite. Quantitative easing is an inflationary policy for various reasons including the following. First, it has increased housing prices, and this increasing housing price has triggered an increase in rent that is the biggest component of the U.S. Consumer Price Index. Second, the free transfer of wealth leads the people of the United States to consume excessively the goods and commodities produced by other countries and thus creates the shortage of commodities and goods globally. That is, it creates global inflation.

The United States can implement quantitative easing because the U.S. dollar is the world's reserve currency, which creates a strong international demand for U.S. dollars, which prevents a sharp decline in their value. If emerging market countries implement quantitative easing, the increasing risk of their default will

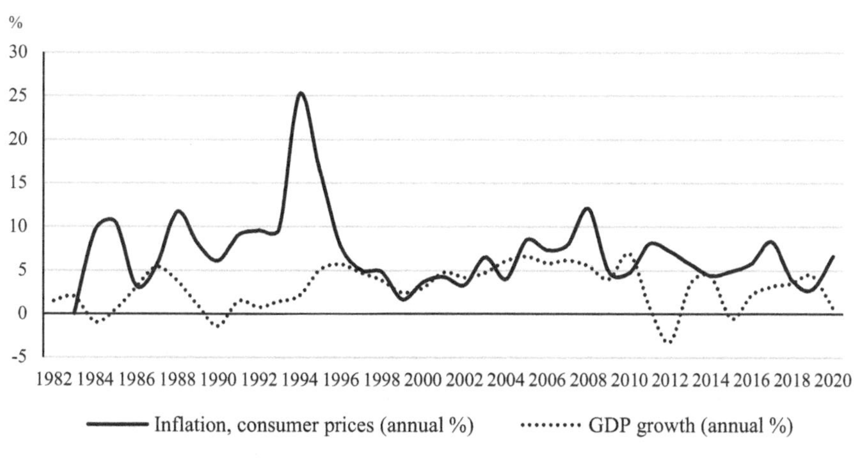

Figure 7.29 GDP Growth and Inflation for Low-Income Countries

Source: World Bank

lead their currency to decline sharply and thus redistributes wealth among different social groups only inside the countries. Thus, quantitative easing can be and has been implemented by the United States and other countries that have *standing* dollar swaps agreements with the Federal Reserve, including Canada, England, the European Union, Japan, and Switzerland. The exception is Australia, but the country is a U.S. ally.

Quantitative easing seems to fracture the world between advanced countries that have implemented quantitative easing and the rest of the world that have not implemented it. Since 2008 when the Western countries began quantitative easing, various forms of conflicts including battles, protests, riots, and explosions have skyrocketed in low-income countries as seen in Figure 7.30. My future research need to examine whether there is a correlation between these skyrocketed conflicts and the wealth transference from the world to the United States by quantitative easing.

The current method by which the United States performs quantitative tightening also inflicts more on developing countries than on the United States. The essence of quantitative tightening is the reduction of the assets of the Federal Reserve, that is, the Federal Reserve's sale of the Treasury securities and mortgage-backed securities. However, the volume of the sale is very small so far: its assets merely decrease from 8.96 trillion dollars in April 2022 to 8.75 trillion dollars in October 5, 2022, and there is almost no sale of mortgage-backed securities. The current main method of the Federal Reserve's quantitative tightening is a sharp increase of short-term interest rates. The United

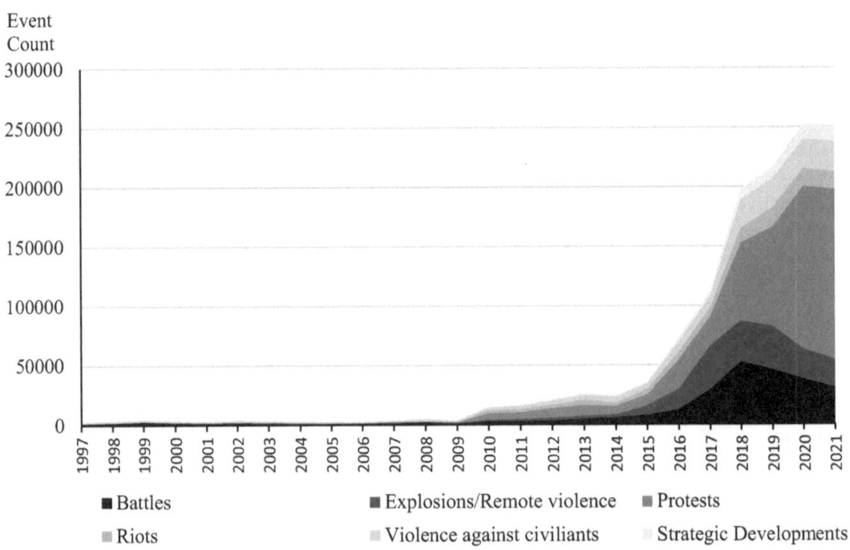

Figure 7.30 Numbers of Conflicts in the World (Cumulative Chart)

Source: The Armed Conflict Location & Event Data Project, acleddata.com

States has taken advantage of the privileges of the World's reserve currency to create its national loan market structure that allows corporations and households to obtain long-term loans at fixed interest rates (home mortgage loans are typically 30 years, and corporate bonds are averaged 10 years). Thus, a sharp short-term rate hike inflicts less on the United States than on other developing countries. Resultantly, emerging and low-income countries will be hit hard, and an economic or foreign exchange crisis is highly likely to occur in these countries. In fact, the rapid increase of interest rate by Federal Reserve has triggered the recurrent crises of foreign exchange in developing countries for the last three decades. This will happen again. This crisis will help the United States maintain its prerogative of the world's reserve currency, because the crisis will increase the international demand for dollars in the long term. Countries that have suffered foreign exchange market crises, like South Korea, have been struggling to accumulate more dollars to avoid future foreign exchange crises.

As Branko Milanovic demonstrates,[28] inequality between countries is more serious than inequality within a country. Around 1870, according to Milanovic, differences in social class within a country explained more than two-thirds of global inequality, while the difference in citizenship explained the rest of it. Around 2000, the difference in citizenship explained more than two-thirds of global inequality, while the difference in social class within countries explained the rest of it. That is, around 1870, peasants in India, workers in England, France, or Germany were invariably poor, "eking out a barely-above-subsistence existence, regardless of the country in which they lived."[29] In 2000, to the contrary, poor people within the United States or the E.U. often had incomes higher than middle-class incomes in poor countries.[30] This inequality between countries has worsened since 2008.

7.8. Genuine Solution?

It seems that we now enter a significant conflictual period internationally and nationally. As Walter Scheidel comments, throughout recorded history, what has flattened such serious inequality as what we face now has always been violent ruptures, including mass mobilization warfare, transformative revolution, state failure, and lethal pandemics.[31] An example was when the serious inequality of the early twentieth century was flattened by a series of two world wars, the Spanish flu killing 25–50 million people, and revolutionary movements. We hope to be allowed to fix inequality through rational and peaceful reform.

Pouring money into the economy and, in so doing, saving wealthy creditors is not a genuine solution for solving financial crises; it only delays the crises and sets the ground for more severe ones in the future, and worsens inequality inside a country and between countries, as seen in the case of quantitative easing. A genuine solution for financial crises would be, as David Graeber identified, (1) first, in the long term, to return to a credit economy that stops using money as a medium of exchange,[32] and (2) second, in the short term, to directly restructure creditor-debtor relations, as happened in credit economies in the form of cancellation of consumer debts or the systematic halt of commercial debt repayment during a debt crisis. The second solution basically restricts the rights of creditors. A detailed discussion of these solutions must be given in future research. Furthermore, to prevent global inflation that would negatively affect the life of people in low-income countries, we should consider replacing the current key reserve currency system with a "commodity reserve currency" system that many well-known economists including Keynes, Friedrich Hayek, and Nicholas Kaldor have supported.[33] According to them, commodity reserve currency is issued by a world commodity bank and anchored to a basket of a wide range of storable commodities.[34]

The U.S. Consumer Price Index skyrocketed to 7 in December 2021. It is at its highest level since 1982. The current level of inflation would affect people's lives more negatively than did the inflation of the 1970s and 1940s. The 1970s was when wealth and income inequality were at their lowest since WWII, and the improved equality of that time allowed people to cope with inflation. The U.S. society since the 1930s had implemented radical social reforms that decreased wealth and income inequality. These reforms included high proportional rates of inheritance tax and income tax, rent control, and many others. Through them, the top income tax rate was an average of 81% from 1932 to 1980, and the highest inheritance tax rate was an average of 75% in the same period. Furthermore, thanks to rent control implemented during 1940s, inflation led real rent to be lowered and was thus bearable to the poor. Consequently, these social reforms had lowered the share of the wealth of the top 1% from 44% in 1930 to 23% by the middle of 1970s.[35] At the present time different from the 1940s, however, social reforms for soaring inequality are not introduced.

Notes

1 Rouse, Zhang, and Tedeschi, "Historical Parallels."
2 Krugman, "History Says."
3 Summers, "On Inflation."
4 Piketty, *Capital,* 103.
5 Bichler and Nitzan, "Oil."
6 Goodhart and Pradhan, *Great Demographic Reversal.*
7 Baines, "Accumulating," 505.
8 Barsky and Kilian, "Do We Really Know," 169.
9 Bašta and Molnár, "Oil Market Volatility," 204.
10 Bichler and Nitzan, "Oil," 72.
11 Goodhart and Pradhan, *Great Demographic Reversal,* 2.
12 Piketty, *Capital,* 79.
13 UN population prospects, https://population.un.org/wpp/, accessed on March 8, 2022.
14 Goodhart and Pradhan, *Great Demographic Reversal.*
15 Bhar and Malliaris, "Oil Prices," 1049; Barsky and Kilian, "Oil," 126.
16 Bichler and Nitzan, "Oil," 63.
17 Bichler and Nitzan, "Oil," 63.
18 Clark, *Petrodollar Warfare.*

19 Ziegler, *Destruction Massive.*
20 Ziegler, *Destruction Massive.*
21 Baines, "Food Crisis," 505.
22 Konings, *American Finance*, 123.
23 Clark, *Petrodollar Warfare*; Spiro, *American Hegemony*; Di Muzio and Robbins, *Debt.*
24 Clark, *Petrodollar Warfare*, 30.
25 Clark, *Petrodollar Warfare*, 28–30.
26 Kruger, "Mortgage Securitization," 586.
27 U.S. Bureau of Labor Statistics, https://fred.stlouisfed.org/graph/?g=KP3b
28 Milanovic, "Global Income Inequality."
29 Milanovic, "Global Income Inequality," 205.
30 Milanovic, "Global Income Inequality," 205.
31 Scheidel, *Great Leveler*, 6.
32 Graeber, *Debt.*
33 Ussher, Hass, Topfer, and Jaeger, "Keynes"; Ussher, "Commodity Reserve Currency."
34 Ussher, "Commodity Reserve Currency," 411.
35 Piketty, *Capital and Ideology*, 423.

Bibliography

Baines, Joseph. "Accumulating Through Food Crisis? Farmers, Commodity Traders and the Distributional Politics of Financialization." *Review of International Political Economy* 24, no. 3 (2017): 497–537.

Barsky, Robert B. and Lutz Kilian. "Do We Really Know that Oil Caused the Great Stagflation? A Monetary Alternative." In *NBER Macroeconomics Annual 2001*, edited by B. S. Bernanke and K. Rogoff. Cambridge, MA: MIT Press, 2004.

Barsky, Robert B. and Lutz Kilian. "Oil and the Macroeconomy since the 1970s." *Journal of Economic Perspectives* 18, no. 4 (2004): 115–134.

Bašta, Milan and Peter Molnár. "Oil Market Volatility and Stock Market Volatility." *Finance Research Letters* 26 (2008): 204–214.

Bhar, Ramaprasad and A. G. Malliaris. "Oil Prices and the Impact of the Financial Crisis of 2007–2009." *Energy Economics* 33 (2011): 1049–1054.

Bichler, Shimshon and Jonathan Nitzan. "Still about Oil?" *Real-World Economics Review* 70 (2014): 49–79.

Clark, William R. *Petrodollar Warfare: Oil, Iraq and the Future of the Dollar*. Gabriola Island, BC: New Society Publishers, 2005.

Di Muzio, Tim and Richard H. Robbins. *Debt as Power*. Manchester: Manchester University Press, 2016.

Goodhart, Charles and Manoj Pradhan. *The Great Demographic Reversal: Ageing Societies, Waning Inequality, and an Inflation Revival*. Cham, Switzerland: Palgrave Macmillan, 2020.

Graeber, David. *Debt: The First 5,000 Years*. Brooklyn, NY: Melville House Publishing, 2011.

Konings, Martijn. *The Development of American Finance*. Cambridge: Cambridge University Press, 2011.

Kruger, Samuel. "The Effect of Mortgage Securitization on Foreclosure and Modification." *Journal of Financial Economics* 53 (2018): 586–607.

Krugman, Paul. "History Says Don't Panic About Inflation." *The New York Times*, November 11, 2021.

Milanovic, Branko. "Global Income Inequality in Numbers: in History and Now." *Global Policy* 4, no. 2 (2013): 198–208.

Piketty, Thomas. *Capital in the Twenty-First Century*. Translated by Arthurs Goldhammers. Cambridge: Harvard University Press, 2014.

Piketty, Thomas. *Capital and Ideology*. Translated by Arthur Goldhammer. Cambridge: Harvard University Press, 2020.

Rouse, Cecilia, Jeffery Zhang, and Ernie Tedeschi. "Historical Parallels to Today's Inflation Episode." *The White House*. Available at www.whitehouse.gov/cea/written-materials/2021/07/06/historical-parallels-to-todays-inflationary-episode. Accessed December 27, 2021

Scheidel, Walter. *The Great Leveler: Violence and the History of Inequality from the Stone Age to the Twenty-First Century*. Princeton and Oxford: Princeton University Press, 2017.

Spiro, David E. *The Hidden Hand of American Hegemony: Petrodollar Recycling and International Markets*. Ithaca and London: Cornell University Press, 1999.

Summers, Lawrence H. "On Inflation, Its' Past Time for Team 'Transitory' to Stand Down." *The Washington Post*, November 15, 2021.

Ussher, Leanne J. "Global Imbalances and the Key Currency Regime: The Case for a Commodity Reserve Currency." *Review of Political Economy* 21, no. 3 (2009): 403–421.

Ussher, Leanne J., Armin Hass, Klaus Topfer, and Carlo C. Jaeger. "Keynes and the International Monetary System: Time for a Tabular Standard?" *The European Journal of the History of Economic Thought* 25, no. 1 (2018): 1–35.

Ziegler, Jean. *Destruction Massive. Géopolitique de La Faim*. Paris: Seuil, 2011.

8 What is to be Done?

Cooperative Basic Capital and the Abolition of the Hybridity

This chapter briefly discusses a principle of reform policy: abolishing the hybridity of property and debt. It also discusses a new method for wealth redistribution that is named "cooperative basic capital." These discussions contribute to setting a direction for possible future research agendas.

8.1. Abolishing the Hybridity

The current financial system creates the boom and bust of economic cycles where the excessive demand and excessive supply of commodities are cyclically made. To meet this cyclic excessive demand, commodity reserve currency would require the maintenance of too large a storage buffer of commodities and thus require the payment of too high storage cost. If we want to introduce commodity reserve currency and make it efficient, we need to reform the current financial system. The main cause of the boom and bust of economic cycles is the hybrid and double-ownership scheme of modern banking and finance. The Austrian School of Economists has offered a persuasive theory of economic cycles. They identify that economic booms and recessions occur because modern banks create additional ownership titles and claims from the same deposits. As Ludwig von Mises, who founded the school in the twentieth century, argues, additional ownership titles and claims

> produce a lowering of the rate of interest, which falls below the level at which it would have been without their intervention. The lowering of the rate of interest stimulates economic activity. Projects which would not have been thought "profitable" if the rate of interest had not been influenced by the manipulations of the banks, and which, therefore, would not have been undertaken, are nevertheless found "profitable" and can be initiated.[1]

Long-term projects that would not have been considered profitable if banks do not create additional ownership titles look now seemingly profitable and are thus undertaken. This creates additional demand for production materials and labor and thus pushes up their prices. However, the existing production

DOI: 10.4324/9781003052210-9

materials and labor required for such long-term projects are not actually available.

> Society is not sufficiently rich to permit the creation of new enterprises. . . . As long as the expansion of [additional ownership titles and claims] is continued this will not be noticed, but this extension cannot be pushed indefinitely. . . . Many enterprises or business endeavors which had been launched thanks to the artificial lowering of the interest rate, and which had been sustained thanks to the equally artificial increase of prices, no longer appear profitable. Some enterprises cut back their scale of operation, others close down or fail.[2]

This failure eventually triggers bank runs in banking and finance, and resultant liquidity crunches will further expand the shutting down and eventual failure of the industry. The current economic cycles that create the excessive demand and excessive supply of commodities are not only harmful to the stability of ordinary people's lives but are also environmentally destructive because they cyclically exploit and discard natural resources.

The Austrian School of Economics has contested the ethics of modern fractional reserve banking. It argues that modern fractional reserve banking is guilty of committing two frauds: embezzlement by a bank against its depositors, and a fraud by a bank and its depositors against third parties.[3] My historical research on the origin of modern banking rejects the first supposed fraud. However, my research has determined that the second type of fraud occurs. A bank and its depositors have contracted to create additional titles and claims to the same quantity of property, and the depositors allow the bank to loan their deposits to third parties. This creation is fraudulent because no one can loan what they do not actually possess.[4] Furthermore, this creation of a hybrid, double-ownership titles and claims exposes the community to a new type of risk that did not exist in the traditional safekeeping business: the risk of illiquidity in the form of bank runs and other types of liquidity crunches. When this illiquidity creates economic recessions, it generates high costs for third parties, including workers, suppliers, consumers, and peripheral countries, who are innocently involved in modern banks' money creating mechanism.[5]

The hybrid and double-ownership scheme of modern banking is one of the main causes of wealth inequality in capitalist societies because it grants undeserved privileged rights to both banks and their clients. By law, the depositors of demand deposits are mere creditors for banks and thus are paid interest from the banks. In practice, however, and similar to property owners, they simultaneously enjoy the property right to withdraw their deposits at any time on demand. Likewise, modern banks formally act as creditors when they loan money to somebody and receive interest, but in essence, they are mere debtors because what they loan out is their promise to pay (IOUs). In this case, the debtors enjoy the creditors' right to be paid interest. Here, banks and depositors can enjoy both disparate rights simultaneously because they contract to create additional titles and claim on one and the same amount of money. As mentioned earlier, this hybrid and double-ownership scheme is also a central nature of the key elements of shadow banking—MMFs and repos—in the twenty-first century where investment banks and their investors' contracts create additional titles and claims on the same amount of money. This creation of additional titles and claims allows banks and their clients to inflate the right to control social resources, which are only available to societies in limited quantities. In this sense, modern banking and finance is a mechanism that redistributes wealth and income between social members; i.e., a free transfer of wealth into financial sectors from non-financial sectors. This wealth redistribution also happens internationally between the United States and the rest of the world. As long as the U.S. dollar is the key reserve currency and the Federal Reserve plays the role of the world's central bank, the creation of additional titles and claims by the Federal Reserve and the U.S. banks will allow them to use a large part of the limited social resources either very cheaply or for free.

I will conclude this book by commenting on a possible reform policy for the current financial system from a new perspective. This comment is brief and incomplete, but I believe it offers a direction for future research. The current discourse focuses on how to externally regulate the greedy and ill-behaved finance sector by adding more regulatory schemes and increasing governmental intervention. However, what this book has discussed thus far infers that we need a more fundamental reform policy.

One of the principles for this reform policy would be to prohibit any propertization of contractual rights; i.e., to prevent financial investors from enjoying both property rights and contractual rights simultaneously. In the case of commercial banking, demand deposit-taking and loan-making should be strictly segregated. In other words, credit banks and deposit banks should be separated. In credit banking, a no-demand clause is granted to promissory notes issued by credit banks. In deposit banking, deposit banks can be modeled on the Bank of Amsterdam in the seventeenth century. As mentioned earlier, the Bank of Amsterdam maintained a 100% reserve ratio, and merchants in Amsterdam during the seventeenth century were legally obliged to present their bills of exchange to the Bank. The debts of the bills were cleared among the merchants by using their funds deposited in the bank. Thus, the financial role of the public deposit banks was to clear the creditor-debtor relations of bills of exchange. Likewise, deposit banks in the future will maintain a 100% reserve ratio, and their role will be to clear creditor-debtor relations among traders and people. Similarly, in the case of MMFs, the redemption rights and voting rights of MMFs shareholders should be abolished, and the shareholders will be re-conceptualized as creditors. Likewise, repo investors will also be re-conceptualized as creditors who would not enjoy property rights. In other words, they would no longer enjoy the ownership rights on collateral or the right to terminate their contract quickly whenever they want. In the same vein, Ireland offers a radical reform policy for correcting corporate irresponsibility.[6] He argues that the policy should strictly divide creditors' rights from property rights, decoupling limited liability from control rights. The shareholders of limited joint-stock corporations would then be re-conceptualized as creditors who do not have voting rights. Abolishing these hybridities will transform the current capitalist money economy into the kind of credit economy David Graeber envisions.

The capitalist money economy has attempted to solve debt crises by pouring money into the economy, thereby saving rich creditors who should have lost money due to debtor default. However, doing this only delays the crisis and lays the ground for more severe ones in the future while worsening inequality both domestically and globally. A proper solution for debt crises would be a systematic halt of commercial debt repayments while the crisis is ongoing. This solution is an extension of the Chapter 11 bankruptcy process for an individual corporation into a whole society of corporations. As explained in Chapter 5, the U.S. bankruptcy process has two procedures: automatic stay and avoidance. Automatic stay prevents creditors from collecting a debtor's assets before a bankruptcy court assesses both the value of the debtor's assets and the full extent of creditors' claims. The process also voids any recent payments made by the firm since payments made just prior to bankruptcy can favor one creditor over others; a procedure known as avoidance. These two procedures lead creditors to share the risk of investment with debtors. The 2008 financial crisis should have been resolved by applying these procedures systematically rather than individually, with international cooperation between governments. A detailed discussion of this solution can be the subject of future research.

8.2. Basic Capital as a New Method of Wealth Redistribution

This section discusses an alternative principle of wealth redistribution, named "cooperative basic capital." The distribution of wealth has been currently done by commercial and investment banks or governments. The distribution by the banks has created inequality and economic booms and busts that endanger the life of workers, while the distribution by government cannot avoid bureaucratic red tapes. An alternative principle of wealth redistribution should overcome the weakness of the experiments of the 1940s when the government played a central role in wealth redistribution by introducing high proportional rates of both inheritance tax and income tax. This heavy taxation system was rapidly dismantled as people began to lose trust in the government by the end of the 1970s. To improve sustainability, there must be a new *liberal* alternative principle of wealth redistribution. Here, liberalism is understood as an idea in which state intervention is minimized as much as possible, and the citizens themselves can make appropriate decisions.

In 1999, Bruce Ackerman and Anne Alstott suggested that the government provide an unconditional endowment of $80,000 of basic capital to every citizen at age 21. Following this, other scholars, including Stuart White, Julian

Le Grand, and Thomas Piketty, have made similar proposals. This idea of a provision of basic capital is considered to be a fairly new idea—traceable in the first instance to Thomas Paine in 1769.[7] However, this is incorrect. This chapter identifies that the ancient thinkers Plato and Mencius both put forward extensive schemes for providing basic capital. The ignorance of these ancient ideas is unfortunate because it prevents modern scholars from learning from them. Plato's and Mencius's ideas for a basic capital scheme differ from the current proposals in three aspects: social inheritance, the protection of basic capital from creditors' claims, and the responsibility to use the capital productively. The basic capital proposals of Ackerman, Alstott, White, Le Grand, and Piketty, and others fail to pose a significant challenge to the capitalist economic system, as Erik Olin Wright indicates.[8] I argue that this failure can be overcome by modernizing the above three distinctive aspects of Plato's and Mencius's basic capital.

By modernizing these aspects, an alternative basic capital proposal (referred to here as cooperative basic capital) consists of the following five aspects. First, it envisions the construction of a new property system that would be simultaneously individual and communal. During the twentieth century, two visions of property systems competed with each other: the capitalist system, which supports private property rights, and the communist system, which nationalizes the main means of production. Separate from these two conventional visions, cooperative basic capital can promote a new property system that makes a means of production something that is both individual and communal.

Second, it allocates basic capital to those who are best able to use it productively, applying it in such a way as to replace the main economic institution of capitalism—the limited-liability joint-stock company—with workers' cooperatives. It imposes on the recipients of basic capital the responsibility of using their endowed basic capital to either set up or join a workers' cooperative. Here, a recipient's total amount of endowed basic capital, whose amount, I suggest, should be 60% of the average adult's wealth, is a kind of membership fee to a worker's cooperative. Additionally, the recipient would be part of only *one* workers' cooperative at a time. If recipients do not use their endowed basic capital for their membership fee, they should instead put it into a time deposit account in a publicly owned full reserve bank, which would then be empowered to loan the deposits to other workers' cooperatives, who would use them productively.

Third, it protects this endowed basic capital from creditors seeking it as repayment of debts, before the basic capital is used for the membership fee. However, it does not prevent the creditors of a cooperative from making claims against the cooperative. This differential treatment of creditors' claims reflects an old perspective, according to which productive loans (investments) and unproductive loans (usury) are treated differently.

Fourth, it does not depend on the resources set aside for social welfare, such as income tax, corporation tax, or value-added tax, meaning that it contributes to maintaining or enhancing social welfare services.

Fifth, it abolishes or restricts inheritance rights to fund basic capital and cyclically redistributes the means of production to those who can use it the most productively. This abolition or restriction of inheritance rights also works against the persistence of inequality across the generations. These five aspects are pro-market but anti-capitalist, because they promote market exchanges but restrict capitalist accumulation.

The current intellectual discussion of basic capital has largely centered on reforms that could set into motion a process of change that would lead to a radically different society. Unfortunately, however, what is lacking in these projects is any explicit discussion of how this different society would appear. This chapter fills this gap. Without the development of an explicit vision, there is no hope of transcending the existing order. In fact, all intellectual projects of reforming a society explicitly or implicitly presuppose their own vision of a good society. For example, Philippe Van Parijs' idea of a basic income is akin to the vision of communism, as argued by him, who asserted that basic income could "move us closer (*ceteris paribus*) to communism."[9] In *The Critique of the Gotha Programme*, Karl Marx argued that in its higher phases, communist society will be organized according to the principle of "from each according to his ability, to each according to his need"—which implies "(1) that everyone's basic needs are adequately met, and (2) that each individual's share is entirely independent of his or her . . . labor contribution."[10] Similar to this principle, Van Parijs' basic income is to be constructed to meet the basic needs of all and is to be distributed to all, independent of their labor contribution. I offer a different vision of the society that basic capital might ultimately lead to. It envisions a different ideal form of society that is quite different from both communism and capitalism. Arguably, this ideal form could be rooted in a property system that would be simultaneously communal and individual, not nationalizing the means of production but cyclically redistributing it to those who can use it the most productively.

This section is organized as follows. First, it critically reviews modern counterparts of basic capital, especially Ackerman and Alstott's and Piketty's.[11] Second, it analyzes Plato's and Mencius's conceptions. Third, it suggests an alternative proposal for basic capital that can undermine the capitalist economy.

Discussions of the ideal form of society have gained urgency as the challenges of the late nineteenth century—extreme wealth and income inequality, financial crises, social strife, and international conflicts—have returned today. In response to those earlier iterations of these crises, many intellectuals, including Marx, began to contemplate a new vision of civilization, involving as communism, guild socialism, the equal distribution of land, and the nationalization of major industries. Marx's vision of communism appealed to many intellectuals and revolutionaries, and his vision was attempted in the Soviet Union and other places. However, the large-scale nationalization of the means of production as part of the communist project of the twentieth century failed, as it concentrated too much power in the technical bureaucracy. Although twenty-first-century civilizations suffer from similar issues to those of the late nineteenth century, there seems to be no current debate regarding a new vision for a better civilization.

Contemporary Proposals for Basic Capital

The most representative proposal for basic capital that has been offered in recent years is that of Ackerman and Alstott. In their vision, every young adult who receives basic capital is free to use it for any purpose they choose: "The money is hers to spend or invest. She may go to college, or not. She may save for a house or a rainy day—or blow her money in Las Vegas."[12] To fund this basic capital, they suggested a flat tax of 2% on each individual's wealth in excess of $230,000 for the first 50 years after the basic capital be introduced.[13]

Piketty extended the scale of this proposal,[14] suggesting that the amount of basic capital given to each young adult, at age 25 in his proposal, be 60% of average adult wealth. To fund this amount, he suggested a proportional annual property tax, a proportional inheritance tax, and a gift tax, in which the proportional tax rates would reach 90% for 10,000 times the average level of adult wealth.[15]

These basic capital proposals have faced the following acute and reasonable criticisms. First, there is a high probability that the recipients of basic capital will waste it, and thus, basic capital proposals would not be able to achieve their primary goal of providing every citizen with the economic means for real autonomy. Even if young adults utilize it to start a business, they may have difficulty succeeding because they do not have adequate business experience within the highly competitive market. In the U.S. market, "50% of small businesses fail within 5 years and two thirds within 10 years."[16] Young adults raised in poverty tend to have less ability to manage their assets than those raised in middle- and upper-class families. Further, while some small businesses, even those founded by people from lower-class families, do beat the odds and survive, they are often subordinated to "credit markets or contractual relations such as franchises, suppliers, subcontractors and so on."[17] Moreover, under the modern imperative that all debts must be repaid, contemporary basic capital proposals allow creditors to take away this basic capital for repayment of debts.

Second, even though the endowed basic capital can be used to pay university tuition or put down a payment on a house, these uses may even promote rather than erode the capitalist market and its commodification of higher education and housing. As Wright argued alternatives that could work against the capitalist market logic here would be "a tuition-free higher education coupled with a graduate surtax for people with higher education if their income rises above the median" and "creating community land-trusts to underwrite low cost housing."[18] Thus, many scholars doubt whether a one-time payment in early adulthood could produce real citizen autonomy and undermine capitalism.

How can we overcome the above weaknesses and make basic capital a means of undermining the capitalist economy? This book suggests investigating ancient ideas on basic capital in Plato and Mencius. Let us first describe their proposals in detail.

Basic Capital in Ancient Times

Plato's Klēros

Plato considered that the communistic idea put forward in his *Republic* would be difficult to realize, so he put the idea of basic capital in his *Laws*.[19] Plato proposed to allocate land, equal in terms both of quality and amount, to each family.[20] This household estate was called *klēros* meaning a lot because it was allocated by lots.

This basic capital system had the following characteristics. First, unlike its modern counterpart, basic capital is here not given to young adults alone but to every family, in the form of a minimum amount of land guaranteed to each family. Second, there was also a legal maximum that each family could possess. By law, no family could possess more than four times the measure of the *klēros*. Third, unlike modern basic capital proposals, Plato offered various methods to protect families from losing the *klēros*. Their possession of it was inscribed on cypress-wood tablets that were publicly maintained, and thus everyone could learn who owned any specific *klēros*. The community elected protectors of the law to maintain the initial status of *klēros* distribution. Moreover, no *klēros* was allowed to be sold or bought.[21] It was also immune to credit claims, and creditors could not take ownership of a *klēros* even if its owner failed to repay his/her debts.[22] Furthermore, Plato suggested that the monetary system be regulated so that no one could become rich enough to exploit another's *klēros*. Fourth, each family was required to use its *klēros* productively. If a family failed to do so, its neighbors could criticize it morally. Fifth, the purpose of basic capital in this form was not only to promote freedom among citizens but also friendship between them. Plato argued that,

> In a state which is desirous of being saved from the greatest of all plagues—not faction, but rather distraction;—there should exist among the citizens neither extreme poverty, nor, again, excess of wealth, for both are productive of both these evils.[23]

Sixth, the dichotomy between the private and the public collapsed in the case of *klēros* ownership.[24] On the one hand, *klēroi* were publicly owned. Plato argued that, "in making the distribution, let the several possessors feel that their particular lots also belong to the whole city."[25] The possessors were not allowed to sell their *klēroi*, and others could not buy them. On the other hand, each *klēros* was privately owned by each family, and each family could exploit it for their well-being. A *klēros* could be inherited by the next generation of the family that owned it, and the state could not directly manage this.

Mencius's Well-Field System

The well-field system is the Confucian basic capital institution. Its name comes from the Chinese character 井, which means "a well" and symbolizes a land division into nine fields. The outlying eight fields around a central one are granted to eight peasant families. Each peasant family owns one of the outlying fields, and all of the families jointly work in the ninth, central field and pay the produce of this field to the government as tax. The well-field system was first described in the writings of the Confucian philosopher Mencius (c 372–289 BC), who argued that this system had been implemented under the Zhou dynasty (c. 1046–256 BC) and should be restored. This system had a large influence on Chinese history, for more than 2000 years: whenever the land system became disturbed and peasants' lives and livelihoods were in crisis, Confucian reformists or the leaders of peasant uprisings repeatedly compared this system to the current government's land practices and urged the government to re-introduce it.

This basic capital system had the following characteristics. First, unlike the modern counterpart but like Plato's conception, basic capital was not given to young adults alone but to every peasant family. Second, again unlike modern ideas but similar to Plato's, mechanisms were put into play to guarantee each family the ability to retain their endowed field. The endowment fields were officially documented by the government and could not be sold or bought. They were immune from the claims of creditors, because the fields were legally owned by the ruler. Third, like Plato's *klēros*, a family was obliged to use its endowed field productively. Fourth, like Plato's *klēros*, the dichotomy between the private and the public collapsed in the case of ownership of the well-field system. On the one hand, its ownership was public: the formal ownership of the endowed field belonged to the ruler who represented the community, and the peasant families could neither sell the land nor give it away themselves. On the other hand, its ownership was private. It practically belonged to each family, who could exploit it for its well-being. It could be inherited by the next generation if the next generation was willing to cultivate it and pay tax to the government, and the government would not directly manage it.

Fifth, the purpose of basic capital was not only to promote the autonomy of citizens but to support other social values as well, such as morality, humane governance, social welfare, taxation, and government finance. Mencius believed that ordinary people could not become moral without possessing basic capital, on the basis of which their economic well-being could be guaranteed. Moreover, if the provision of basic capital were to improve people's morality, rulers could avoid having to punish them and thus could establish humane governance. The well-field system would also reduce the tax burden on peasant families. In this system, the tax burden is lowered to one ninth of the total product because only the goods produced in a ninth of the total area, within the central field, were paid to the state. This system also ensured that the tax burden was flexible, rising or falling in according with the overall productivity of a given year. In a bad year, it was lower, while in a good year, it was increased.

The well-field system also expanded the total tax revenues that the government could gather. If this system became disturbed and a few powerful families came to own a majority of the land, the government would have difficulty in collecting tax from them because they control the government tax policy, and many of them were exempt from taxes. Furthermore, land in the well-field system was not allotted to the aristocratic class, who could not work on it, but only to peasant families, who could. Because, in this system, land is assigned only to those who could use it the most efficiently, social productivity could be enhanced, and thus government could collect more tax. Through the enhancements to government finance and social productivity achieved in this way, the well-field system allows the government to expand its social welfare services to reach minority groups, such as widows, orphans, elderly widowers, and the elderly without offspring.[26]

Breaking Down the Dichotomy between the Private and the Public

A main difference between the ancient conceptions reviewed here and contemporary basic capital proposals is that the former imposed an obligation of productive use on the recipients while the latter do not. In fact, Ackerman and Alstott were certainly opposed to imposing any such obligation on the recipients of basic capital. For Ackerman and Alstott, to inherit basic capital was "the birthright of every liberal citizen—not a scarce commodity to be doled out by the community as a reward for proper behavior."[27] Thus, the imposition of any obligations on its use is "paternalism," which contradicts or restricts this individual birthright.[28] Paternalism can be legitimately exercised only when an individual "lacks the capacities of self-government—of rationality and self-discipline—that citizens are assumed in general to have."[29]

Does the imposition of such responsibility contradict or restrict individual liberty? In other words, is basic capital a birthright, to which any social obligations and restrictions cannot be attached, as Ackerman and Alstott argue?[30] To answer this question, we must address the question whether there are any rights that we can consider birthrights. The idea of birthright began to significantly affect the English society where capitalism came into being earlier than other regions. In England the idea developed together with the linguistic development of the English term "property." This book discussed it in Chapter 2. Let me briefly explain it again. In an English dictionary, the word "property" is given two meanings: an attribute of something and a thing that can be owned. For example, in the case of humans, their attributes are liberty, body, actions, and life, and the things that humans can own are land and other things. English intellectuals, including Locke, in the seventeenth century tend to conflate the two senses of the word, mixing attributes and things. This conflation leads them to treat the right to possess land and things as a birthright. That is, the right to possess land and things is considered to be the same as the right to possess the natural attributes of human beings such as liberty and life. This assumption helped English intellectuals form the modern ideology that human beings are assumed to have a birthright to possess property understood as not only liberty and body but also land and goods. Previously, in the Middle Ages, land appertained to various stakeholders: it was formally the property of the Crown, but peasants had the right to cultivate it and enjoy its products, and the aristocracy had judicial power over certain areas and the right to enjoy the part of its product. However, in the seventeenth century, the nobility began to claim that land was their birthright. This birthright ideology had direct practical impact after Parliament employed it in its struggle against the Crown in seventeenth-century England. This modern concept of property as birthright has given the wealthy an excuse to turn public land into exclusively private property and to exploit others' basic capital. As a result, vast lands were concentrated in the hands of a few nobles, and many independent farmers became vagabonds, ultimately being transformed into free laborers who do not have their own means of production, as Marx set out in *Capital I*.[31]

This ideology of private property is justifiable, only when human attributes such as body can be considered *exclusively private*. Is the body exclusively private? Historically, this belief has not been universal, as explained in Chapter 2. More to the point, the body, which is a main attribute of a human being, is both private and public. It is public in that it is the closest environment to me or an assemblage of what nature offers to a person. At the same time, it is private: as property, it should belong to a person. Without her own property, including both her body and assets, a person would have to subordinate herself to others. Here, the dichotomy between the private and the public collapses in the concept of property, as in Plato's and Mencius's versions of basic capital. This collapse justifies the cooperative basic capital proposal to attach various obligations to endowed basic capital to promote various social values, including individual freedom, friendship, morality, social productivity, government finance, and social welfare. It is only when we promote all these values together, without impeding any one of them that we can realize freedom for individuals. Otherwise, an exclusively private concept of property leads to the exploitation of others' basic capital, as has happened since the early modern times. This study suggests that assigning to the recipients of basic capital the responsibility of using it productively should not be understood as a paternalism that contradicts or restricts individual freedom but as a recovery of the traditional economic principle of basic capital, through which the main means of production can be cyclically redistributed to those who are willing to embrace the obligation to use it the most productively.

Cooperative Basic Capital

Duty to use Productively: Workers' Cooperatives

We must consider three other issues that pertain to productive use: first, whether the recipients of basic capital should be restricted to young adults or not; second, how much basic capital is to be granted to each; and third, the best way to use basic capital productively in modern industrialized society. This study suggests that the recipients be all adult individuals who are willing and able to use basic capital productively, following the principle of our ancient models. Moreover, a sufficient amount of basic capital should be granted to allow the recipient to plan out her long-term career. Thus, the amount should be set to 60% of average adult wealth, as Piketty suggested.

Furthermore, this study proposes that basic capital be directly used to promote workers' cooperatives and thus enhance workers' democratic control of industry.[32] This would make a significant difference from previous basic capital proposals, and this difference is reflected in the name for this approach, which is thus called "cooperative basic capital." White suggested that the promotion of workers' cooperatives be one component of the egalitarian toolkit that also includes basic capital.[33] Piketty argued for capping large shareholder voting rights and strengthening workers' ownership in firms.[34] However, unfortunately, these two theorists did not consider whether to impose on the recipients of basic capital the responsibility of using basic capital as a membership fee of a workers' cooperative.

Workers' cooperatives are democratically managed enterprises owned by workers themselves—not shareholders. Cooperative business, therefore, should not be driven by profit alone but by a range of values, including fairness, equality, social justice, solidarity, and sustainability. However, current work organizations—limited liability joint-stock companies—treat workers as temporarily employed *outsiders* and mere tools for profit-making. These companies are undemocratically controlled by the wealthy and only pursue maximum profit at the cost of other social values such as fairness, social justice, solidarity, and environmental protection. This is a distortion introduced by the unbalanced rights and responsibilities appertaining to shareholders, as examined in detail in Chapter 6.

To solve the lack of balance between rights and responsibilities among shareholders, some political economists, including Kenneth W. Wedderburn and Paddy Ireland, have argued that shareholders should have their voting rights removed.[35] This reform policy would transform shareholders into mere creditors who receive interest payments in the form of dividends but do not have voting rights. If this is implemented, workers and their representative managers can make informed decisions about management and business *independently*. Even though this reform policy moves in the right direction, there is something that should be improved, something about whether workers and their representative managers are able to take responsibility in proportion to their enhanced authority. They would lose their jobs if the company went bankrupt. However, this would not be enough to bring them to take active responsibility as owners. They must also lose their membership fees when their company goes bankrupt, as shareholders do.

Workers' cooperatives can also contribute to enhancing the moral sentiments of the subjects who are responsible for important decisions about management and business. Currently, shareholders can hide their identities behind computer screens, and they can simply click to see only trends in rates of profitability of companies. Due to their anonymity and their sole concern for the maximization of profit, shareholders feel little moral sentiment toward those who are negatively affected by the unethical business of their corporation. As Graeber writes,

> [A limited liability joint-stock company] is a structure designed to eliminate all moral imperatives but profit. The executives who make decisions can argue—and regularly do—that, if it were their own money, of course they would not fire lifelong employees a week before retirement, or dump carcinogenic waste next to schools. Yet they are morally bound to ignore such considerations, because they are mere employees whose only responsibility is to provide the maximum return on investment for the company's stockholders. (The stockholders, of course, are not given any say.)[36]

However, this structure that eliminates all moral imperatives but profit does not exist in a workers' cooperative where those who make the decisions and those who own the company are the same people. Furthermore, Mencius would consider that this unification will enhance the moral sentiments of the decision makers in a company because it fits the moral sentiments of human beings. He argues,

> Here is why I say that all human beings have a mind that commiserates with others. Now, if anyone were suddenly to see a child about to fall into a well, his mind would be filled with alarm, distress, pity, and compassion. That he would react accordingly is not because he would hope to use the opportunity to ingratiate himself with the child's parents, nor because he would seek commendation from neighbors and friends, nor because he would hate the adverse reputation [that could come from not reacting accordingly]. From this it may be seen that one who lacks a mind that feels pity and compassion would not be human.[37]

The main point that Mencius emphasizes here is that the person we are imagining has seen a child about to fall into a well firsthand. Of course, human compassion does not always appear. A person with a certain intention in mind in advance may not show any compassion while seeing a child falling into a well. However, if a person is not working with any such intention and is only looking at the child, compassion will naturally appear. We often see this happening all around us. For example, in 2003, during the U.S. invasion of Iraq, CNN broadcast a scene of an airstrike in Baghdad, in which fighter jets were dropping bombs in a dark night, like a scene from a computer game. There was no compassion in the hearts of those who watched this scene as if they were watching a war game movie, and American public opinion supported the war. However, if CNN had broadcast footage of Iraqi citizens bleeding from the dropped bombs, public opinion in the United States would have been very different. In fact, as the Iraq War progressed and the plight of Iraqi citizens was more faithfully reported, American public opinion changed to oppose the war. Those who control economic organizations must also be in a better position to express human compassion: workers who can directly see how their work affects other people enjoy such a position.

Distinguishing Unproductive Debts from Productive Debts

Cooperative basic capital draws on the lessons of a long tradition of distinguishing between productive and unproductive debts and of treating them differently. Productive debts are those that borrowers invest to make a profit. These debts were (and are) called "commercial loans" because they were often invested in commerce. Because this investment is made with the intention of producing a profit, debtors usually have no difficulty repaying such debts. Unproductive debts (often called "consumer loans") are those that borrowers require for their living expenses, such as, purchasing daily necessities, paying rental fees, or buying a house. Because no profit is made from these debts, debtors often have difficulty repaying them. Historically, rich creditors have used these unproductive debts to exploit impoverished debtors. If debtors failed to repay their creditors, creditors would often take debtors' wives and daughters as debt peons, or take away their land. In this way, historically, unproductive debts have generated inequality and destroyed reciprocity and solidarity among community members. In ancient Israel, productive debts were called *tarbit*, meaning "increase," while unproductive debts were called *neshek*, meaning "bite"; the former were encouraged because they were considered to increase well-being, while the latter were cancelled cyclically, as was also done in nearby societies, including the Mesopotamian culture of Babylonia.[38] In ancient Israel, this cyclic cancellation of unproductive debts occurred every Sabbatical year and in the Jubilee year. Likewise, in the European Middle Ages, unproductive debt was called "usury" and was prohibited, while productive debt was not. Plato also strongly opposed interest-bearing loans, arguing, "nor shall he lend money upon interest; and the borrower should be under no obligation to repay either capital or interest."[39] Here it remains unclear whether Plato distinguished productive and unproductive loans. Nevertheless, he would undoubtedly agree with my suggestion that the two be distinguished, as his reform policy drew on the above ancient practices of Mesopotamia in which the two forms of debts were treated differently.

The loss of a distinction between consumer loans and commercial loans was a major case of the 2007 financial crisis in the United States. During the Golden Age of capitalism between 1960s and 1970s, the U.S. government established several rules that would put the two loans on different footings to protect borrowers of consumer loans. For example, in the 1960s several state governments including Wisconsin acted a new consumer act that stipulated that consumer loans, including mortgage loans, were no longer subject to the legal rule of "holder in due course," a rule that had been introduced to protect the creditors in commercial loan agreements and thus could be inequitable to their debtors.[40] However, when this act was repealed and thus when the debtors of consumer loans could no longer defend themselves even in cases where their original debt contracts were found to have been made fraudulently, the securitization of consumer loans has rapidly expanded since the late 1970s. This expansion was one of the causes of the financial crisis of 2007.

In the ideals put forward by ancient and medieval tradition, society should protect debtors from unproductive loans while encouraging productive loans. In a cooperative basic capital, if an individual has debts before she uses her basic capital as a membership fee for a workers' cooperative, those debts are regarded as unproductive, and thus the basic capital is protected from creditors. However, once it is used as a membership fee of a workers' cooperative, if this cooperative begins to owe money, the basic capitals can be used to repay the debts of the cooperative, because these debts are productive. Here, the proposal of combining basic capital with workers' cooperatives transforms the unproductive debts of individuals into the productive debts of a cooperative. A cooperative's debts are productive in the same way as traditional productive debts: cooperatives use the debts to make profit rather than simply to consume. Because the business of workers' cooperatives, where the basic capital of the members is put together, is likely to be more successful than that of a similar small business, profits will be more secure, and the cooperatives will be more likely repay their debts.

Treating productive and unproductive loans differently is in strikingly contrast with Ackerman and Alstott's attitude toward debt obligations. Without acknowledging that unproductive debts are a major cause of wealth inequality, these theorists consider that adults would be morally irresponsible if they failed to repay all forms of debt,[41] and by this move, these theorists allow rich creditors to exploit the basic capital of the poor.

Financing Basic Capital: Social Inheritance

Le Grand suggests that basic capital be financed with a reformation of the inheritance tax, which John Stuart Mill first proposed in the nineteenth century.[42] This suggestion has now been adopted by many theorists of basic capital including White, Anthony Atkinson, and Piketty.[43] Mill suggested that we shift the basis for inheritance tax from the donor to the recipient and extend it to include all inheritance and gifts over the course of the lifetime of a recipient. This new system would give everyone a lifetime gift and inheritance allowance that could be received free of tax, after which the system can levy taxes at highly progressive rates for any amount exceeding the allowance.[44] This reformed tax, the "lifetime capital receipts tax," could give the wealthy an incentive to spread their wealth among those who have benefited little from any inheritance or gift.[45]

Cooperative basic capital modifies Le Grand's suggestion to follow the practice of the ancient basic capital, which did not rely on taxation. Cooperative basic capital sets the above allowance to 60% of the average adult wealth, and no one receives basic capital beyond this amount. However, a person can receive up to seven times the average adult wealth from inheritance or gift from the parents or spouse. Here, the amount of seven times the average adult wealth is merely an example. The amount of allowance should be decided by consensus in the population. A donor can choose recipients, and these recipients must be adults who can, and are willing to, use the allowance productively.

For example, suppose that you want to give your property to your nephew. You cannot do this if your nephew has already inherited or received 60% of average adult wealth (for example, U.S. $144,000 [60% of U.S. $240,000] in the case of the United States) from someone else or if he is under the age of 20. If you have three daughters, each one of your daughters can receive up to U.S. $1,008,000 (7 x U.S. $144,000) from you after she reaches the age of 20. If she has already received $144,000 from someone else, you can grant her up to $864,000. Consequently, you can hand over to your three daughters up to $3,024,000 (3 x U.S. $1,008,000) in total if they receive nothing from other sources. If your total wealth is valued at more than $3,024,000, you can distribute the rest of it to others as you choose.

Cooperative basic capital differs from Le Grand's suggestion in four respects. First, Le Grand allows a donor to give a recipient more than the amount of the allowance but imposes a progressive tax rate in response. However, cooperative basic capital forbids a donor to give a recipient more than the amount of the allowance. Second, for Le Grand, anyone—including those under the age of 20—can receive inheritance and gifts, while for cooperative basic capital, the recipients must be over 20 years old. This is because the recipients must be able to use the inheritance or gifts productively. Third, cooperative basic capital requires the recipients to use basic capital to become members of a cooperative, while Le Grand does not.[46] Fourth, in Le Grand's system, the government collects the tax and grants basic capital to citizens, while in cooperative basic capital, the donor can herself choose the recipients and grant them basic capital. This is a liberal characteristic of cooperative basic capital, if liberalism is understood as an idea in which the state's intervention is reduced as far as possible, and the citizens themselves can make appropriate decisions. Because the donors hope that their wealth will be applied the most usefully, they are more cautious than anyone else when choosing who will inherit or receive their wealth. Furthermore, donors who are shareholders in a company are encouraged to choose the employees of the company as inheritors of their wealth and to transform the company into a workers' cooperative. In this way, social inheritance will help promote workers' cooperatives.

Piketty's idea of basic capital relies on an annual property tax and inheritance/gift tax whose total annual amount reached 5% of gross domestic product. In 2018, the average income of governments from property taxes among OECD countries was approximately 1.86% of GDP,[47] and to implement Piketty's proposal, an additional 3.14% of GDP of property tax should be collected. Historically, however, resistance to property tax has often driven governments out of power, as Piketty himself acknowledges, citing, for example, the 1978 property tax revolt in California, "which was in some ways a harbinger of Reagan's successful run for the presidency two years later."[48]

The liberal characteristics of social inheritance has some advantages that Piketty's proposal does not. Piketty's proposal relies on heavy taxation that would easily break down when people lose trust in government, as happened at the end of 1970s. By contrast, our liberal aspect of social inheritance does not have this weakness, because the government does not intervene in the distribution of basic capital. Moreover, this distribution is made when the donors have less concern regarding the accumulation of wealth in their life cycle, that is, when they face death. The wealthy turn their attention to philanthropic giving, usually as retirement or death approaches. Furthermore, because they are allowed to choose the recipients of their wealth, that is, to receive honor as donors, the resistance will not reach the strength that it did for property taxes.

Table 8.1 describes the features of the proposal in comparison with ancient and contemporary equivalents.

The proposal for cooperative basic capital presented in this chapter seeks to modernize Plato's and Mencius's schemes by rethinking the three modern institutions of property rights, inheritance rights, and debt obligations, which constitute the foundation of modern capitalism. A key method of the

Table 8.1 Basic Capital Proposals

	Ancient basic capital	*Ackerman & Alstott's or Piketty's basic capital*	*Cooperative basic capital*
Form of basic capital	Land (a means of production in an agricultural society)	Money that can be used for any purpose	Money that must be used for getting means of production
Method of getting resources for basic capital	Dividing common land to each peasant family	Taxation	Social inheritance
Recipients	All peasant families	Adult individuals at a particular age	All adult individuals who can use basic capital productively
Protection from credit claims	Protected	Not protected	Protected
Inheritance	An heir could inherit only basic capital and should use it productively (Mencius) or could inherit no more than four times the basic capital (Plato)	Inheritance rights are restricted	An heir can inherit no more than seven times of "average adult wealth" from her/his parent.

modernization is to organically synthesize basic capital with such institutions as the restriction of inheritance rights, the distinction of investment from usury, and workers' cooperatives. This can help revitalize workers' cooperatives enough to compete against the current undemocratic work organizations—limited liability joint-stock companies—and to expand workers' autonomy, workplace democracy, and social productivity. It also can help contribute to distinguishing unproductive loans, which are a major cause of wealth inequality and social discord, from productive loans, thus increasing social productivity. Furthermore, cooperative basic capital is expected to increase current government's welfare services and make them more efficient. Cooperative basic capital does not use such tax resources as income tax, corporation tax, or value-added tax, because it takes the reformed inheritance practices as the means of funding basic capital. This means that after basic capital is implemented, the government could continue the current welfare services without being restricted by loss of tax revenue (except the current inheritance tax). Furthermore, once citizens have received basic capital and used it productively, poverty will be decreased significantly, and the government will be able to collect more taxes in the normal round due to enhanced economic activities. This will allow the government to expand and diversify its welfare services.

Cooperative basic capital will indirectly contribute to reducing global inequality. In order to mitigate domestic inequality, many rich countries have transferred wealth from the outside to the inside of their countries by, for example, implementing quantitative easing, exporting military weapons to poor countries, monopolistically controlling global supply chains, and managing the privileged power of their currencies internationally. However, cooperative basic capital will allow rich countries to forbear complete reliance on these methods because they can compensate for the inequality within their borders by cyclically redistributing wealth among their citizens and using it productively.

Notes

1 Mises, "Austrian Theory," 28.
2 Mises, "Austrian Theory," 29.
3 Huerta de Soto, *Money*.
4 Huerta de Soto, *Money*.
5 Huerta de Soto, *Money*.
6 Ireland, "Limited Liability."
7 Cunliffe and Erreygers, "Introduction," x; Ackerman and Alstott, "Why Stakeholding?"; Le Grand, "Implementing Stakeholder Grants," 120.
8 Wright, "Eroding Capitalism."
9 Van der Veen and Van Parijs, "Road to Communism," 642.
10 Van der Veen and Van Parijs, "Road to Communism," 642–643.
11 Ackerman and Alstott, "Why Stakeholding?"; Piketty, *Capital and Ideology*.
12 Ackerman and Alstott, "Why Stakeholding?" 45.
13 Ackerman and Alstott, "Why Stakeholding?" 45.

14 Piketty, *Capital and Ideology*, 983.
15 Piketty, *Capital and Ideology*, 982.
16 Wright, "Eroding Capitalism," 439.
17 Wright, "Basic Income," 96.
18 Wright, "Eroding Capitalism," 437.
19 A form of this idea was actually practiced in most of ancient Greek city-states, with the exception of a few, such as Sparta.
20 Plato, *Laws*, 736e.
21 Plato, *Laws*, 741c.
22 Plato, *Laws*, 742c.
23 Plato, *Laws*, 744c.
24 Moore, *Sex and the Second-Best City*, 113.
25 Plato, *Laws*, 740a.
26 Mencius, *Mencius*, 19.
27 Ackerman and Alstott, "Why Stakeholding?" 43.
28 Ackerman and Alstott, "Why Stakeholding?" 44.
29 White, *Civic Minimum*, 148.
30 Ackeman and Alstott, "Why Stakeholding?" 43.
31 Marx, *Capital I*.
32 This is the same vision as that of guild socialism that developed in England in the first two decades of the twentieth century.
33 White, "Basic Capital," 422.
34 Piketty, *Capital and Ideology*, 975.
35 Wedderburn, *Company Law Reform*; Ireland, "Limited Liability."
36 Graeber, *Debt,* 320.
37 Mencius, *Mencius,* 35.
38 Hudson, "Origins of Interest-Bearing Debt."
39 Plato, *Laws*, 742c.
40 Erickson, "Demise of Holder," 248–249.
41 Ackerman and Alstott, "Why Stakeholding?" 49.
42 Le Grand, "Markets," 210.
43 White, "Basic Capital"; Atkinson, *Inequality*, 170, 194–196; Piketty, *Capital and Ideology*.
44 Le Grand, "Implementing Stakeholder Grants," 123.
45 Le Grand, "Implementing Stakeholder Grants," 123.
46 Nissan and Le Grand, *Capital Idea*.
47 OECD Data, https://data.oecd.org/tax/tax-on-property.htm. Property tax here is defined as recurrent and non-recurrent taxes on the use, ownership or transfer of property. These include taxes on immovable property or net wealth, taxes on the change of ownership of property through inheritance or gift and taxes on financial and capital transactions.
48 Piketty, *Capital and Ideology*, 836.

Bibliography

Atkinson, B. Anthony. *Inequality: What Can Be Done?* Cambridge, MA: Harvard University Press, 2015.

Ackerman, Bruce and Anne Alstott. "Why Stakeholding?" In *Redesigning Distribution: Basic Income and Stakeholder Grants as Alternative Cornerstones for a More Egalitarian Capitalism*, edited by Erik Olin Wright, 43–65. London and New York: Verso, 2006.

Cunliffe, John and Guido Erreygers. "Introduction." In *The Origins of Universal Grants: An Anthology of Historical Writings on Basic Capital and Basic Income*, edited by John Cunliffe and Guido Erreygers. New York: Palgrave Macmillan, 2004.

Erickson, Myron L. "Demise of Holder in Due Course, Waiver of Defense, and Interlocking Loan Lender Defenses in Consumer Transactions." *South Texas Law Journal* 15, no. 3 (1973): 236–261.

Graeber, David. *Debt: The First 5,000 Years*. Brooklyn, NY: Melville House Publishing, 2011.

Horsefield, J. K. "The Beginnings of Paper Money in England." *Journal of European Economic History* 6, no. 1 (1977): 117–133.

Hudson, Michael. "Reconstructing the Origins of Interest-Bearing Debt and the Logic of Clean Slates." In *Debt and Economic Renewal in the Ancient Near East*, edited by Michael Hudson. 7–58. Marc Van de Mieroop, Bethesda, MD: CDL Press, 2002.

Huerta de Soto, Jesús. *Money, Bank Credit, and Economic Cycles*. Auburn, AL: Ludwig von Mises Institute, 2009.

Ireland, Paddy. "Limited Liability, Shareholder Rights and the Problem of Corporate Irresponsibility." *Cambridge Journal of Economics* 34, no. 5 (2010), 837–856.

Kruger, Samuel. "The Effect of Mortgage Securitization on Foreclosure and Modification." *Journal of Financial Economics* 53 (2018): 586–607.

Le Grand, Julian. "Markets, Welfare and Equality." In *Market Socialism*, edited by Julian Le Grand and Saul Estrin. Oxford: Oxford University Press, 1989.

Le Grand, Julian. "Implementing Stakeholder Grants: the British Case." In *Redesigning Distribution: Basic Income and Stakeholder Grants as Alternative Cornerstones for a More Egalitarian Capitalism*, edited by Erik Olin Wright. London and New York: Verso, 2006.

Marx, Karl. *Capital*. Vol. 1. Penguin Classics, 1992.

Mencius *Mencius*. Translated by Irene Boom. New York: Columbia University Press, 2009.

Mises, Ludwig von. "The 'Austrian' Theory of the Trade Cycle." In *The Austrian Theory of the Trade Cycle and Other Essays*. Auburn, AL: Ludwig von Mises Institute, 1996.

Moore, Kenneth Royce. *Sex and the Second-Best City: Sex and Society in the Laws of Plato*. London and New York: Routledge, 2016.

Nissan, David and Julian Le Grand. *A Capital Idea: Start-up Grants for Young People*. London: Fabian Society, 2000.

Piketty, Thomas. *Capital and Ideology*. Translated by Arthur Goldhammer. Cambridge: Harvard University Press, 2020.

Plato. *Laws*. Translated by Benjamin Jowett. Mineola, New York: Dover Publications, Inc., 2006. Available at http://classics.mit.edu/Plato/laws.html.

Van der Veen, R. and P. Van Parijs. "A Capitalist Road to Communism." *Theory and Society* 15, no. 5 (1986): 635–655.

Wedderburn, K. W. *Company Law Reform*. London: The Fabian Society, 1969.

White, Stuart. *The Civic Minimum: On The Rights and Obligations of Economic Citizenship*. Oxford: Oxford University Press, 2003.

White, Stuart. "Basic Capital in the Egalitarian Toolkit?" *Journal of Applied Philosophy* 32, no. 4 (2015): 417–431.

Wright, Erik Olin. "Basic Income, Stakeholder Grants, and Class Analysis." In *Redesigning Distribution: Basic Income and Stakeholder Grants as Alternative Cornerstones for a More Egalitarian Capitalism*, edited by Erik Olin Wright. London and New York: Verso, 2006.

Wright, Erik Olin. "Eroding Capitalism: A Comment on Stuart White's "Basic Capital in the Egalitarian Toolkit." *Journal of Applied Philosophy* 32, no. 4 (2015): 432–439.

Index